# Oracle Database Transactions and Locking Revealed

Building High Performance Through Concurrency

Second Edition

**Darl Kuhn**
**Thomas Kyte**

**Apress®**

*Oracle Database Transactions and Locking Revealed: Building High Performance Through Concurrency*

Darl Kuhn
Morrison, CO, USA

Thomas Kyte
Denver, CO, USA

ISBN-13 (pbk): 978-1-4842-6424-9
https://doi.org/10.1007/978-1-4842-6425-6

ISBN-13 (electronic): 978-1-4842-6425-6

Managing Director, Apress Media LLC: Welmoed Spahr
Acquisitions Editor: Jonathan Gennick
Development Editor: Laura Berendson
Coordinating Editor: Jill Balzano

Cover image designed by Freepik (www.freepik.com)

Distributed to the book trade worldwide by Springer Science+Business Media LLC, 1 New York Plaza, Suite 4600, New York, NY 10004. Phone 1-800-SPRINGER, fax (201) 348-4505, e-mail orders-ny@springer-sbm.com, or visit www.springeronline.com. Apress Media, LLC is a California LLC and the sole member (owner) is Springer Science + Business Media Finance Inc (SSBM Finance Inc). SSBM Finance Inc is a **Delaware** corporation.

For information on translations, please e-mail booktranslations@springernature.com; for reprint, paperback, or audio rights, please e-mail bookpermissions@springernature.com.

Apress titles may be purchased in bulk for academic, corporate, or promotional use. eBook versions and licenses are also available for most titles. For more information, reference our Print and eBook Bulk Sales web page at http://www.apress.com/bulk-sales.

Any source code or other supplementary material referenced by the author in this book is available to readers on GitHub via the book's product page, located at www.apress.com/9781484264249. For more detailed information, please visit http://www.apress.com/source-code.

Printed on acid-free paper

# Table of Contents

# About the Authors

**Darl Kuhn** is a senior-level database administrator with decades of experience. He handles all facets of database administration from design and development to production support. He enjoys documenting and sharing knowledge and has authored several books on Oracle technology.

**Thomas Kyte** is a former vice president of the Core Technologies Group at Oracle Corporation. He is the same Tom who created the "Ask Tom" website and the *Oracle Magazine* column of the same name. He has a long history of answering questions about the Oracle database and tools that developers and database administrators struggle with every day.

# About the Technical Reviewer

**Charles Bell** conducts research in emerging technologies. He is a member of the Oracle MySQL Development team and is a senior software developer for the MySQL Enterprise Backup team. He lives in a small town in rural Virginia with his loving wife. He received his Doctor of Philosophy in Engineering from Virginia Commonwealth University in 2005.

Charles is an expert in the database field and has extensive knowledge and experience in software development and systems engineering. His research interests include three-dimensional printers, microcontrollers, three-dimensional printing, database systems, software engineering, high-availability systems, cloud, and sensor networks. He spends his limited free time as a practicing maker, focusing on microcontroller projects and refinement of three-dimensional printers.

# Acknowledgments

I'd like to thank Tom for inviting me to work with him on this book. I'd also like to acknowledge Jonathan Gennick; his guidance (over many years and books) laid the foundation for me being able to work on a book like this one. And I'd like to thank Heidi, Brandi, Lisa, Evan Saxton, Mike Tanaka, Simon Ip, Laurie Bourgeois, Jeff Beacham, Greg Buchanan, and Kevin Bayer; without their support, I could not have successfully participated.

—Darl Kuhn

I would like to thank many people for helping me complete this book. First, I would like to thank you, the reader of this book. There is a high probability that if you are reading this book, you have participated in my site http://asktom.oracle.com in some fashion, perhaps by asking a question or two. It is that act—the act of asking questions, and of questioning the answers—that provides me with the material for the book and the knowledge behind the material. Without the questions, I would not be as knowledgeable about the Oracle database as I am. So, it is ultimately you who makes this book possible.

Second, at Oracle, I work with the best and brightest people I have ever known, and they all have contributed in one way or another.

Lastly, but most important, I would like to acknowledge the unceasing support I've received from my family. You know you must be important to someone when you try to do something that takes a lot of "outside of work hours" and that someone lets you know about it. Without the continual support of my wife Melanie (who also was a technical reviewer on the book), son Alan, and daughter Megan, I don't see how I could have finished this book.

—Tom Kyte

# Introduction

I've been asked many times, "What is the key to building highly concurrent and scalable database applications?" Invariably, my response is "Begin with the basics, start with thoroughly understanding how Oracle manages transactions."

When designing and creating database applications, understanding how the underlying database manages transactions will enable you to make intelligent architectural decisions that result in highly concurrent and scalable applications. Without knowledge of how the database handles transactions, you'll invariably make poor design choices and end up with code that will never perform well. If you're going to be building systems that use an Oracle database, it's critical that you understand Oracle's transaction management architecture.

## Who This Book Is For

The target audience for this book is anyone who develops applications with Oracle as the database back end. It is a book for professional Oracle developers who need to know how to get things done in the database. The practical nature of the book means that many sections should also be very interesting to the DBA. Most of the examples in the book use SQL*Plus to demonstrate the key features, so you won't find out how to develop a really cool GUI—but you will find out how Oracle handles transaction management. As the title suggests, *Oracle Database Transactions and Locking Revealed* focuses on the core database topics of how transactions work, as well as locking. Related to those topics is Oracle's use of redo and undo. I'll explain what each of these is and why it is important for you to know about these features.

## Source Code and Updates

The best way to digest the material in this book is to thoroughly work through and understand the hands-on examples. As you work through the examples in this book, you may decide that you prefer to type all the code by hand. Many readers choose to do this because it is a good way to get familiar with the coding techniques that are being used.

Whether you want to type the code or not, all the source code for this book is available in the Source Code section of the Apress website (`www.apress.com`). If you like to type the code, you can use the source code files to check the results you should be getting—they should be your first stop if you think you might have typed an error. If you don't like typing, then downloading the source code from the Apress website is a must! Either way, the code files will help you with updates and debugging.

# Errata

Apress makes every effort to make sure that there are no errors in the text or the code. However, to err is human, and as such, we recognize the need to keep you informed of any mistakes as they're discovered and corrected. Errata sheets are available for all our books at `www.apress.com`. If you find an error that hasn't already been reported, please let us know. The Apress website acts as a focus for other information and support, including the code from all Apress books, sample chapters, previews of forthcoming titles, and articles on related topics.

# Setting Up Your Environment

In this section, I will cover how to set up an environment capable of executing the examples in this book, specifically:

- Instantiating a database with Oracle VM VirtualBox

- How to set up the `YODA` account used for many of the examples in this book

- How to set up the `SCOTT/TIGER` demonstration schema properly

- The environment you need to have up and running

- Configuring AUTOTRACE, a SQL*Plus facility

- Installing Statspack

- Creating the `BIG_TABLE` table

- The coding conventions I use in this book

All of the non-Oracle supplied scripts are available for download from the `www.apress.com` website. If you download the scripts, there will be a chNN folder that contains the scripts for each chapter (where NN is the number of the chapter). The ch00 folder contains the scripts listed here in the "Setting Up Your Environment" section.

# Creating a Database with Oracle VM VirtualBox

One of the quickest ways to gain access to a fully functional Oracle database is to download and install Oracle VM VirtualBox and use it with a prebuilt database VM. You can literally have a working database within a few minutes of downloading and installing the required software. All of the examples in this book will be run on a prebuilt database VM using the latest version of Oracle.

First, you must download and install VirtualBox. To do this, go to this link and download and install the software:

`www.virtualbox.org/wiki/Downloads`

After you have downloaded and installed VirtualBox, download a prebuilt database VM and follow the instructions for instantiating it within VirtualBox. Use this link to download the prebuilt VM:

`www.oracle.com/downloads/developer-vm/community-downloads.html`

For the examples in this book, I used the `Database App Development` VM. This VM contains a container database named `CDB$ROOT`. Within this container database, there is a pluggable database named `ORCL`. Where applicable, in the examples in this book, I'll specify whether I'm connecting to the root container or the pluggable database.

When logging onto the Database App Development VM, I use the Oracle OS account and run the following commands to set up the environment:

```
export ORACLE_SID=orclcdb
export ORACLE_HOME=/u01/app/oracle/product/version/db_1
export PATH=$ORACLE_HOME/bin:$PATH
set -o vi
export EDITOR=vi
export TWO_TASK=
```

> **Note** When using the Database App Development VM database, the TWO_TASK variable needs to be unset before you can connect to the root using sqlplus / as sysdba.

# Setting Up the YODA Schema

The YODA user is used for most of the examples in this book. This is simply a schema that has been granted the DBA role and granted execute and select on certain objects owned by SYS. This example assumes that you're using a container database that contains a pluggable database. The pluggable database that I'm using in this book is named ORCL. In the following code, you'll have to specify the name of the pluggable database that you're using:

```
sqlplus / as sysdba
alter session set container=orcl;
define username=yoda
define usernamepwd=foo
create user &&username identified by &&usernamepwd;
grant dba to &&username;
grant execute on dbms_stats to &&username;
grant select on V_$STATNAME to &&username;
grant select on V_$MYSTAT to &&username;
grant select on V_$LATCH to &&username;
grant select on V_$TIMER to &&username;
conn &&username/&&usernamepwd@localhost:1521/orcl
```

In the previous code, if you're not using a container/pluggable database, there's no need to alter your session to set it to a container. Also, if not using a container/pluggable database, then you can connect directly to the user you created via

```
SQL> conn &&username/&&usernamepwd
```

> **Note** You can set up whatever user (schema) you want to run the examples in this book. I picked the username YODA simply because I'm a Star Wars fan.

# Setting Up the SCOTT/TIGER Schema

The SCOTT/TIGER schema will sometimes already exist in your database. This schema is often used to show basic examples especially when you require a couple of tables with primary and foreign key relationships (the EMP and DEPT tables). There is nothing magic about using the SCOTT account. You could install the EMP/DEPT tables directly into your own database account if you wish.

Having said that, many of my examples in this book draw on the tables in the SCOTT schema. If you would like to be able to work along with them, you will need these tables. If you are working on a shared database, it would be advisable to install your own copy of these tables in some account other than SCOTT to avoid side effects caused by other users mucking about with the same data.

You can use the following script to create the SCOTT user in a pluggable database. You'll need to change the pluggable database name and connection string to match your environment:

```
sqlplus / as sysdba

alter session set container=orcl;

GRANT CONNECT,RESOURCE,UNLIMITED TABLESPACE TO SCOTT IDENTIFIED BY tiger;

CONNECT SCOTT/tiger@localhost:1521/orcl

CREATE TABLE DEPT
       (DEPTNO NUMBER(2) CONSTRAINT PK_DEPT PRIMARY KEY,
       DNAME VARCHAR2(14) ,
       LOC VARCHAR2(13) ) ;
CREATE TABLE EMP
       (EMPNO NUMBER(4) CONSTRAINT PK_EMP PRIMARY KEY,
       ENAME VARCHAR2(10),
       JOB VARCHAR2(9),
       MGR NUMBER(4),
       HIREDATE DATE,
       SAL NUMBER(7,2),
       COMM NUMBER(7,2),
       DEPTNO NUMBER(2) CONSTRAINT FK_DEPTNO REFERENCES DEPT);
```

INTRODUCTION

```
INSERT INTO DEPT VALUES
      (10,'ACCOUNTING','NEW YORK');
INSERT INTO DEPT VALUES (20,'RESEARCH','DALLAS');
INSERT INTO DEPT VALUES
      (30,'SALES','CHICAGO');
INSERT INTO DEPT VALUES
      (40,'OPERATIONS','BOSTON');
INSERT INTO EMP VALUES
(7369,'SMITH','CLERK',7902,to_date('17-12-1980','dd-mm-yyyy'),800,NULL,20);
INSERT INTO EMP VALUES
(7499,'ALLEN','SALESMAN',7698,to_date('20-2-1981','dd-mm-yyyy'),1600,300,30);
INSERT INTO EMP VALUES
(7521,'WARD','SALESMAN',7698,to_date('22-2-1981','dd-mm-yyyy'),1250,500,30);
INSERT INTO EMP VALUES
(7566,'JONES','MANAGER',7839,to_date('2-4-1981','dd-mm-yyyy'),2975,NULL,20);
INSERT INTO EMP VALUES
(7654,'MARTIN','SALESMAN',7698,to_date('28-9-1981','dd-mm-yyyy'),1250,1400,30);
INSERT INTO EMP VALUES
(7698,'BLAKE','MANAGER',7839,to_date('1-5-1981','dd-mm-yyyy'),2850,NULL,30);
INSERT INTO EMP VALUES
(7782,'CLARK','MANAGER',7839,to_date('9-6-1981','dd-mm-yyyy'),2450,NULL,10);
INSERT INTO EMP VALUES
(7788,'SCOTT','ANALYST',7566,to_date('13-JUL-87','dd-mm-rr')-85,3000,NULL,20);
INSERT INTO EMP VALUES
(7839,'KING','PRESIDENT',NULL,to_date('17-11-1981','dd-mm-yyyy'),5000,NULL,10);
INSERT INTO EMP VALUES
(7844,'TURNER','SALESMAN',7698,to_date('8-9-1981','dd-mm-yyyy'),1500,0,30);
INSERT INTO EMP VALUES
(7876,'ADAMS','CLERK',7788,to_date('13-JUL-87', 'dd-mm-rr')-51,1100,NULL,20);
INSERT INTO EMP VALUES
(7900,'JAMES','CLERK',7698,to_date('3-12-1981','dd-mm-yyyy'),950,NULL,30);
INSERT INTO EMP VALUES
(7902,'FORD','ANALYST',7566,to_date('3-12-1981','dd-mm-yyyy'),3000,NULL,20);
INSERT INTO EMP VALUES
(7934,'MILLER','CLERK',7782,to_date('23-1-1982','dd-mm-yyyy'),1300,NULL,10);
```

```
CREATE TABLE BONUS
      (
      ENAME VARCHAR2(10)        ,
      JOB VARCHAR2(9)   ,
      SAL NUMBER,
      COMM NUMBER
      ) ;
CREATE TABLE SALGRADE
      ( GRADE NUMBER,
      LOSAL NUMBER,
      HISAL NUMBER );
INSERT INTO SALGRADE VALUES (1,700,1200);
INSERT INTO SALGRADE VALUES (2,1201,1400);
INSERT INTO SALGRADE VALUES (3,1401,2000);
INSERT INTO SALGRADE VALUES (4,2001,3000);
INSERT INTO SALGRADE VALUES (5,3001,9999);
COMMIT;
EXIT
```

After running the prior code, you should be able to connect as SCOTT to your pluggable database and describe the tables, for example:

```
sqlplus scott/tiger@locahost:1521/orcl
```

```
SQL> desc dept
 Name                                      Null?    Type
 ----------------------------------------- -------- --------------------------
 DEPTNO                                    NOT NULL NUMBER(2)
 DNAME                                              VARCHAR2(14)
 LOC                                                VARCHAR2(13)
```

# Setting Up AUTOTRACE in SQL*Plus

AUTOTRACE is a facility within SQL*Plus to show us the explain plan of the queries we've executed and the resources they used. This book makes extensive use of this facility. There is more than one way to get AUTOTRACE configured. In many databases, AUTOTRACE will already be enabled. If that's the case, then (of course) there's no need to perform the setup steps described in the following subsections. You can check to see if AUTOTRACE is enabled by connecting to the database and running the following code:

```
SQL> set autotrace on explain
SQL> select 'x' from dual;

'
-
x
```

If you see output as shown next, then AUTOTRACE is already enabled:

```
Execution Plan
----------------------------------------------------------
Plan hash value: 1388734953

----------------------------------------------------------
| Id  | Operation        | Name | Rows | Cost (%CPU)| Time     |
----------------------------------------------------------
|   0 | SELECT STATEMENT |      |    1 |     2  (0)| 00:00:01 |
|   1 |   FAST DUAL      |      |    1 |     2  (0)| 00:00:01 |
----------------------------------------------------------
```

If you don't see the prior output, then proceed to the next section that details the initial setup.

## Initial Setup

AUTOTRACE relies on a table named PLAN_TABLE being available. The SYS schema contains a global temporary table named PLAN_TABLE$. All required privileges to this table have been granted to PUBLIC and there is a public synonym (named PLAN_TABLE that points to SYS.PLAN_TABLE$). This means any user can access this table.

---

**Note**  If you're using a very old version of Oracle, you can manually create the PLAN_TABLE by executing the $ORACLE_HOME/rdbms/admin/utlxplan.sql script.

---

You must also create and grant the PLUSTRACE role:

- `cd $ORACLE_HOME/sqlplus/admin`

- Log into SQL*Plus as SYS or as a user granted the SYSDBA privilege

- Run `@plustrce`

- Run `GRANT PLUSTRACE TO PUBLIC;`

You can replace `PUBLIC` in the `GRANT` command with some user if you want.

## Controlling the Report

You can automatically get a report on the execution path used by the SQL optimizer and the statement execution statistics. The report is generated after successful SQL DML (i.e., `SELECT`, `DELETE`, `UPDATE`, `MERGE`, and `INSERT`) statements. It is useful for monitoring and tuning the performance of these statements.

You can control the report by setting the AUTOTRACE system variable:

- `SET AUTOTRACE OFF`: No AUTOTRACE report is generated. This is the default.

- `SET AUTOTRACE ON EXPLAIN`: The AUTOTRACE report shows only the optimizer execution path.

- `SET AUTOTRACE ON STATISTICS`: The AUTOTRACE report shows only the SQL statement execution statistics.

- `SET AUTOTRACE ON`: The AUTOTRACE report includes both the optimizer execution path and the SQL statement execution statistics.

- `SET AUTOTRACE TRACEONLY`: Like `SET AUTOTRACE ON`, but suppresses the printing of the user's query output, if any.

- `SET AUTOTRACE TRACEONLY EXPLAIN`: Like `SET AUTOTRACE ON`, but suppresses the printing of the user's query output (if any), and also suppresses the execution statistics.

# Setting Up Statspack

Statspack is designed to be installed when connected as SYS (CONNECT/AS SYSDBA) or as a user granted the SYSDBA privilege. In many installations, installing Statspack will be a task that you must ask the DBA or administrators to perform. Installing Statspack is trivial. You simply run @spcreate.sql. This script will be found in $ORACLE_HOME/rdbms/admin and should be executed when connected as SYS via SQL*Plus.

You'll need to know the following three pieces of information before running the spcreate.sql script:

- The password you would like to use for the PERFSTAT schema that will be created

- The default tablespace you would like to use for PERFSTAT

- The temporary tablespace you would like to use for PERFSTAT

Running the script will look something like this:

```
$ sqlplus / as sysdba

SQL> @spcreate

Choose the PERFSTAT user's password
-----------------------------------
Not specifying a password will result in the installation FAILING
Enter value for perfstat_password:
... <output omitted for brevity> ...
```

The script will prompt you for the needed information as it executes. In the event you make a typo or inadvertently cancel the installation, you should use spdrop.sql found in $ORACLE_HOME/rdbms/admin to remove the user and installed views prior to attempting another install of Statspack. The Statspack installation will create a file called spcpkg. lis. You should review this file for any possible errors that might have occurred. The user, views, and PL/SQL code should install cleanly, however, as long as you supplied valid tablespace names (and didn't already have a user PERFSTAT).

---

**Tip** Statspack is documented in the following text file: $ORACLE_HOME/rdbms/admin/spdoc.txt.

---

# Big_Table

For examples throughout this book, I use a table called BIG_TABLE. Depending on which system I use, this table has between one record and four million records and varies in size from 200MB to 800MB. In all cases, the table structure is the same. To create BIG_TABLE, I wrote a script that does the following:

- Creates an empty table based on ALL_OBJECTS. This dictionary view is used to populate the BIG_TABLE.

- Makes this table NOLOGGING. This is optional. I did it for performance. Using NOLOGGING mode for a test table is safe; you won't use it in a production system, so features like Oracle Data Guard will not be enabled.

- Populates the table by seeding it with the contents of ALL_OBJECTS and then iteratively inserting into itself, approximately doubling its size on each iteration.

- Creates a primary key constraint on the table.

- Gathers statistics.

To build the BIG_TABLE table, you can run the following script at the SQL*Plus prompt and pass in the number of rows you want in the table. The script will stop when it hits that number of rows.

```
create table big_table
as
select rownum id, OWNER, OBJECT_NAME, SUBOBJECT_NAME, OBJECT_ID,
DATA_OBJECT_ID, OBJECT_TYPE, CREATED, LAST_DDL_TIME, TIMESTAMP,
STATUS, TEMPORARY, GENERATED, SECONDARY, NAMESPACE, EDITION_NAME
 from all_objects
 where 1=0
/
```

INTRODUCTION

```sql
alter table big_table nologging;

declare
 l_cnt number;
 l_rows number := &numrows;
begin
 insert /*+ append */
 into big_table
 select rownum id, OWNER, OBJECT_NAME, SUBOBJECT_NAME, OBJECT_ID,
 DATA_OBJECT_ID, OBJECT_TYPE, CREATED, LAST_DDL_TIME, TIMESTAMP,
 STATUS, TEMPORARY, GENERATED, SECONDARY, NAMESPACE, EDITION_NAME
 from all_objects
 where rownum <= &numrows;
 --
 l_cnt := sql%rowcount;
 commit;
 while (l_cnt < l_rows)
 loop
  insert /*+ APPEND */ into big_table
  select rownum+l_cnt,OWNER, OBJECT_NAME, SUBOBJECT_NAME, OBJECT_ID,
  DATA_OBJECT_ID, OBJECT_TYPE, CREATED, LAST_DDL_TIME, TIMESTAMP,
  STATUS, TEMPORARY, GENERATED, SECONDARY, NAMESPACE, EDITION_NAME
  from big_table a
  where rownum <= l_rows-l_cnt;
  l_cnt := l_cnt + sql%rowcount;
  commit;
 end loop;
end;
/

alter table big_table add constraint
big_table_pk primary key(id);

exec dbms_stats.gather_table_stats( user, 'BIG_TABLE', estimate_percent=> 1);
```

I estimated baseline statistics on the table. The index associated with the primary key will have statistics computed automatically when it is created.

## Coding Conventions

The one coding convention I use in this book that I would like to point out is how I name variables in PL/SQL code. For example, consider a package body like this:

```
create or replace package body my_pkg
as
  g_variable varchar2(25);

  procedure p( p_variable in varchar2 )
  is
   l_variable varchar2(25);
  begin
   null;
  end;
end;
/
```

Here, I have three variables: a global package variable, G_VARIABLE; a formal parameter to the procedure, P_VARIABLE; and a local variable, L_VARIABLE. I name my variables after the scope they are contained in. All globals begin with G_, parameters with P_, and local variables with L_. The main reason for this is to distinguish PL/SQL variables from columns in a database table. For example, a procedure such as the following would always print out every row in the EMP table where ENAME is not null:

```
create procedure p( ENAME in varchar2 )
as
begin
  for x in ( select * from emp where ename = ENAME ) loop
   Dbms_output.put_line( x.empno );
  end loop;
end;
```

SQL sees ename = ENAME and compares the ENAME column to itself (of course). We could use ename = P.ENAME; that is, qualify the reference to the PL/SQL variable with the procedure name; but this is too easy to forget, leading to errors.

I just always name my variables after the scope. That way, I can easily distinguish parameters from local variables and global variables, in addition to removing any ambiguity with respect to column names and variable names.

# CHAPTER 1

# Getting Started

I spend a great deal of time working with Oracle technology. I'm often called in to assist with diagnosing and resolving performance issues. Many of the applications I've worked with have experienced problems in part due to the developers (and to some degree database administrators) treating the database as if it was a black box. In other words, the team hadn't spent any time becoming familiar with the database technology that was at the core of their application. In this regard, a fundamental piece of advice I have is *do not* treat the database as a nebulous piece of software to which you simply feed queries and receive results. The database is the most critical piece of most applications. Trying to ignore its internal workings and database vendor–specific features results in architectural decisions from which high performance cannot be achieved.

Having said that, at the core of understanding how a database works is a solid comprehension of how its transactional control mechanisms are implemented. The key to gaining maximum utility from an Oracle database is based on understanding how Oracle concurrently manages transactions while simultaneously providing consistent point-in-time results to queries. This knowledge forms the foundation from which you can make intelligent decisions resulting in highly concurrent and well-performing applications. Also important is that every database vendor implements transaction and concurrency control features differently. If you don't recognize this, your database will give "wrong" answers, and you will have large contention issues, leading to poor performance and limited scalability.

© Darl Kuhn and Thomas Kyte 2021
D. Kuhn and T. Kyte, *Oracle Database Transactions and Locking Revealed*,
https://doi.org/10.1007/978-1-4842-6425-6_1

# Background

There are several topics underpinning how Oracle handles concurrent access to data. I've divided these into the following categories:

- Locking

- Concurrency Control

- Multiversioning

- Transactions

- Redo and Undo

These features are the focus of this book. Since these concepts are all interrelated, it's difficult to pick which topic to discuss first. For example, in order to discuss locking, you must understand what a transaction is, and vice versa. Understanding these topics is a prerequisite for being able to successfully implement scalable and robust applications utilizing Oracle databases. The order in which these are introduced here in this chapter is also the order these topics are covered in subsequent chapters in the book.

# Locking

The database uses *locks* to ensure that, at most, one transaction is modifying a given piece of data at any given time. Basically, locks are the mechanism that allows for concurrency—without some locking model to prevent concurrent updates to the same row, for example, multiuser access would not be possible in a database. However, if overused or used improperly, locks can inhibit concurrency. If you or the database itself locks data unnecessarily, fewer people will be able to concurrently perform operations. Thus, understanding what locking is and how it works in your database is vital if you are to develop a scalable, correct application.

What is also vital is that you understand that each database implements locking differently. Some have page-level locking, others row-level; some implementations escalate locks from row level to page level, some do not; some use read locks, others don't; some implement serializable transactions via locking and others via read-consistent views of data (no locks). These small differences can balloon into huge performance issues or downright bugs in your application if you don't understand how they work.

The following points sum up Oracle's locking policy:

- Oracle locks data at the row level on modification. There is no lock escalation to a block or table level.

- Oracle never locks data just to read it. There are no locks placed on rows of data by simple reads.

- A writer of data does not block a reader of data. Let me repeat: *reads* are not blocked by *writes*. This is fundamentally different from many other databases, where reads are blocked by writes. While this sounds like an extremely positive attribute (and it generally is), if you do not understand this thoroughly and you attempt to enforce integrity constraints in your application via application logic, *you are most likely doing it incorrectly.*

- A writer of data is blocked only when another writer of data has already locked the row it was going after. A reader of data never blocks a writer of data.

You must take these facts into consideration when developing your application and you must also realize that this policy is unique to Oracle; every database has subtle differences in its approach to locking. Even if you go with lowest common denominator SQL in your applications, the locking and concurrency control models employed by each vendor assure something will be different. A developer who does not understand how his or her database handles concurrency will certainly encounter data integrity issues. This is particularly common when a developer moves from another database to Oracle, or vice versa, and neglects to take the differing concurrency mechanisms into account in the application. Chapters 2 and 3 in this book will provide you an in-depth technical discussion of locking.

# Concurrency Control

*Concurrency control* ensures that no two transactions modify the same piece of data at the same time. This is an area where databases differentiate themselves. Concurrency control is an area that sets a database apart from a file system and databases apart from each other. As a programmer, it is vital that your database application works correctly under concurrent access conditions, and yet time and time again, this is something people fail to test. Techniques that work well if everything happens consecutively do not necessarily work so well when everyone does them simultaneously. If you don't have a good grasp of how your particular database implements concurrency control mechanisms, then you will

- Corrupt the integrity of your data

- Have applications run slower than they should with a small number of users

- Decrease your applications' ability to scale to a large number of users and transactions

Notice I don't say, "you might…" or "you run the risk of…," but rather that invariably you *will* do these things. You will do these things without even realizing it. Without correct concurrency control, you will corrupt the integrity of your database because something that works in isolation will not work as you expect in a multiuser situation. Your application will run slower than it should because you'll end up waiting for data. Your application will lose its ability to scale because of locking and contention issues. As the queues to access a resource get longer, the wait gets longer and longer.

An analogy here would be a backup at a tollbooth. If cars arrive in an orderly, predictable fashion, one after the other, there won't ever be a backup. If many cars arrive simultaneously, queues start to form. Furthermore, the waiting time does not increase linearly with the number of cars at the booth. After a certain point, considerable additional time is spent "managing" the people who are waiting in line, as well as servicing them (the parallel in the database would be context switching).

Concurrency issues are the hardest to track down; the problem is similar to debugging a multithreaded program. The program may work fine in the controlled, artificial environment of the debugger, but it crashes horribly in the real world. For example, under race conditions, you find that two threads can end up modifying the same data structure simultaneously. These kinds of bugs are extremely difficult to track down and fix. If you only test your application in isolation and then deploy it to dozens of concurrent users, you are likely to be (painfully) exposed to an undetected concurrency issue.

So, if you are used to the way other databases work with respect to query consistency and concurrency, or you never had to grapple with such concepts (i.e., you have no real database experience), you can now see how understanding how this works will be important to you. In order to maximize Oracle's potential, and to implement correct code, you *need* to understand these issues as they pertain to Oracle—not how they are implemented in other databases. Oracle concurrency control internals are covered in detail in Chapter 4.

# Multiversioning

Multiversioning is related to concurrency control, as it forms the foundation for Oracle's concurrency control mechanism. Oracle operates a multiversion, read-consistent concurrency model. In Chapter 4, we'll cover the technical aspects in more detail, but, essentially, it is the mechanism by which Oracle provides for the following:

- *Read-consistent queries*: Queries that produce consistent results with respect to a point in time.

- *Nonblocking queries*: Queries are never blocked by writers of data, as they are in other databases.

These are two especially important concepts in the Oracle database. The term *multiversioning* basically describes Oracle's ability to simultaneously maintain multiple versions of the data in the database. The term *read consistency* reflects the fact that a query in Oracle will return results from a consistent point in time. Every block used by a query will be "as of" the same exact point in time—even if it was modified or locked while you performed your query.

If you understand how multiversioning and read consistency work together, you will always understand the answers you get from the database. Before we explore in a little more detail how Oracle does this, we'll *demonstrate* how Oracle implements multiversioning. Table 1-1 contains the timing and operations of this demonstration.

*Table 1-1.*  *Demonstrating Multiversioning in Oracle*

| Time | Operation |
| --- | --- |
| Time 1 | Create table T and populate it with data. |
| Time 2 | Open cursor X for select from table T. |
| Time 3 | Delete all rows from table T and commit. |
| Time 4 | Select from table T showing no rows are in the table. |
| Time 5 | Fetch data from cursor X showing rows as they existed in table T at time 2. |

**Note**    In the following examples, you may not get the exact results as shown here. That's to be expected depending on what version of the database you have installed and what features and components are enabled.

In the following code, we first connect to the root container as SYS and perform the operations described in Table 1-1:

```
sqlplus / as sysdba

SQL> -- Time 1
SQL> create table t as select username from all_users where username like
'SYS%';
Table created.

SQL> -- Time 2
SQL> set autoprint off
SQL> variable x refcursor;
SQL> begin
        open :x for select * from t;
        end;
        /
PL/SQL procedure successfully completed.

SQL> -- Time 3
SQL> declare
        pragma autonomous_transaction;
        -- you could do this in another
        -- sqlplus session as well, the
        -- effect would be identical
    begin
        delete from t;
          commit;
      end;
        /
  PL/SQL procedure successfully completed.
```

```
SQL> -- Time 4
SQL> select * from t;
no rows selected

SQL -- Time 5
SQL> print x
USERNAME
---------------
SYS
SYSTEM
SYSBACKUP
SYSDG
SYSKM
SYSRAC
SYS$UMF
SYSMAN

8 rows selected.
```

At time 1, we created a test table, T, and loaded it with some data from the ALL_USERS table. At time 2, we opened a cursor on that table. We fetched *no data* from that cursor, we just opened the cursor and kept it open.

---

**Note**  Bear in mind that Oracle does not "pre-answer" the query. It does not copy the data anywhere when you open a cursor—imagine how long it would take to open a cursor on a one-billion-row table if it did. The cursor opens instantly and it answers the query as it goes along. In other words, the cursor just reads data from the table as you fetch from it.

---

At time 3, the same session (or maybe another session would do this; it would work as well), we proceed to delete all data from the table. We even go as far as to COMMIT work on that delete action.

After committing, at time 4 we select from table T and the rows are gone—but are they? In fact, they are retrievable via the cursor (or via a FLASHBACK query using the AS OF clause). The fact is that the resultset returned to us at time 5 by the PRINT command was preordained at the point in time we opened the cursor. We had not touched a single block of data in that table during the open, but the answer was already fixed in stone. We have no way of knowing what the answer will be until we fetch the data; however, the result is immutable from our cursor's perspective. It is not that Oracle copied all of the preceding data to some other location when we opened the cursor; it was actually the DELETE command that preserved our data for us by placing it (the before image copies of rows as they existed before the DELETE) into a data area called an undo or rollback segment (more on this shortly).

# Transactions

A *transaction* comprises a unit of database work. Transactions are a core feature of database technology. They are part of what distinguishes a database from a file system. And yet, they are often misunderstood and many developers do not even know that they are accidentally not using them.

Transactions take the database from one consistent state to the next consistent state. When you issue a COMMIT, you are assured that all your changes have been successfully saved and that any data integrity checks and rules have been validated. Oracle's transactional control architecture ensures that consistent data is provided every time, under highly concurrent data access conditions. Transactions are the focus of Chapter 5.

# Redo and Undo

Key to Oracle's durability (recovery) mechanism is redo, and core to multiversioning (read consistency) is undo. Oracle uses *redo* to capture how the transaction changed the data; this allows you to replay the transaction (in the event of an instance crash or a media failure). Oracle uses *undo* to store the before image of a modified block; this allows you to reverse or roll back a transaction. Undo also is a key part of implementing read consistency. Recall previously in the chapter when we demonstrated how Oracle implements multiversioning. Figure 1-1 shows how read consistency is implemented through accessing undo.

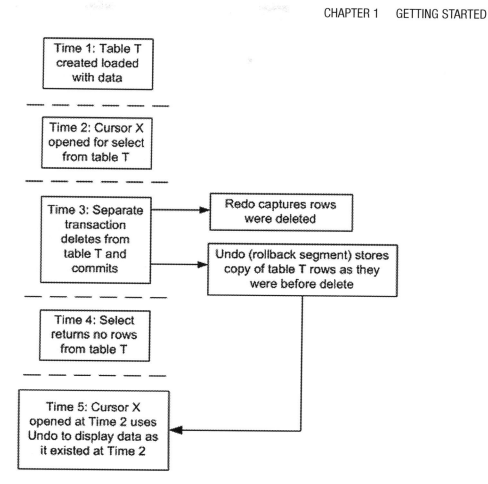

**Figure 1-1.** *Implementing read consistency via undo*

It can be said that developers do not need to understand the details of redo and undo as much as DBAs, but developers do need to know the role they play in the database. It's vital to understand how redo and undo are related to a COMMIT or ROLLBACK statement. It's also important to understand that generating redo and undo consumes database resources, and it's essential to be able to measure and manage that resource consumption. Chapters 6 and 7 do a deep dive into redo and undo internals.

# Summary

In the following chapters, we'll discover that different databases have different ways of doing things. What works well in SQL Server may not work as well in Oracle and vice versa. We'll also see that understanding how Oracle implements locking, concurrency control, and transactions is absolutely vital to the success of your application. This book first discusses Oracle's basic approach to these issues, the types of locks that can be applied (DML, DDL, and latches), and the problems that can arise if locking is not implemented carefully (deadlocking, blocking, and escalation).

We'll also explore my favorite Oracle feature, multiversioning, and how it affects concurrency controls and the very design of an application. Here we will see that all databases are *not* created equal and that their very implementation can have an impact on the design of our applications. We'll start by reviewing the various transaction isolation levels as defined by the ANSI SQL standard and see how they map to the Oracle implementation (as well as how the other databases map to this standard). Then we'll look at what implications multiversioning, the feature that allows Oracle to provide nonblocking reads in the database, might have for us.

This book also examines how transactions should be used in Oracle and exposes some bad habits that may have been picked up when developing with other databases. In particular, we look at the implications of atomicity and how it affects statements in Oracle. We also discuss transaction control statements (COMMIT, SAVEPOINT, and ROLLBACK), integrity constraints, distributed transactions (the two-phase commit, or 2PC), and autonomous transactions.

The last few chapters of this book delve into redo and undo. After first defining redo, we examine what exactly a COMMIT does. We discuss how to find out how much redo is being generated and how to significantly reduce the amount of redo generated for certain operations using the NOLOGGING clause. We also investigate redo generation in relation to issues such as block cleanout and log contention. In the undo section of the chapter, we examine the role of undo data and the operations that generate the most/least undo. Finally, we'll look at common techniques to troubleshoot issues such as the infamous ORA-01555: snapshot too old error, blocking, and locking sessions, possible causes of these issues, and how to avoid associated problems.

# CHAPTER 2

# Locking and Blocking

One of the key challenges in developing multiuser, database-driven applications is to maximize concurrent access and, at the same time, ensure that each user is able to read and modify the data in a consistent fashion. The locking mechanisms that allow this to happen are key features of any database, and Oracle excels in providing them. However, Oracle's implementation of these features is specific to Oracle—just as SQL Server's implementation is to SQL Server—and it is up to you, the application developer, to ensure that when your application performs data manipulation, it uses these mechanisms correctly. If you fail to do so, your application will behave in an unexpected way, and inevitably the integrity of your data will be compromised.

---

**Note** Ensure that you review the material in the "Setting Up Your Environment" section of the "Introduction" of this book. It contains setup information that lays the foundation for the code used in many examples in this book such as the SCOTT and YODA schemas.

---

## What Are Locks?

*Locks* are mechanisms used to regulate concurrent access to a shared resource. Note how I used the term "shared resource" and not "database row." It is true that Oracle locks table data at the row level, but it also uses locks at many other levels to provide concurrent access to various resources. For example, while a stored procedure is executing, the procedure itself is locked in a mode that allows others to execute it, but it will not permit another user to alter that instance of that stored procedure in any way. Locks are used in the database to permit concurrent access to these shared resources while at the same time providing data integrity and consistency.

© Darl Kuhn and Thomas Kyte 2021
D. Kuhn and T. Kyte, *Oracle Database Transactions and Locking Revealed*,
https://doi.org/10.1007/978-1-4842-6425-6_2

In a single-user database, locks are not necessary. There is, by definition, only one user modifying the information. However, when multiple users are accessing and modifying data or data structures, it is crucial to have a mechanism in place to prevent concurrent modification of the same piece of information. This is what locking is all about.

It is very important to understand that there are as many ways to implement locking in a database as there are databases. Just because you have experience with the locking model of one particular relational database management system (RDBMS) does not mean you know everything about locking. For example, before I got heavily involved with Oracle, I used other databases including Sybase, Microsoft SQL Server, and Informix. All three of these databases provide locking mechanisms for concurrency control, but there are deep and fundamental differences in the way locking is implemented in each one.

To demonstrate this, I'll outline my progression from a Sybase SQL Server developer to an Informix user and finally to an Oracle developer. This happened many years ago, and the SQL Server fans out there will tell me "But we have row-level locking now!" It is true: SQL Server may now use row-level locking, but the way it is implemented is totally different from the way it is done in Oracle. It is a comparison between apples and oranges, and that is the key point.

As a SQL Server programmer (many years ago), I would hardly ever consider the possibility of multiple users inserting data into a table concurrently. It was something that just didn't often happen in that database. At that time, SQL Server provided only for page-level locking, and since all the data tended to be inserted into the last page of nonclustered tables, concurrent inserts by two users was simply not going to happen.

---

**Note**    A SQL Server clustered table (a table that has a clustered index) is in some regard similar to, but very different from, an Oracle cluster. SQL Server used to only support page (block)-level locking; if every row inserted was to go to the "end" of the table, you would never have had concurrent inserts or concurrent transactions in that database. The clustered index in SQL Server was used to insert rows all over the table, in sorted order by the cluster key, and as such improved concurrency in that database.

---

Exactly the same issue affected concurrent updates (since an UPDATE was really a DELETE followed by an INSERT in SQL Server). Perhaps this is why SQL Server, by default, commits or rolls back immediately after execution of each statement, compromising transactional integrity in an attempt to gain higher concurrency.

So in most cases, with page-level locking, multiple users could not simultaneously modify the same table. Compounding this was the fact that while a table modification was in progress, many queries were also effectively blocked against that table. If I tried to query a table and needed a page that was locked by an update, I waited (and waited and waited). The locking mechanism was so poor that providing support for transactions that took more than a second was deadly—the entire database would appear to freeze. I learned a lot of bad habits as a result. I learned that transactions were "bad" and that you ought to commit rapidly and never hold locks on data. Concurrency came at the expense of consistency. You either wanted to get it right or get it fast. I came to believe that you couldn't have both.

When I moved on to Informix, things were better, but not by much. As long as I remembered to create a table with row-level locking enabled, then I could actually have two people simultaneously insert data into that table. Unfortunately, this concurrency came at a high price. Row-level locks in the Informix implementation were expensive, both in terms of time and memory. It took time to acquire and unacquire (release) them, and each lock consumed real memory. Also, the total number of locks available to the system had to be computed prior to starting the database. If you exceeded that number, you were just out of luck. Consequently, most tables were created with page-level locking anyway, and, as with SQL Server, both row- and page-level locks would stop a query in its tracks. As a result, I found that once again I would want to commit as fast as I could. The bad habits I picked up using SQL Server were simply reinforced, and furthermore, I learned to treat a lock as a very scarce resource—something to be coveted. I learned that you should manually escalate locks from row level to table level to try to avoid acquiring too many of them and bringing the system down, and bring it down I did—many times.

When I started using Oracle, I didn't really bother reading the manuals to find out how locking worked in this particular database. After all, I had been using databases for quite a while and was considered something of an expert in this field (in addition to Sybase, SQL Server, and Informix, I had used Ingress, DB2, Gupta SQLBase, and a variety of other databases). I had fallen into the trap of believing that I knew how things *should* work, so I thought of course they *would* work in that way. *I was wrong in a big way.*

It was during a benchmark that I discovered just how wrong I was. In the early days of these databases (around 1992/1993), it was common for the vendors to benchmark for really large procurements to see who could do the work the fastest, the easiest, and with the most features.

The benchmark was between Informix, Sybase SQL Server, and Oracle. Oracle went first. Their technical people came on-site, read through the benchmark specs, and started setting it up. The first thing I noticed was that the technicians from Oracle were going to use a database table to record their timings, even though we were going to have many dozens of connections doing work, each of which would frequently need to insert and update data in this log table. Not only that, but they were going to *read* the log table during the benchmark as well! Being a nice guy, I pulled one of the Oracle technicians aside to ask him if they were crazy. Why would they purposely introduce another point of contention into the system? Wouldn't the benchmark processes all tend to serialize around their operations on this single table? Would they jam the benchmark by trying to read from this table as others were heavily modifying it? Why would they want to introduce all of these extra locks that they would need to manage? I had dozens of "Why would you even consider that?"–type questions. The technical folks from Oracle thought I was a little daft at that point. That is, until I pulled up a window into either Sybase SQL Server or Informix, and showed them the effects of two people inserting into a table, or someone trying to query a table with others inserting rows (the query returns zero rows per second). The differences between the way Oracle does it and the way almost every other database does it are phenomenal—they are night and day.

Needless to say, neither the Informix nor the SQL Server technicians were too keen on the database log table approach during their attempts. They preferred to record their timings to flat files in the operating system. The Oracle people left with a better understanding of exactly how to compete against Sybase SQL Server and Informix: just ask the audience "How many rows per second does your current database return when data is locked?" and take it from there.

The moral to this story is twofold. First, *all databases are fundamentally different.* Second, when designing an application for a new database platform, you must make no assumptions about how that database works. *You must approach each new database as if you had never used a database before.* Things you would do in one database are either not necessary or simply won't work in another database.

In Oracle, you will learn that

- Transactions are what databases are all about. They are a good thing.

- You should defer committing until the correct moment. You should not do it quickly to avoid stressing the system, as it does not stress the system to have long or large transactions. The rule is *commit when you must, and not before.* Your transactions should only be as small or as large as your business logic dictates.

- You should hold locks on data as long as you need to. They are tools for you to use, not things to be avoided. Locks are not a scarce resource. Conversely, you should hold locks on data only as long as you need to. Locks may not be scarce, but they can prevent other sessions from modifying information.

- There is no overhead involved with row-level locking in Oracle— *none*. Whether you have 1 row lock or 1,000,000 row locks, the number of resources dedicated to locking this information will be the same. Sure, you'll do a lot more work modifying 1,000,000 rows rather than 1 row, but the number of resources needed to lock 1,000,000 rows is the same as for 1 row; it is a fixed constant.

- You should never escalate a lock (e.g., use a table lock instead of row locks) because it would be "better for the system." In Oracle, it won't be better for the system—it will save no resources. There are times to use table locks, such as in a batch process, when you know you will update the entire table and you do not want other sessions to lock rows on you. But you are not using a table lock to make it easier for the system by avoiding having to allocate row locks; you are using a table lock to ensure you can gain access to all of the resources your batch program needs in this case.

- Concurrency and consistency can be achieved simultaneously. You can get it fast and correct, every time. *Readers of data are not blocked by writers of data. Writers of data are not blocked by readers of data.* This is one of the fundamental differences between Oracle and most other relational databases.

Before we discuss the various types of locks that Oracle uses (in Chapter 3), it is useful to look at some locking issues, many of which arise from badly designed applications that do not make correct use (or make no use) of the database's locking mechanisms.

# Lost Updates

A lost update is a classic database problem. Actually, it is a problem in all multiuser computer environments. Simply put, a lost update occurs when the following events occur, in the order presented here:

1.  A transaction in Session1 retrieves (queries) a row of data into local memory and displays it to an end user, User1.

2.  Another transaction in Session2 retrieves that same row, but displays the data to a different end user, User2.

3.  User1, using the application, modifies that row and has the application update the database and commit. Session1's transaction is now complete.

4.  User2 modifies that row also and has the application update the database and commit. Session2's transaction is now complete.

This process is referred to as a *lost update* because all of the changes made in Step 3 will be lost. Consider, for example, an employee update screen that allows a user to change an address, work number, and so on. The application itself is very simple: a small search screen to generate a list of employees and then the ability to drill down into the details of each employee. This should be a piece of cake. So, we write the application with no locking on our part, just simple SELECT and UPDATE commands.

Then, an end user (User1) navigates to the details screen, changes an address on the screen, clicks Save, and receives confirmation that the update was successful. Fine, except that when User1 checks the record the next day to send out a tax form, the old address is still listed. How could that have happened? Unfortunately, it can happen all too easily. In this case, another end user (User2) queried the same record just after User1 did—after User1 read the data, but before User1 modified it. Then, after User2 queried the data, User1 performed her update, received confirmation, and even requeried to see the change for herself. However, User2 then updated the work telephone number field and clicked Save, blissfully unaware of the fact that he just overwrote User1's changes to the address field with the old data! The reason this can happen *in this case* is that the application developer wrote the program such that when one particular field is updated, all fields for that record are refreshed (simply because it's easier to update all the columns instead of figuring out exactly which columns changed and only updating those).

Note that for this to happen, User1 and User2 didn't even need to be working on the record at the exact same time. They simply needed to be working on the record at *about* the same time.

I've seen this database issue crop up time and again when GUI programmers with little or no database training are given the task of writing a database application. They get a working knowledge of SELECT, INSERT, UPDATE, and DELETE and set about writing the application. When the resulting application behaves in the manner just described, it completely destroys a user's confidence in it, especially since it seems so random, so sporadic, and totally irreproducible in a controlled environment (leading the developer to believe it must be user error).

Many tools, such as Oracle Forms and APEX, transparently protect you from this behavior by ensuring the record is unchanged from the time you query it and locked before you make any changes to it (known as *optimistic locking*); but many others (such as a handwritten Visual Basic or a Java program) do not. What the tools that protect you do behind the scenes, or what the developers must do themselves, is use one of two types of locking strategies: *pessimistic* or *optimistic*.

# Pessimistic Locking

The pessimistic locking method would be put into action the instant before a user modifies a value on the screen. For example, a row lock would be placed as soon as the user indicates his intention to perform an update on a specific row that he has selected and has visible on the screen (by clicking a button on the screen, say). That row lock would *persist* until the application applied the user's modifications to the row in the database and committed.

Pessimistic locking is useful only in a stateful or connected environment—that is, one where your application has a continual connection to the database and you are the only one using that connection for at least the life of your transaction. This was the prevalent way of doing things in the early to mid-1990s with client/server applications. Every application would get a direct connection to the database to be used solely by that application instance. This method of connecting, in a stateful fashion, has become less common (though it is not extinct), especially with the advent of application servers in the mid to late 1990s.

Assuming you are using a stateful connection, you might have an application that queries the data without locking anything. Let's connect to the SCOTT schema in the pluggable database ORCL and demonstrate this:

```
sqlplus scott/tiger@localhost:1521/orcl
```

```
SQL> select empno, ename, sal from emp where deptno = 10;
```

```
    EMPNO ENAME            SAL
---------- ---------- ----------
      7782 CLARK           2450
      7839 KING            5000
      7934 MILLER          1300
```

---

**Note**    The SCOTT and YODA schemas are used extensively in code examples throughout this book. Reference the front matter of this book for examples of how to create these schemas.

---

Eventually, the user picks a row she would like to update. Let's say in this case, she chooses to update the MILLER row. Our application will, at that point (before the user makes any changes on the screen but after the row has been out of the database for a while), bind the values the user selected so we can query the database and make sure the data hasn't been changed yet. In SQL*Plus, to simulate the bind calls the application would make, we can issue the following:

```
SQL> variable empno number
SQL> variable ename varchar2(20)
SQL> variable sal number
SQL> exec :empno := 7934; :ename := 'MILLER'; :sal := 1300;
PL/SQL procedure successfully completed.
```

Now in addition to simply querying the values and verifying that they have not been changed, we are going to lock the row using FOR UPDATE NOWAIT. The application will execute the following query:

```
SQL> select empno, ename, sal
       from emp
      where empno = :empno
        and decode( ename, :ename, 1 ) = 1
        and decode( sal, :sal, 1 ) = 1
      for update nowait
      /

    EMPNO ENAME              SAL
---------- ---------- ----------
     7934 MILLER            1300
```

---

**Note**   Why did we use "decode( column, :bind_variable, 1 ) = 1"? It is simply a shorthand way of expressing "where (column = :bind_variable OR (column is NULL and :bind_variable is NULL)". You could code either approach, the decode() is just more compact in this case, and since NULL = NULL is never true (nor false!) in SQL, one of the two approaches would be necessary if either of the columns permitted NULLs.

---

The application supplies values for the bind variables from the data on the screen (in this case 7934, MILLER, and 1300) and requeries this same row from the database, this time locking the row against updates by other sessions; hence, this approach is called *pessimistic* locking. We lock the row before we attempt to update because we doubt—*we are pessimistic*—that the row will remain unchanged otherwise.

Since all tables *should* have a primary key (the preceding SELECT will retrieve at most one record since it includes the primary key, EMPNO) and primary keys should be immutable (we should never update them), we'll get one of three outcomes from this statement:

- If the underlying data has not changed, we will get our MILLER row back, and this row will be locked from updates (but not reads) by others.

- If another user is in the process of modifying that row, we will get an
  ORA-00054 resource busy error. We must wait for the other user to
  finish with it.

- If, in the time between selecting the data and indicating our intention
  to update, someone has already changed the row, then we will get
  zero rows back. That implies the data on our screen is stale. To avoid
  the lost update scenario previously described, the application needs
  to *requery* and lock the data before allowing the end user to modify
  it. With pessimistic locking in place, when User2 attempts to update
  the telephone field, the application would now recognize that the
  address field had been changed and would *requery* the data. Thus,
  User2 would not overwrite User1's change with the old data in that
  field.

Once we have locked the row successfully, the application will bind the new values,
issue the update, and commit the changes:

```
SQL> update emp
        set ename = :ename, sal = :sal
        where empno = :empno;

1 row updated.

SQL> commit;
Commit complete.
```

We have now very safely changed that row. It is not possible for us to overwrite
someone else's changes, as we verified the data did not change between when we initially
read it out and when we locked it—our verification made sure no one else changed it
before we did, and our lock ensures no one else can change it while we are working with it.

# Optimistic Locking

The second method, referred to as *optimistic* locking, defers all locking up to the point right
before the update is performed. In other words, we will modify the information on the
screen without a lock being acquired. We are *optimistic* that the data will not be changed
by some other user; hence, we wait until the very last moment to find out if we are right.

This locking method works in all environments, but it does increase the probability that a user performing an update will lose. That is, when that user goes to update her row, she finds that the data has been modified, and she has to start over.

One popular implementation of optimistic locking is to keep the old and new values in the application and, upon updating the data, use an update like this:

```
Update table
   Set column1 = :new_column1, column2 = :new_column2, ....
Where primary_key = :primary_key
   And decode( column1, :old_column1, 1 ) = 1
   And decode( column2, :old_column2, 1 ) = 1
   ...
```

Here, we are optimistic that the data doesn't get changed. In this case, if our update updates one row, we got lucky; the data didn't change between the time we read it and the time we got around to submitting the update. If we update zero rows, we lose; someone else changed the data and now we must figure out what we want to do to continue in the application. Should we make the end user rekey the transaction after querying the new values for the row (potentially causing the user frustration, as there is a chance the row will have changed yet again)? Should we try to merge the values of the two updates by performing update conflict-resolution based on business rules (lots of code)?

The preceding UPDATE will, in fact, avoid a lost update, but it does stand a chance of being blocked, hanging while it waits for an UPDATE of that row by another session to complete. If all your applications use optimistic locking, then using a straight UPDATE is generally OK since rows are locked for a very short duration as updates are applied and committed. However, if some of your applications use pessimistic locking, which will hold locks on rows for relatively long periods of time, or if there is any application (such as a batch process) that might lock rows for a long period of time (more than a second or two is considered long), then you should consider using a SELECT FOR UPDATE NOWAIT instead to verify the row was not changed, and lock it immediately prior to the UPDATE to avoid getting blocked by another session.

There are many methods of implementing optimistic concurrency control. We've discussed one whereby the application will store all of the before images of the row in the application itself. In the following sections, we'll explore two others, namely:

- Using a special column that is maintained by a database trigger or application code to tell us the "version" of the record

- Using a checksum or hash that was computed using the original data

21

# Optimistic Locking Using a Version Column

This is a simple implementation that involves adding a single column to each database table you wish to protect from lost updates. This column is generally either a NUMBER or DATE/TIMESTAMP column. It is typically maintained via a row trigger on the table, which is responsible for incrementing the NUMBER column or updating the DATE/TIMESTAMP column every time a row is modified.

---

**Note**    I said it was typically maintained via a row trigger. I did not, however, say that was the best way or right way to maintain it. I would personally prefer this column be maintained by the UPDATE statement itself, not via a trigger because triggers that are not absolutely necessary (as this one is) should be avoided. For background on why I avoid triggers, refer to my "The Trouble with Triggers" article from *Oracle Magazine*, found on the Oracle Technology Network at https://blogs.oracle.com/oraclemagazine/the-trouble-with-triggers.

---

The application you want to implement optimistic concurrency control would need only to save the value of this additional column, not all of the before images of the other columns. The application would only need to verify that the value of this column in the database at the point when the update is requested matches the value that was initially read out. If these values are the same, then the row has not been updated.

Let's look at an implementation of optimistic locking connecting to the YODA user and creating a copy of the SCOTT.DEPT table. We could use the following Data Definition Language (DDL) to create the table:

```
sqlplus yoda/foo@localhost:1521/orcl

SQL> create table dept
   ( deptno     number(2),
     dname      varchar2(14),
     loc        varchar2(13),
     last_mod   timestamp with time zone
                default systimestamp
                not null,
     constraint dept_pk primary key(deptno)
   )
 /
```

Table created.

Then we INSERT a copy of the DEPT data into this table:

```
SQL> insert into dept( deptno, dname, loc )
        select deptno, dname, loc
        from scott.dept;

4 rows created.


SQL> commit;
Commit complete.
```

That code re-creates the DEPT table, but with an additional LAST_MOD column that uses the TIMESTAMP WITH TIME ZONE data type. We have defined this column to be NOT NULL so that it must be populated, and its default value is the current system time.

This TIMESTAMP data type has the highest precision available in Oracle, typically going down to the microsecond (millionth of a second). For an application that involves user think time, this level of precision on the TIMESTAMP is more than sufficient, as it is highly unlikely that the process of the database retrieving a row and a human looking at it, modifying it, and issuing the update back to the database could take place within a fraction of a second. The odds of two people reading and modifying the same row in the same fraction of a second are very small indeed.

Next, we need a way of maintaining this value. We have two choices: either the application can maintain the LAST_MOD column by setting its value to SYSTIMESTAMP when it updates a record, or a trigger/stored procedure can maintain it. Having the application maintain LAST_MOD is definitely more performant than a trigger-based approach, since a trigger will add additional processing on top of that already done by Oracle. However, this does mean that you are relying on all of the applications to maintain LAST_MOD consistently in all places that they modify this table. So, if each application is responsible for maintaining this field, it needs to consistently verify that the LAST_MOD column was not changed and set the LAST_MOD column to the current SYSTIMESTAMP. For example, if an application queries the row where DEPTNO=10:

```
SQL> variable deptno   number
SQL> variable dname    varchar2(14)
SQL> variable loc      varchar2(13)
SQL> variable last_mod varchar2(50)
```

```
SQL>
SQL> begin
        :deptno := 10;
        select dname, loc, to_char( last_mod, 'DD-MON-YYYY HH.MI.SSXFF AM TZR' )
          into :dname,:loc,:last_mod
          from dept
        where deptno = :deptno;
    end;
    /
PL/SQL procedure successfully completed.
```

which we can see is currently

```
SQL> select :deptno dno, :dname dname, :loc loc, :last_mod lm from dual;

DNO     DNAME        LOC       LM
------  -----------  --------  ----------------------------------------
10      ACCOUNTING   NEW YORK  28-APR-2020 09.32.17.919485 PM -04:00
```

The value in the LAST_MOD column will be used in the next update statement to modify the information. The last line does the very important check to make sure the timestamp has not changed and uses the built-in function TO_TIMESTAMP_TZ (tz is short for time zone) to convert the string we saved in from the SELECT statement back into the proper data type. Additionally, line 3 of the UPDATE statement updates the LAST_MOD column to be the current time if the row is found to be updated:

```
SQL> update dept
        set dname = initcap(:dname),
        last_mod = systimestamp
      where deptno = :deptno
      and last_mod = to_timestamp_tz(:last_mod, 'DD-MON-YYYY HH.MI.SSXFF
                        AM TZR' );

1 row updated.
```

As you can see, one row was updated, the row of interest. We updated the row by primary key (DEPTNO) and verified that the LAST_MOD column had not been modified by any other session between the time we read it first and the time we did the update. If we were to try to update that same record again, using the same logic but without retrieving the new LAST_MOD value, we would observe the following:

```
SQL> update dept
        set dname = upper(:dname),
        last_mod = systimestamp
     where deptno = :deptno
     and last_mod = to_timestamp_tz(:last_mod, 'DD-MON-YYYY HH.MI.SSXFF
                        AM TZR' );

0 rows updated.
```

Notice how 0 rows updated is reported this time because the predicate on LAST_MOD was not satisfied. While DEPTNO 10 still exists, the value at the moment we wish to update no longer matches the timestamp value at the moment we queried the row. So, the application knows that the data has been changed in the database, based on the fact that no rows were modified—and it must now figure out what it wants to do about that.

You would not rely on each application to maintain this field for a number of reasons. For one, it adds code to an application, and it is code that must be repeated and correctly implemented anywhere this table is modified. In a large application, that could be in many places. Furthermore, every application developed in the future must also conform to these rules. There are many chances to miss a spot in the application code and thus not have this field properly used. So, if the application code itself isn't responsible for maintaining this LAST_MOD field, then I believe that the application shouldn't be responsible for checking this LAST_MOD field either (if it can do the check, it can certainly do the update). So, in this case, I suggest *encapsulating the update logic in a stored procedure* and not allowing the application to update the table directly at all. If it cannot be trusted to maintain the value in this field, then it cannot be trusted to check it properly either. So, the stored procedure would take as inputs the bind variables we used in the previous updates and do exactly the same update. Upon detecting that zero rows were updated, the stored procedure could raise an exception back to the client to let the client know the update had, in effect, failed.

CHAPTER 2 LOCKING AND BLOCKING

An alternate implementation uses a trigger to maintain this LAST_MOD field, but for something as simple as this, my recommendation is to avoid the trigger and let the DML take care of it. Triggers introduce a measurable amount of overhead, and in this case, they would be unnecessary. Furthermore, the trigger would not be able to confirm that the row has not been modified (it would only be able to supply the value for LAST_MOD, not check it during the update); hence, the application has to be made painfully aware of this column and how to properly use it. So the trigger is not by itself sufficient.

# Optimistic Locking Using a Checksum

This is very similar to the previous version column method, but it uses the base data itself to compute a "virtual" version column. I'll quote the *Oracle Database PL/SQL Packages and Types Reference* manual (before showing how to use one of the supplied packages) to help explain the goal and concepts behind a checksum or hash function:

> *A one-way hash function takes a variable-length input string, the data, and converts it to a fixed-length (generally smaller) output string called a hash value. The hash value serves as a unique identifier (like a fingerprint) of the input data. You can use the hash value to verify whether data has been changed or not.*
>
> *Note that a one-way hash function is a hash function that isn't easily reversible. It is easy to compute a hash value from the input data, but it is hard to generate data that hashes to a particular value.*

We can use these hashes or checksums in the same way that we used our version column. We simply compare the hash or checksum value we obtain when we read data out of the database with what we obtain before modifying the data. If someone modified the row's values after we read it out, but before we updated it, then the hash or checksum will almost certainly be different.

There are many ways to compute a hash or checksum. I'll list several of these and demonstrate one in this section. All of these methods are based on supplied database functionality.

- DBMS_CRYPTO.HASH: This method is available in Oracle 10*g* Release 1 and up. It is capable of computing a Secure Hash Algorithm 1 (SHA-1) or MD4/MD5 message digests. It is recommended that you use the SHA-1 algorithm.

- DBMS_SQLHASH.GETHASH: This method is available in Oracle 10*g* Release 2 and up. It supports hash algorithms of SHA-1, MD4, and MD5. As a SYSDBA privileged user, you must grant execute on this package to a user before they can access it. This package is documented in the *Oracle Database Security Guide*.

- ORA_HASH: This method is available in Oracle 10*g* Release 1 and up. This is a built-in SQL function that takes a VARCHAR2 value as input and (optionally) another pair of inputs that control the return value. The returned value is a number—by default a number between 0 and 4294967295.

- STANDARD_HASH: This method is available in Oracle 12*c* Release 1 and up. This is a built-in SQL function that computes a hash value on an expression using standard hash algorithms such as SHA1 (default), SHA256, SHA384, SHA512, and MD5. The returned value is a RAW data type.

---

**Note**   An array of hash and checksum functions are available in many programming languages, so there may be others at your disposal outside the database. That said, if you use built-in database capabilities, you will have increased your portability (to new languages, new approaches) in the future.

---

The following example shows how you might use the ORA_HASH built-in function to compute these hashes/checksums. The technique would also be applicable for the other listed approaches; the logic would not be very much different, but the APIs you call would be. First, we'll start by removing the column we used in the previous example:

```
SQL> alter table dept drop column last_mod;
Table altered.
```

And then have our application query and display the information for department 10. Note that while we query the information, we compute the hash using the ORA_HASH built-in. This is the version information that we retain in our application. The following is our code to query and display:

```
SQL> variable deptno number
```

```
SQL> variable dname varchar2(14)
SQL> variable loc varchar2(13)
SQL> variable hash number

SQL> begin
    select deptno, dname, loc,
           ora_hash( dname || '/' || loc ) hash
      into :deptno, :dname, :loc, :hash
      from dept
     where deptno = 10;
    end;
    /
PL/SQL procedure successfully completed.

SQL> select :deptno, :dname, :loc, :hash  from dual;

  :DEPTNO :DNAME      :LOC               :HASH
---------- ---------- ---------- ----------
        10 Accounting NEW YORK    2721972020
```

As you can see, the hash is just some number. It is the value we would want to use before updating. To update that row, we would lock the row in the database as it exists right now and then compare the hash value of that row with the hash value we computed when we read the data out of the database. The logic for doing so could look like the following:

```
SQL> exec :dname := lower(:dname);
PL/SQL procedure successfully completed.

SQL> update dept
        set dname = :dname
      where deptno = :deptno
        and ora_hash( dname || '/' || loc ) = :hash
    /
1 row updated.

SQL> select dept.*,
           ora_hash( dname || '/' || loc ) hash
```

```
    from dept
  where deptno = :deptno;

   DEPTNO DNAME        LOC              HASH
---------- ---------- ---------- ----------
        10 accounting NEW YORK   2818855829
```

Upon requerying the data and computing the hash again after the update, we can see that the hash value is different. If someone had modified the row before we did, our hash values would not have compared. We can see this by attempting our update again, using the *old* hash value we read out the first time:

```
SQL> update dept
       set dname = :dname
     where deptno = :deptno
       and ora_hash( dname || '/' || loc ) = :hash
   /

0 rows updated.
```

As you see, there were zero rows updated, since our hash value did not match the data currently in the database.

In order for this hash-based approach to work properly, we must ensure every application uses the same approach when computing the hash, specifically they must concatenate dname with '/' with loc—in that order. To make that approach universal, I would suggest adding a virtual column to the table or using a view to add a column, so that the function is hidden from the application itself. Adding a column would look like this:

```
SQL> alter table dept
       add hash as
     ( ora_hash(dname || '/' || loc ) );
Table altered.

SQL> select *
       from dept
     where deptno = :deptno;

   DEPTNO DNAME        LOC              HASH
---------- ---------- ---------- ----------
        10 accounting NEW YORK   2818855829
```

The added column is a virtual column and as such incurs no storage overhead. The value is not computed and stored on disk. Rather, it is computed upon retrieval of the data from the database.

This example showed how to implement optimistic locking with a hash or checksum. You should bear in mind that computing a hash or checksum is a somewhat CPU-intensive operation; it is computationally expensive. On a system where CPU bandwidth is a scarce resource, you must take this fact into consideration. However, this approach is much more network-friendly because the transmission of a relatively small hash instead of a before-and-after image of the row (to compare column by column) over the network will consume much less of that resource.

# Optimistic or Pessimistic Locking?

So which method is best? In my experience, pessimistic locking works very well in Oracle (but perhaps not so well in other databases) and has many advantages over optimistic locking. However, it requires a stateful connection to the database, like a client/server connection. This is because locks are not held across connections. This single fact makes pessimistic locking unrealistic in many cases today. In the past, with client/server applications and a couple dozen or hundred users, it would have been my first and only choice. Today, however, optimistic concurrency control is what I would recommend for most applications. Having a connection for the entire duration of a transaction is just too high a price to pay.

Of the methods available, which do I use? I tend to use the version column approach with a timestamp column. It gives me the extra update information in a long-term sense. Furthermore, it's less computationally expensive than a hash or checksum, and it doesn't run into the issues potentially encountered with a hash or checksum when processing LONG, LONG RAW, CLOB, BLOB, and other very large columns (LONG and LONG RAW are obsolete, I only mention them here because they're still used in the Oracle data dictionary).

If I had to add optimistic concurrency controls to a table that was still being used with a pessimistic locking scheme (e.g., the table was accessed in both client/server applications and over the Web), I would opt for the ORA_HASH approach. The reason is that the existing legacy application might not appreciate a new column appearing. Even if we took the additional step of hiding the extra column, the application might suffer from the overhead of the necessary trigger. The ORA_HASH technique would be nonintrusive and lightweight in that respect. The hashing/checksum approach can be very database independent, especially if we compute the hashes or checksums outside of the database. However, by performing the computations in the middle tier rather than the database, we will incur higher resource usage penalties in terms of CPU usage and network transfers.

# Blocking

*Blocking* occurs when one session holds a lock on a resource that another session is requesting. As a result, the requesting session will be blocked—it will hang until the holding session gives up the locked resource. In almost every case, blocking is avoidable. In fact, if you do find that your session is blocked in an interactive application, then you have probably been suffering from the lost update bug as well, perhaps without realizing it. That is, your application logic is flawed and that is the cause of the blocking.

The five common DML statements that will block in the database are INSERT, UPDATE, DELETE, MERGE, and SELECT FOR UPDATE. The solution to a blocked SELECT FOR UPDATE is trivial: simply add the NOWAIT clause and it will no longer block. Instead, your application will report a message back to the end user that the row is already locked. The interesting cases are the remaining four DML statements. We'll look at each of them and see why they should not block and how to correct the situation if they do.

# Blocked Inserts

There are few times when an INSERT will block. The most common scenario is when you have a table with a primary key or unique constraint placed on it and two sessions attempt to insert a row with the same value. One of the sessions will block until the other session either commits (in which case the blocked session will receive an error about a duplicate value) or rolls back (in which case the blocked session succeeds). Another case involves tables linked together via referential integrity constraints. An INSERT into a child table may become blocked if the parent row it depends on is being created or deleted.

Blocked INSERTs typically happen with applications that allow the end user to generate the primary key/unique column value. This situation is most easily avoided by using a sequence or the SYS_GUID() built-in function to generate the primary key/ unique column value. Sequences/SYS_GUID() were designed to be highly concurrent methods of generating unique keys in a multiuser environment. In the event that you cannot use either and must allow the end user to generate a key that might be duplicated, you can use the following technique, which avoids the issue by using manual locks implemented via the built-in DBMS_LOCK package.

---

**Note**    The following example demonstrates how to prevent a session from blocking on an insert statement due to a primary key or unique constraint. It should be stressed that the fix demonstrated here should be considered a short-term solution while the application architecture itself is inspected. This approach adds obvious overhead and should not be implemented lightly. A well-designed application would not encounter this issue (e.g., you wouldn't have transactions that last for hours in a concurrent environment). This should be considered a last resort and is definitely not something you want to do to every table in your application "just in case."

---

With inserts, there's no existing row to select and lock; there's no way to prevent others from inserting a row with the same value, thus blocking our session and causing an indefinite wait. Here is where DBMS_LOCK comes into play. To demonstrate this technique, we will create a table with a primary key and a trigger that will prevent two (or more) sessions from inserting the same values simultaneously. The trigger will use DBMS_UTILITY.GET_HASH_VALUE to hash the primary key into some number between 0 and 1,073,741,823 (the range of lock ID numbers permitted for our use by Oracle). In this example, I've chosen a hash table of size 1,024, meaning we will hash our primary keys into one of 1,024 different lock IDs. Then we will use DBMS_LOCK.REQUEST to allocate an exclusive lock based on that ID. Only one session at a time will be able to do that, so if someone else tries to insert a record into our table with the same primary key, that person's lock request will fail (and the error resource busy will be raised).

---

**Note**    To successfully compile this trigger, execute permission on DBMS_LOCK must be granted directly to your schema. The privilege to execute DBMS_LOCK may not come from a role.

---

The following example first connects to the pluggable database ORCL as the SCOTT user and then executes the code:

```
sqlplus scott/tiger@localhost:1521/orcl

SQL> create table demo ( x int primary key );
Table created.

SQL> create or replace trigger demo_bifer
     before insert on demo
    for each row
    declare
        l_lock_id    number;
        resource_busy    exception;
        pragma exception_init( resource_busy, -54 );
    begin
        l_lock_id :=
            dbms_utility.get_hash_value( to_char( :new.x ), 0, 1024 );
        if ( dbms_lock.request
                  ( id                 => l_lock_id,
                    lockmode           => dbms_lock.x_mode,
                    timeout            => 0,
                    release_on_commit => TRUE ) not in (0,4) )
        then
            raise resource_busy;
        end if;
    end;
   /
Trigger created.

SQL> insert into demo(x) values (1);
1 row created.
```

Now, to demonstrate us catching this blocking INSERT problem in a single session, we'll use an AUTONOMOUS_TRANSACTION so that it seems as if this next block of code was executed in another SQL*Plus session. In fact, if you use another session, the behavior will be the same. Here we go:

```
SQL> declare
        pragma autonomous_transaction;
```

33

```
    begin
        insert into demo(x) values (1);
        commit;
    end;
    /
declare
*
ERROR at line 1:
ORA-00054: resource busy and acquire with NOWAIT specified or timeout
expired
ORA-06512: at "SCOTT.DEMO_BIFER", line 14
ORA-04088: error during execution of trigger 'SCOTT.DEMO_BIFER'
ORA-06512: at line 4
```

The concept here is to take the supplied primary key value of the table protected by the trigger and put it in a character string. We can then use DBMS_UTILITY.GET_HASH_VALUE to come up with a mostly unique hash value for the string. As long as we use a hash table smaller than 1,073,741,823, we can lock that value exclusively using DBMS_LOCK.

After hashing, we take that value and use DBMS_LOCK to request that lock ID to be exclusively locked with a timeout of ZERO (this returns immediately if someone else has locked that value). If we time out or fail for any reason, we raise ORA-00054 Resource Busy. Otherwise, we do nothing—it is okay to insert, we won't block. Upon committing our transaction, all locks, including those allocated by this DBMS_LOCK call, will be released.

Of course, if the primary key of your table is an INTEGER and you don't expect the key to go over 1 billion, you can skip the hash and just use the number as the lock ID.

You'll need to play with the size of the hash table (1,024 in this example) to avoid artificial resource busy messages due to different strings hashing to the same number. The size of the hash table will be application (data)-specific, and it will be influenced by the number of concurrent insertions as well. You might also add a flag to the trigger to allow people to turn the check on and off. If I were going to insert hundreds or thousands of records, for example, I might not want this check enabled.

# Blocked Merges, Updates, and Deletes

In an interactive application—one where you query some data out of the database, allow an end user to manipulate it, and then put it back into the database—a blocked UPDATE or DELETE indicates that you probably have a lost update problem in your code. (I'll call it a bug in your code if you do.) You are attempting to UPDATE a row that someone else is already updating (in other words, one that someone else already has locked). You can avoid the blocking issue by using the SELECT FOR UPDATE NOWAIT query to

- Verify the data has not changed since you queried it out (preventing lost updates)

- Lock the row (preventing the UPDATE or DELETE from blocking)

As discussed earlier, you can do this regardless of the locking approach you take. Both pessimistic and optimistic locking may employ the SELECT FOR UPDATE NOWAIT query to verify the row has not changed. Pessimistic locking would use that SELECT FOR UPDATE NOWAIT statement the instant the user indicated her intention to modify the data. Optimistic locking would use that statement immediately prior to updating the data in the database. Not only will this resolve the blocking issue in your application, but it'll also correct the data integrity issue.

Since a MERGE is simply an INSERT and UPDATE (and in 10g and above, with the enhanced MERGE syntax, it's a DELETE as well), you would use both techniques simultaneously.

# Deadlocks

*Deadlocks* occur when you have two sessions, each of which is holding a resource that the other wants. For example, if I have two tables, A and B, in my database, and each has a single row in it, I can demonstrate a deadlock easily. All I need to do is open two sessions (e.g., two SQL*Plus sessions). In session A, I update table A. In session B, I update table B. Now, if I attempt to update table A in session B, I will become blocked. Session A has this row locked already. This is not a deadlock; it is just blocking. I have not yet deadlocked because there is a chance that session A will commit or roll back, and session B will simply continue at that point.

If I go back to session A and then try to update table B, I will cause a deadlock. One of the two sessions will be chosen as a victim and will have its statement rolled back. For example, the attempt by session B to update table A may be rolled back, with an error such as the following:

```
update a set x = x+1
       *
ERROR at line 1:
ORA-00060: deadlock detected while waiting for resource
```

The previously described deadlock scenario is depicted in Figure 2-1.

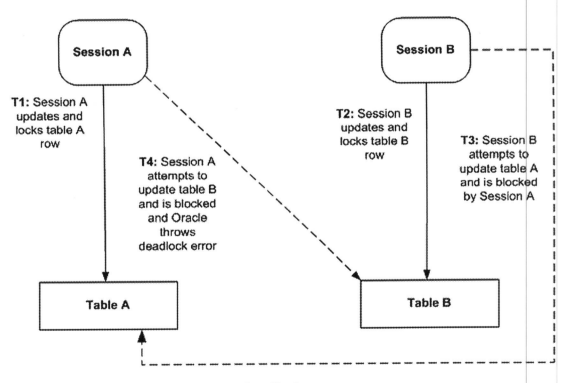

***Figure 2-1.*** *Example of creating a deadlock*

Session A's attempt to update table B will remain blocked—Oracle will not roll back the entire transaction. Only one of the statements that contributed to the deadlock is rolled back. Session B still has the row in table B locked, and session A is patiently waiting for the row to become available.

After receiving the deadlock message, session B must decide whether to commit the outstanding work on table B, roll it back, or continue down an alternate path and commit later. As soon as this session does commit or roll back, the other blocked session will continue on as if nothing happened.

Oracle considers deadlocks to be so rare and unusual that it creates a trace file on the server each time one does occur. The contents of the trace file will look something like this:

```
DEADLOCK DETECTED ( ORA-00060 )
See Note 60.1 at My Oracle Support for Troubleshooting ORA-60 Errors

[Transaction Deadlock]

The following deadlock is not an ORACLE error. It is a
deadlock due to user error in the design of an application
or from issuing incorrect ad-hoc SQL.
```

Obviously (from the prior message), Oracle considers these application deadlocks a self-induced error on the part of the application, and for the most part, Oracle is correct. Unlike in many other RDBMSs, deadlocks are so rare in Oracle they can be considered almost nonexistent. Typically, you must come up with artificial conditions to get one.

The number one cause of deadlocks in the Oracle database, in my experience, is unindexed foreign keys. (The number two cause is bitmap indexes on tables subject to concurrent updates.) Oracle will place a full table lock on a child table after modification of the parent table in two scenarios:

- If you update the parent table's primary key (a very rare occurrence if you follow the rule of relational databases stating that primary keys should be immutable), the child table will be locked in the absence of an index on the foreign key.

- If you delete a parent table row, the entire child table will be locked (in the absence of an index on the foreign key) as well.

These full table locks are a short-term occurrence, meaning they need to be taken for the duration of the DML operation, not the entire transaction. Even so, they can and do cause large locking issues. As a demonstration of the first point, if we have a pair of tables set up as follows, nothing untoward happens yet:

```
SQL> create table p ( x int primary key );
Table created.

SQL> create table c ( x references p );
Table created.

SQL> insert into p values ( 1 );
1 row created.

SQL> insert into p values ( 2 );
1 row created.

SQL> commit;
Commit complete.

SQL> insert into c values ( 2 );
1 row created.
```

But if we go into another session and attempt to delete the first parent record, we'll find that session gets immediately blocked.

```
SQL> delete from p where x = 1;
```

It is attempting to gain a full table lock on table C before it does the delete. Now, no other session can initiate a DELETE, INSERT, or UPDATE of any rows in C (the sessions that had already started may continue, but no new sessions may start to modify C).

This blocking would happen with an update of the primary key value as well. Because updating a primary key is a huge no-no in a relational database, this is generally not an issue with updates. However, I have seen this updating of the primary key become a serious issue when developers use tools that generate SQL for them, and those tools update every single column, regardless of whether the end user actually modified that column or not. For example, say that we use Oracle Forms and create a default layout on any table. Oracle Forms by default will generate an update that modifies every single column in the table we choose to display. If we build a default layout on the DEPT table and include all three fields, Oracle Forms will execute the following command whenever we modify any of the columns of the DEPT table:

```
update dept set deptno=:1,dname=:2,loc=:3 where rowid=:4
```

In this case, if the EMP table has a foreign key to DEPT and there is no index on the DEPTNO column in the EMP table, then the entire EMP table will be locked during an update to DEPT. This is something to watch out for carefully if you are using any tools that generate SQL for you. Even though the value of the primary key does not change, the child table EMP will be locked after the execution of the preceding SQL statement. In the case of Oracle Forms, the solution is to set that table's UPDATE CHANGED COLUMNS ONLY property to YES. Oracle Forms will generate an UPDATE statement that includes only the changed columns (not the primary key).

Problems arising from deletion of a row in a parent table are far more common. As I demonstrated, if I delete a row in table P, then the child table, C, will become locked during the DML operation, thus preventing other updates against C from taking place for the duration of the transaction (assuming no one else was modifying C, of course; in which case the delete will wait). This is where the blocking and deadlock issues come in. By locking the entire table C, I have seriously decreased the concurrency in my database to the point where no one will be able to modify anything in C. In addition, I have increased the probability of a deadlock, since I now own lots of data until I commit. The probability that some other session will become blocked on C is now much higher; any session that tries to modify C will get blocked. Therefore, I'll start seeing lots of sessions that hold some preexisting locks on other resources getting blocked in the database. If any of these blocked sessions are, in fact, locking a resource that my session also needs, we will have a deadlock. The deadlock in this case is caused by my session preventing access to many more resources (in this case, all of the rows in a single table) than it ever needed.

---

**Note**    See Chapter 9 for a query that reports on unindexed foreign keys.

---

# Lock Escalation

When lock escalation occurs, the system is decreasing the granularity of your locks. An example would be the database system turning your 100 row-level locks against a table into a single table-level lock. You are now using one lock to lock everything, and typically, you are also locking a whole lot more data than you were before. Lock escalation is used frequently in databases that consider a lock to be a scarce resource and overhead to be avoided.

**Note**   Oracle will never escalate a lock. Never.

Oracle never escalates locks, but it does practice lock conversion or lock promotion, terms that are often confused with lock escalation.

**Note**   The terms *lock conversion* and *lock promotion* are synonymous. Oracle typically refers to the process as *lock conversion*.

Oracle will take a lock at the lowest level possible (i.e., the least restrictive lock possible) and convert that lock to a more restrictive level if necessary. For example, if you select a row from a table with the FOR UPDATE clause, two locks will be created. One lock is placed on the row(s) you selected (and this will be an exclusive lock; no one else can lock that specific row in exclusive mode). The other lock, a ROW SHARE TABLE lock, is placed on the table itself. This will prevent other sessions from placing an exclusive lock on the table and thus prevent them from altering the structure of the table, for example. Another session can modify any other row in this table without conflict. As many commands as possible that could execute successfully given there is a locked row in the table will be permitted.

Lock escalation is not a database "feature." It is not a desired attribute. The fact that a database supports lock escalation implies there is some inherent overhead in its locking mechanism and significant work is performed to manage hundreds of locks. In Oracle, the overhead to have 1 lock or 1 million locks is the same: none.

# Summary

This chapter covered a lot of material that, at times, may have made you scratch your head. While locking is rather straightforward, some of its side effects are not. However, it is vital that you understand these issues. For example, if you were not aware of the table lock Oracle uses to enforce a foreign key relationship when the foreign key is not indexed, then your application would suffer from poor performance. If you did not understand how to review the data dictionary to see who was locking whom, you might never figure that one out. You would just assume that the database hangs sometimes. These issues can be resolved via a proper indexing strategy.

# CHAPTER 3

# Locks, Latches, and Mutexes

In this chapter, we'll take a detailed look at how Oracle locks both data (e.g., rows in tables) and shared data structures (such as those found in the SGA). We'll investigate the granularity to which Oracle locks data and what that means to you, the developer. When appropriate, I'll contrast Oracle's locking scheme with other popular implementations, mostly to dispel the myth that row-level locking adds overhead; in reality, it adds overhead only if the implementation adds overhead. In the next chapter, we'll continue this discussion and investigate Oracle's multiversioning techniques and how locking strategies interact with them.

The three general classes of locks in Oracle are as follows:

- *DML locks*: DML stands for *Data Manipulation Language*. In general, this means SELECT, INSERT, UPDATE, MERGE, and DELETE statements. DML locks are the mechanism that allows for concurrent data modifications. DML locks will be, for example, locks on a specific row of data or a lock at the table level that locks every row in the table.

- *DDL locks*: DDL stands for *Data Definition Language* (CREATE and ALTER statements, and so on). DDL locks protect the definition of the structure of objects.

- *Internal locks and latches*: Oracle uses these locks to protect its internal data structures. For example, when Oracle parses a query and generates an optimized query plan, it will latch the library cache to put that plan in there for other sessions to use. A latch is a lightweight, low-level serialization device employed by Oracle, similar in function to a lock. Do not confuse or be misled by the

D. Kuhn and T. Kyte, *Oracle Database Transactions and Locking Revealed*,
https://doi.org/10.1007/978-1-4842-6425-6_3

term *lightweight*; latches are a common cause of contention in the database, as you will see. They are lightweight in their implementation, but not their effect.

We will now take a more detailed look at the specific types of locks within each of these general classes and the implications of their use. There are more lock types than I can cover here. The ones I cover in the sections that follow are the most common and are held for a long duration. The other types of locks are generally held for very short periods of time.

# DML Locks

DML locks are used to ensure that only one person at a time modifies a row and that no one can drop a table upon which you are working. Oracle will place these locks for you, more or less transparently, as you do work.

## TX (Transaction) Locks

A *TX lock* is acquired when a transaction initiates its first change. The transaction is automatically initiated at this point (you don't explicitly start a transaction in Oracle). The lock is held until the transaction performs a COMMIT or ROLLBACK. It is used as a queuing mechanism so that other sessions can wait for the transaction to complete. Each and every row you modify or SELECT FOR UPDATE in a transaction will point to an associated TX lock for that transaction. While this sounds expensive, it is not. To understand why this is, you need a conceptual understanding of where locks live and how they are managed. In Oracle, locks are stored as an attribute of the data. Oracle does not have a traditional lock manager that keeps a long list of every row that is locked in the system. Many other databases do it that way because, for them, locks are a scarce resource, the use of which needs to be monitored. The more locks are in use, the more these systems have to manage, so it is a concern in these systems if too many locks are being used.

In a database with a traditional memory-based lock manager, the process of locking a row would resemble the following:

1.  Find the address of the row you want to lock.

2.  Get in line at the lock manager (which must be serialized, as it is a common in-memory structure).

3.  Lock the list.

4.  Search through the list to see if anyone else has locked this row.

5.  Create a new entry in the list to establish the fact that you have locked the row.

6.  Unlock the list.

Now that you have the row locked, you can modify it. Later, as you commit your changes, you must continue the procedure as follows:

1.  Get in line again.

2.  Lock the list of locks.

3.  Search through the list and release all of your locks.

4.  Unlock the list.

As you can see, the more locks acquired, the more time spent on this operation, both before and after modifying the data. Oracle does not do it that way. Oracle's process looks like this:

1.  Find the address of the row you want to lock.

2.  Go to the row.

3.  Lock the row right there, right then—at the location of the row, not in a big list somewhere (waiting for the transaction that has it locked to end if it is already locked, unless you are using the NOWAIT option).

That's it. Since the lock is stored as an attribute of the data, Oracle does not need a traditional lock manager. The transaction will simply go to the data and lock it (if it is not locked already). The interesting thing is that the data may appear locked when you get to it, even if it's not. When you lock rows of data in Oracle, the row points to a copy of the transaction ID that is stored with the block containing the data, and when the lock is released, that transaction ID is left behind. This transaction ID is unique to your transaction and represents the undo segment number, slot, and sequence number. You leave that on the block that contains your row to tell other sessions that you own this data (not all of the data on the block—just the one row you are modifying). When another session comes along, it sees the transaction ID, and using the fact that it represents a transaction, it can quickly see if the transaction holding the lock is still active. If the lock is not active, the session is allowed access to the data. If the lock is still active, that session will ask to be notified as soon as the lock is released. Hence, you have a queuing mechanism: the session requesting the lock will be queued up waiting for that transaction to complete, and then it will get the data.

Here is a small example showing how this happens, using three V$ tables:

- V$TRANSACTION, which contains an entry for every active transaction.

- V$SESSION, which shows the sessions logged in.

- V$LOCK, which contains an entry for all enqueue locks being held as well as for sessions that are waiting on locks. You will not see a row in this view for each row locked by a session. As stated earlier, that master list of locks at the row level doesn't exist. If a session has one row in the EMP table locked, there will be one row in this view for that session indicating that fact. If a session has millions of rows in the EMP table locked, there will still be just one row in this view. This view shows what enqueue locks individual sessions have.

First, let's get a copy of the EMP and DEPT tables. If you already have these tables in your schema, replace them with the following definitions:

```
SQL> create table dept  as select * from scott.dept;
Table created.
```

```
SQL> create table emp  as select * from scott.emp;
Table created.
```

```
SQL> alter table dept
     add constraint dept_pk
     primary key(deptno);
Table altered.
```

```
SQL> alter table emp
      add constraint emp_pk
      primary key(empno);
Table altered.
```

```
SQL> alter table emp
       add constraint emp_fk_dept
       foreign key (deptno)
       references dept(deptno);

Table altered.

SQL> create index emp_deptno_idx  on emp(deptno);
Index created.
```

Let's start a transaction now:

```
SQL> update dept  set dname = initcap(dname);
4 rows updated.
```

Now, let's look at the state of the system at this point. This example assumes a single-user system; otherwise, you may see many rows in V$TRANSACTION. Even in a single-user system, do not be surprised to see more than one row in V$TRANSACTION, as many of the background Oracle processes may be performing a transaction as well. First, let's look at the lock being held:

```
SQL> select username,
            v$lock.sid,
            trunc(id1/power(2,16)) rbs,
            bitand(id1,to_number('ffff','xxxx'))+0 slot,
            id2 seq,
           lmode,
            request,
            block
       from v$lock, v$session
       where v$lock.type = 'TX'
     and v$lock.sid = v$session.sid
     and v$session.username = USER;
```

| USERNAME | SID | RBS | SLOT | SEQ | LMODE | REQUEST | BLOCK |
|----------|-----|-----|------|-----|-------|---------|-------|
| YODA | 36 | 19 | 8 | 567 | 6 | 0 | 0 |

Now, let's look at the transaction information:

```
SQL> select XIDUSN, XIDSLOT, XIDSQN from v$transaction;

    XIDUSN    XIDSLOT    XIDSQN
---------- ---------- ----------
        19          8        567
```

The interesting points to note here are as follows:

- The LMODE is 6 in the V$LOCK table and the REQUEST is 0. If you refer to the definition of the V$LOCK table in the *Oracle Database Reference* manual, you will find that LMODE=6 is an exclusive lock. A value of 0 in the request means you are not making a request; you have the lock.

- There is only one row in this table. This V$LOCK table is more of a queuing table than a lock table. Many people expect four rows in V$LOCK since we have four rows locked. Remember, however, that Oracle does not store a master list of every row locked anywhere. To find out if a row is locked, we must go to that row.

- I took the ID1 and ID2 columns and performed some manipulation on them. Oracle needed to save three 16-bit numbers, but only had two columns in order to do it. So, the first column ID1 holds two of these numbers. By dividing by 2^16 with trunc(id1/power(2,16)) rbs, and by masking out the high bits with bitand(id1,to_number('ffff','xxxx'))+0 slot, I am able to get back the two numbers that are hiding in that one number.

- The RBS, SLOT, and SEQ values match the V$TRANSACTION information. This is my transaction ID.

Now we'll start another session using the same username, update some rows in EMP, and then try to update DEPT:

```
SQL> update emp set ename = upper(ename);
14 rows updated.

SQL> update dept set deptno = deptno-10;
```

We're now blocked in this session. Running the following V$ queries in the session that is not blocked, we see the following:

```
SQL> select username,
            v$lock.sid,
            trunc(id1/power(2,16)) rbs,
            bitand(id1,to_number('ffff','xxxx'))+0 slot,
            id2 seq,
            lmode,
            request,
            block
     from v$lock, v$session
     where v$lock.type = 'TX'
     and v$lock.sid = v$session.sid
     and v$session.username = USER;
```

| USERNAME | SID | RBS | SLOT | SEQ | LMODE | REQUEST | BLOCK |
|----------|-----|-----|------|-----|-------|---------|-------|
| YODA | 6 | 16 | 31 | 571 | 6 | 0 | 0 |
| YODA | 6 | 19 | 8 | 567 | 0 | 6 | 0 |
| YODA | 36 | 19 | 8 | 567 | 6 | 0 | 1 |

```
SQL> select XIDUSN, XIDSLOT, XIDSQN from v$transaction;
```

| XIDUSN | XIDSLOT | XIDSQN |
|--------|---------|--------|
| 16 | 31 | 571 |
| 19 | 8 | 567 |

What we see here is that a new transaction has begun, with a transaction ID of (16,31,571). Our new session, SID=6, has two rows in V$LOCK this time. One row represents the locks that it owns (where LMODE=6). It also has a row that shows a REQUEST with a value of 6. This is a request for an exclusive lock. The interesting thing to note here is that the RBS/SLOT/SEQ values of this request row are the transaction ID of the *holder* of the lock. The transaction with SID=36 is blocking the transaction with SID=6. We can see this more explicitly simply by doing a self-join of V$LOCK:

```
SQL> select
            (select username from v$session where sid=a.sid) blocker,
             a.sid,
            ' is blocking ',
             (select username from v$session where sid=b.sid) blockee,
                b.sid
       from v$lock a, v$lock b
      where a.block = 1
        and b.request > 0
      and a.id1 = b.id1
      and a.id2 = b.id2;
```

| BLOCKER | SID | 'ISBLOCKING' | BLOCKEE | SID |
|---|---|---|---|---|
| YODA | 36 | is blocking | YODA | 6 |

We can also view which session is waiting for another session to release a lock via the DBA_WAITERS view. This useful view shows all sessions waiting for a lock, for example:

```
SQL> select holding_session, waiting_session, lock_type, mode_held,
mode_requested
        from dba_waiters;
```

| HOLDING_SESSION | WAITING_SESSION | LOCK_TYPE | MODE_HELD | MODE_REQUE |
|---|---|---|---|---|
| 36 | 6 | Transaction | Exclusive | Exclusive |

Now, if we commit our original transaction, SID=36, and rerun our lock query, we find that the request row has gone:

```
SQL> select username,
            v$lock.sid,
            trunc(id1/power(2,16)) rbs,
            bitand(id1,to_number('ffff','xxxx'))+0 slot,
            id2 seq,
            lmode,
            request,
            block
```

```
from v$lock, v$session
where v$lock.type = 'TX'
and v$lock.sid = v$session.sid
and v$session.username = USER;
```

| USERNAME | SID | RBS | SLOT | SEQ | LMODE | REQUEST | BLOCK |
|----------|-----|-----|------|-----|-------|---------|-------|
| YODA     | 6   | 16  | 31   | 571 | 6     | 0       | 0     |

```
SQL> select XIDUSN, XIDSLOT, XIDSQN from v$transaction;
```

| XIDUSN | XIDSLOT | XIDSQN |
|--------|---------|--------|
| 16     | 31      | 571    |

The request row disappeared the instant the other session gave up its lock. That request row was the queuing mechanism. The database is able to wake up the blocked sessions the instant the transaction is completed. There are prettier displays with various GUI tools, but in a pinch, having knowledge of the tables you need to look at is very useful.

However, before we can say that we have a good understanding of how the row locking in Oracle works, we must look at one additional topic: how the locking and transaction information is managed with the data itself. It is part of the block overhead. At the top of a database block is some leading overhead space in which to store a transaction table for that block. This transaction table contains an entry for each real transaction that has locked some data in that block. The size of this structure is controlled by two physical attribute parameters on the CREATE statement for an object:

- INITRANS: The initial, preallocated size of this structure. This defaults to 2 for indexes and tables.

- MAXTRANS: MAXTRANS is always 255.

Each block starts life with, by default, two transaction slots. The number of simultaneous active transactions that a block can ever have is constrained by the value of MAXTRANS and by the availability of space on the block. You may not be able to achieve 255 concurrent transactions on the block if there is not sufficient space to grow this structure.

We can artificially demonstrate how this works by creating a table with lots of rows packed into a single block such that the block is very full from the start; there will be very little room left on the block after we initially load our data. The presence of these rows will limit how large the transaction table can grow, due to the lack of space. I was using an 8KB block size and I tested this particular example in all versions of Oracle from version 9 through 19 with the same results (so, if you have an 8KB block size, you should be able to reproduce this). We'll start by creating our packed table. I played around with different lengths of data until I arrived at this very special size:

```
SQL> -- First drop table T if it exists
SQL> drop table t;

SQL> create table t
     ( x int primary key,
       y varchar2(4000)
     )
     /
Table created.

SQL> insert into t (x,y)
     select rownum, rpad('*',148,'*')
      from dual
     connect by level <= 46;
46 rows created.

SQL> select length(y),
            dbms_rowid.rowid_block_number(rowid) blk,
            count(*), min(x), max(x)
       from t
      group by length(y), dbms_rowid.rowid_block_number(rowid);

LENGTH(Y)        BLK   COUNT(*)     MIN(X)      MAX(X)
---------- ---------- ---------- ---------- ----------
      148      46438         46          1         46
```

So, our table has 46 rows, all on the same block. I chose 148 characters because if it was one character more, we'd need two blocks to hold these same 46 records. Now, we need a way to see what happens when many transactions try to lock data on this single block simultaneously. For that, we'll use an AUTONOMOUS_TRANSACTION again, just so we can use a single session and not have to run lots of concurrent SQL*Plus sessions. Our stored procedure will lock a row in the table by the primary key starting with a primary key value of 1 (the first record inserted). If our procedure gets the lock on this row without having to wait (without getting blocked), it will simply increase the primary key value by 1 and, using recursion, do it all over again. So, the second call will try to lock record 2, the third call record 3, and so on. If the procedure is made to wait, it will raise an ORA-54 resource busy error and we'll print out "locked out trying to select row <primary key value>". That will indicate we ran out of transaction slots on this block before we ran out of rows to lock. On the other hand, if we find no row to lock, that means we've already locked every row on this block and we print out success (meaning, the transaction table in the block header was able to grow to accommodate all of the transactions). Here is that stored procedure:

```
SQL> create or replace procedure do_update( p_n in number )
    as
        pragma autonomous_transaction;
        l_rec t%rowtype;
        resource_busy exception;
        pragma exception_init( resource_busy, -54 );
    begin
        select *
          into l_rec
          from t
        where x = p_n
          for update NOWAIT;

        do_update( p_n+1 );
        commit;
    exception
    when resource_busy
    then
        dbms_output.put_line( 'locked out trying to select row ' || p_n );
        commit;
```

```
    when no_data_found
    then
        dbms_output.put_line( 'we finished - no problems' );
        commit;
    end;
/
Procedure created.
```

The magic is on line 14 where we recursively call ourselves with a new primary key value to lock over and over. If you run the procedure after populating the table with 148 character strings, you should observe:

```
SQL> set serverout on
SQL> exec do_update(1);
locked out trying to select row 38
PL/SQL procedure successfully completed.
```

This output shows that we were able to lock 37 rows but ran out of transaction slots for the 38th row. For this given block, a maximum of 37 transactions can concurrently access it. If we redo the example with a slightly smaller string, we'll see that if finishes with no problems:

```
SQL> truncate table t;
Table truncated.

SQL> insert into t (x,y)
     select rownum, rpad('*',147,'*')
      from dual
     connect by level <= 46;
46 rows created.

SQL> select length(y),
            dbms_rowid.rowid_block_number(rowid) blk,
            count(*), min(x), max(x)
       from t
      group by length(y), dbms_rowid.rowid_block_number(rowid);
```

| LENGTH(Y) | BLK | COUNT(*) | MIN(X) | MAX(X) |
|---|---|---|---|---|
| ---------- | ---------- | ---------- | ---------- | ---------- |
| 147 | 48135 | 46 | 1 | 46 |

```
SQL> set serverout on
SQL> exec do_update(1);
```
**we finished - no problems**
```
PL/SQL procedure successfully completed.
```

This time we completed successfully—the difference a single byte makes! In this case, having the extra 46 bytes of space free on the block (each of the 46 strings was just one byte smaller) allowed us to have at least nine more transactions active on the block.

This example demonstrates what happens when many transactions attempt to access the same block simultaneously—a wait on the transaction table may occur if there is an extremely high number of concurrent transactions. Blocking may occur if the INITRANS is set low and there is not enough space on a block to dynamically expand the transaction. In most cases, the default of 2 for INITRANS is sufficient, as the transaction table will dynamically grow (space permitting), but in some environments you may need to increase this setting (to reserve more room for slots) to increase concurrency and decrease waits.

An example of when you might need to increase the setting would be on a table or, even more frequently, on an index (since index blocks can get many more rows on them than a table can typically hold) that is frequently modified and has a lot of rows per block on average. You may need to increase either PCTFREE or INITRANS to set aside ahead of time sufficient space on the block for the number of expected concurrent transactions. This is especially true if you anticipate the blocks will be nearly full to begin with, meaning there is no room for the dynamic expansion of the transaction structure on the block.

One last note on INITRANS. A couple of times I've stated that the default value for this attribute is 2. However, if you examine the data dictionary after creating a table, you'll notice that INITRANS displays a value of 1:

```
SQL> -- First drop table T if it exists
SQL> drop table t;
SQL> create table t ( x int );
SQL> select ini_trans from user_tables where table_name = 'T';
```

```
 INI_TRANS
----------
        1
```

So is the default number of transaction slots 1 or 2? Even though the data dictionary is showing a value of 1, we can demonstrate that it really is 2. Consider this experiment. First, generate one transaction for table T by inserting a single record:

```
SQL> insert into t values ( 1 );
```

Now, verify that one block is consumed by table T:

```
SQL> select dbms_rowid.ROWID_BLOCK_NUMBER(rowid)  from t;

DBMS_ROWID.ROWID_BLOCK_NUMBER(ROWID)
------------------------------------
                               48446
```

Next, place into the variables—B and F—the block number and the data file number of the block used by table T:

```
SQL> column b new_val B
SQL> column f new_val F
SQL> select dbms_rowid.ROWID_BLOCK_NUMBER(rowid) B,
            dbms_rowid.ROWID_TO_ABSOLUTE_FNO( rowid, user, 'T' ) F
        from t;
```

Now, dump the block being used by table T:

```
SQL> alter system dump datafile &F block &B;
```

Next, place into a variable named TRACE the location and name of the trace file containing the dump information for the block:

```
SQL> column trace new_val TRACE

SQL> select c.value || '/' || d.instance_name || '_ora_' || a.spid ||
'.trc' trace
        from v$process a, v$session b, v$diag_info c, v$instance d
      where a.addr = b.paddr
        and b.audsid = userenv('sessionid')
        and c.name = 'Diag Trace';
```

You should see some output similar to this:

```
TRACE
----------------------------------------------------------------------
/u01/app/oracle/diag/rdbms/orclcdb/orclcdb/trace/orclcdb_ora_18604.trc
```

Now, terminate the session and edit the trace file:

```
SQL> disconnect
SQL> edit &TRACE
```

Searching the trace file for the value of Itl, we see there are two transaction slots that have been initialized (even though there has only been one transaction issued for this table):

```
Itl          Xid                  Uba             Flag  Lck     Scn/Fsc
0x01   0x001a.008.00000002   0x03c0046a.0000.14  --U-   1   fsc 0x0000.00443058
0x02   0x0000.000.00000000   0x00000000.0000.00  ----   0   fsc 0x0000.00000000
```

The INITRANS value of 1 reported in the data dictionary is most likely a legacy value and it really should display a value of 2 for more current versions of Oracle.

## TM (DML Enqueue) Locks

TM locks are used to ensure that the structure of a table is not altered while you are modifying its contents. For example, if you have updated a table, you will acquire a TM lock on that table. This will prevent another user from executing DROP or ALTER commands on that table. If another user attempts to perform DDL on the table while you have a TM lock on it, he'll receive the following error message:

```
drop table dept
        *
ERROR at line 1:
ORA-00054: resource busy and acquire with NOWAIT specified
```

> **Note**    In Oracle 11*g* Release 2 and above, you may set DDL_LOCK_TIMEOUT
> in order to have DDL wait. This is achieved typically via the ALTER SESSION
> command. For example, you could issue ALTER SESSION SET DDL_LOCK_
> TIMEOUT=60; before issuing the DROP TABLE command. The DROP TABLE
> command issued would then wait 60 seconds before returning an error (or it could
> succeed, of course, as well).

The ORA-00054 message is a confusing message at first, since there is no direct method to specify NOWAIT or WAIT on a DROP TABLE at all. It is just the generic message you get when you attempt to perform an operation that would be blocked, but the operation does not permit blocking. As you've seen before, it's the same message you get if you issue a SELECT FOR UPDATE NOWAIT against a locked row.

The following shows how these locks would appear in the V$LOCK table:

```
SQL> create table t1 ( x int );
Table created.

SQL> create table t2 ( x int );
Table created.

SQL> insert into t1 values ( 1 );
1 row created.

SQL> insert into t2 values ( 1 );
1 row created.

SQL> select (select username
              from v$session
            where sid = v$lock.sid) username,
          sid,
          id1,
          id2,
          lmode,
          request, block, type
      from v$lock
   where sid = sys_context('userenv','sid');
```

| USERNAME | SID | ID1 | ID2 | LMODE | REQUEST | BLOCK | TY |
|----------|-----|-----|-----|-------|---------|-------|----|
| YODA | 451 | 134 | 2832289441 | 4 | 0 | 0 | AE |
| YODA | 451 | 80449 | 0 | 3 | 0 | 0 | TM |
| YODA | 451 | 2228240 | 2 | 6 | 0 | 0 | TX |
| YODA | 451 | 80448 | 0 | 3 | 0 | 0 | TM |

From the preceding output, the rows with the lock type of TM use the corresponding ID1 columns in this query:

```
SQL> select object_name, object_id
       from user_objects
       where object_id in (80449,80448);
```

```
OBJECT_NAME      OBJECT_ID
---------------  ----------
T1                   80448
T2                   80449
```

---

**Note**    The AE lock is an edition lock, available in Oracle 11*g* and above. It is part of the Edition-based redefinition feature (not covered in this particular book). ID1 is the object ID of the edition that SID is using currently. This edition lock protects the referenced edition from modification (dropping of the edition, for example) in much the same way the TM locks protect the tables they point to from structural modification.

---

Whereas we get only one TX lock per transaction, we can get as many TM locks as the objects we modify. Here, the interesting thing is that the ID1 column for the TM lock is the object ID of the DML-locked object, so it is easy to find the object on which the lock is being held.

An interesting aside to the TM lock: the total number of TM locks allowed in the system is configurable by you (for details, see the DML_LOCKS parameter definition in the *Oracle Database Reference* manual). It may, in fact, be set to zero. This does not mean that your database becomes a read-only database (no locks), but rather that DDL is not permitted. This is useful in very specialized applications, such as RAC implementations, to reduce the amount of intra-instance coordination that would otherwise take place.

You can also remove the ability to gain TM locks on an object-by-object basis using the `ALTER TABLE <TABLENAME> DISABLE TABLE LOCK` command. This is a quick way to make it harder to accidentally drop a table, as you will have to reenable the table lock before dropping the table. It can also be used to detect a full table lock as a result of the unindexed foreign key we discussed previously.

# DDL Locks

DDL locks are automatically placed against objects during a DDL operation to protect them from changes by other sessions. For example, if I perform the DDL operation `ALTER TABLE T`, the table T will *in general* have an exclusive DDL lock placed against it, preventing other sessions from getting DDL locks and TM locks on this table.

---

**Note**    Oracle 11*g* has modified what used to be a rule. In the past, ALTER TABLE T would have an exclusive DDL lock placed against it. In this example, table T prevents other sessions from performing DDL and acquiring TM locks (used to modify the contents of the table). Now, many ALTER commands can be performed online—without preventing modifications.

---

DDL locks are held for the duration of the DDL statement and are released immediately afterward. This is done, in effect, by always wrapping DDL statements in implicit commits (or a commit/rollback pair). For this reason, DDL always commits in Oracle. Every `CREATE`, `ALTER`, and so on statement is really executed as shown in this pseudocode:

```
Begin
    Commit;
    DDL-STATEMENT
    Commit;
Exception
    When others then rollback;
End;
```

So, DDL will always commit, even if it is unsuccessful. DDL starts by committing; be aware of this. It commits first so that if it has to roll back, it will not roll back your transaction. If you execute DDL, it will make permanent any outstanding work you have performed, even if the DDL is not successful. If you need to execute DDL, but you do not want it to commit your existing transaction, you may use an autonomous transaction.

---

**Note**    Because a DDL statement will always commit, there's no need to put a COMMIT statement after the DDL statement. Sometimes, developers and DBAs do this, whereas there is no need for this.

---

There are three types of DDL locks:

- *Exclusive DDL locks*: These prevent other sessions from gaining a DDL lock or TM (DML) lock themselves. This means that you may query a table during a DDL operation, but you may not modify it in any way.

- *Share DDL locks*: These protect the structure of the referenced object against modification by other sessions, but allow modifications to the data.

- *Breakable parse locks*: These allow an object, such as a query plan cached in the shared pool, to register its reliance on some other object. If you perform DDL against that object, Oracle will review the list of objects that have registered their dependence and invalidate them. Hence, these locks are breakable—they do not prevent the DDL from occurring.

Most DDL takes an exclusive DDL lock. If you issue a statement such as

```
Alter table t move;
```

the table T will be unavailable for modifications during the execution of that statement. The table may be queried using SELECT during this time, but most other operations will be prevented, including all other DDL statements. In Oracle, some DDL operations may now take place without DDL locks. For example, I can issue the following:

```
Create index t_idx on t(x) ONLINE;
```

The ONLINE keyword modifies the method by which the index is actually built. Instead of taking an exclusive DDL lock, preventing modifications of data, Oracle will only attempt to acquire a low-level (mode 2) TM lock on the table. This will effectively prevent other DDL from taking place, but it will allow DML to occur normally. Oracle accomplishes this feat by keeping a record of modifications made to the table during the DDL statement and applying these changes to the new index as it finishes the CREATE action. This greatly increases the availability of data. To see this for yourself, you could create a table of some size:

```
SQL> create table t as select * from all_objects;
Table created.

SQL> select object_id from user_objects where object_name = 'T';

 OBJECT_ID
----------
    244277
```

And then run the create index against that table:

```
SQL> create index t_idx on t(owner,object_type,object_name) ONLINE;
```

while at the same time running this query in another session to see the locks taken against that newly created table (remember, ID1=244277 is specific to my example, you'll want to use *your* object ID).

```
SQL> select (select username
               from v$session
              where sid = v$lock.sid) username,
          sid,
          id1,
          id2,
          lmode,
          request, block, type
      from v$lock
   where id1 = 244277
  /
```

| USERNAME | SID | ID1 | ID2 | LMODE | REQUEST | BLOCK | TY |
|----------|-----|-----|-----|-------|---------|-------|-----|
| YODA | 451 | 80470 | 0 | 4 | 0 | 0 | OD |
| YODA | 451 | 80470 | 0 | 3 | 0 | 0 | DL |
| YODA | 451 | 80470 | 0 | 3 | 0 | 0 | DL |
| YODA | 451 | 80470 | 0 | 2 | 0 | 0 | TM |

So, here we see four locks taken out against our object. The two DL locks are *direct load* locks. They are used to prevent a direct path load into our base table while the index creation is taking place (which implies, of course, that you cannot directly path load the table AND create the index simultaneously). The OD lock is a lock type first appeared with Oracle 11*g* that permits truly online DDL. In the past (10*g* and before), online DDL such as CREATE INDEX ONLINE was not 100 percent online. It would take a lock at the beginning and end of the CREATE statement—preventing other concurrent activities (modifications of the base table data). It was *mostly online* but not *completely online*. Starting with 11*g*, the CREATE INDEX ONLINE command is completely online; it does not require exclusionary locks at the beginning/end of the command. Part of the implementation to accomplish this feat was the introduction of the OD (online DDL) lock; it is used internally to allow truly online DDL operations.

Other types of DDL take share DDL locks. These are taken out against dependent objects when you create stored, compiled objects, such as procedures and views. For example, if you execute the following, share DDL locks will be placed against both EMP and DEPT while the CREATE VIEW command is being processed:

```
Create view MyView
as
select emp.empno, emp.ename, dept.deptno, dept.dname
  from emp, dept
 where emp.deptno = dept.deptno;
```

You can modify the contents of these tables, but you cannot modify their structure.

The last type of DDL lock is a breakable parse lock. When your session parses a statement, a parse lock is taken against every object referenced by that statement. These locks are taken in order to allow the parsed, cached statement to be invalidated (flushed) in the shared pool if a referenced object is dropped or altered in some way.

A view that is invaluable for looking at this information is DBA_DDL_LOCKS. There is no V$ view. The DBA_DDL_LOCKS view is built on the more mysterious X$ tables, and by default, it might not be installed in your database. You can install this and other locking views by running the `catblock.sql` script found in the directory `[ORACLE_HOME]/rdbms/admin`. This script must be executed as the user `SYS` in order to succeed. Once you have executed this script, you can run a query against the view. For example, in a freshly connected session, I might see the following when connecting to my pluggable database:

```
sqlplus yoda/foo@localhost:1521/orcl
```

```
SQL> set linesize 1000
SQL> select session_id sid, owner, name, type,
          mode_held held, mode_requested request
    from dba_ddl_locks
    where session_id = (select sid from v$mystat where rownum=1)
    /
```

| SID | OWNER | NAME | TYPE | HELD | REQUEST |
|-----|-------|------|------|------|---------|
| 451 | | YODA | 73 | Share | None |
| 451 | YODA | YODA | 18 | Null | None |
| 451 | SYS | DBMS_OUTPUT | Body | Null | None |
| 451 | SYS | DBMS_APPLICATION_INFO | Body | Null | None |
| 451 | SYS | DBMS_OUTPUT | Table/Procedure/Type | Null | None |
| 451 | SYS | DBMS_APPLICATION_INFO | Table/Procedure/Type | Null | None |
| 451 | SYS | DATABASE | 18 | Null | None |

These are all the objects that my session is locking. I have breakable parse locks on a couple of the DBMS_* packages. These are a side effect of using SQL*Plus; it might call DBMS_APPLICATION_INFO, for example, when you initially log in (to enable/disable DBMS_OUTPUT via the SET SERVEROUTPUT command). I may see more than one copy of various objects here; this is normal, and it just means I have more than one thing I'm using in the shared pool that references these objects. Note that in the view, the OWNER column is not the owner of the lock; rather, it is the owner of the object being locked. This is why you see many SYS rows. SYS owns these packages, but they all *belong* to my session.

To see a breakable parse lock in action, let's first create and run a stored procedure, P:

```
SQL> create or replace procedure p
     as
     begin
      null;
     end;
    /
Procedure created.

SQL> exec p
PL/SQL procedure successfully completed.
```

The procedure, P, will now show up in the DBA_DDL_LOCKS view. We have a parse lock on it:

```
SQL> select session_id sid, owner, name, type,
            mode_held held, mode_requested request
       from dba_ddl_locks
      where session_id = (select sid from v$mystat where rownum=1)
    /
```

| SID | OWNER | NAME | TYPE | HELD | REQUEST |
|-----|-------|------|------|------|---------|
| 451 | SYS | DBMS_STANDARD | Table/Procedure/Type | Null | None |
| 451 |  | YODA | 73 | Share | None |
| 451 | YODA | YODA | 18 | Null | None |
| 451 | YODA | P | Table/Procedure/Type | Null | None |

We then recompile our procedure and query the view again:

```
SQL> alter procedure p compile;
Procedure altered.

SQL> select session_id sid, owner, name, type,
            mode_held held, mode_requested request
       from dba_ddl_locks
      where session_id = (select sid from v$mystat where rownum=1)
    /
```

| SID | OWNER | NAME | TYPE | HELD | REQUEST |
|------|--------|------|------|------|---------|
| 451 | SYS | DBMS_STANDARD | Table/Procedure/Type | Null | None |
| 451 | | YODA | 73 | Share | None |
| 451 | YODA | YODA | 18 | Null | None |

We find that P is now missing from the view. Our parse lock has been broken.

This view is useful to you, as a developer, when it is found that some piece of code won't compile in the test or development system—it hangs and eventually times out. This indicates that someone else is using it (actually running it), and you can use this view to see who that might be. The same will happen with GRANT statements and other types of DDL against the object. You cannot grant EXECUTE on a procedure that is running, for example. You can use the same method to discover the potential blockers and waiters.

---

**Note**    Oracle 11*g* Release 2 and above introduce the *feature* Edition-based redefinition (EBR). With EBR, you can, in fact, grant EXECUTE and/or recompile code in the database without interfering with users currently executing the code. EBR allows you to have multiple versions of the same stored procedure in a schema at once. This allows you to work on a copy of the procedure in a new edition (version) without contending with the current version of the procedure being used by other users. We will not be covering EBR in this book, however, just mentioning it when it changes the rules.

---

# Latches

*Latches* are lightweight serialization devices used to coordinate multiuser access to shared data structures, objects, and files. Latches are locks designed to be held for extremely short periods of time—for example, the time it takes to modify an in-memory data structure. They are used to protect certain memory structures, such as the database block buffer cache or the library cache in the shared pool. Latches are typically requested internally in a *willing to wait* mode. This means that if the latch is not available, the requesting session will sleep for a short period of time and retry the operation later. Other latches may be requested in an immediate mode, which is similar in concept to a

SELECT FOR UPDATE NOWAIT, meaning that the process will go do something else, such as try to grab an equivalent sibling latch that may be free, rather than sit and wait for this latch to become available. Since many requestors may be waiting for a latch at the same time, you may see some processes waiting longer than others. Latches are assigned rather randomly, based on the luck of the draw, if you will. Whichever session asks for a latch right after it was released will get it. There is no line of latch waiters—just a mob of waiters constantly retrying.

Oracle uses atomic instructions like "test and set" and "compare and swap" for operating on latches. Since the instructions to set and free latches are atomic, the operating system itself guarantees that only one process gets to test and set the latch even though many processes may be going for it simultaneously. Since the instruction is only one instruction, it can be quite fast (but the overall latching algorithm itself is many CPU instructions). Latches are held for short periods of time and provide a mechanism for cleanup in case a latch holder dies abnormally while holding it. This cleanup process would be performed by PMON.

Enqueues, which we discussed earlier, are another, more sophisticated serialization device used when updating rows in a database table, for example. They differ from latches in that they allow the requestor to queue up and wait for the resource. With a latch request, the requestor session is told right away whether or not it got the latch. With an enqueue lock, the requestor session will be blocked until it can actually attain it.

---

**Note**    Using SELECT FOR UPDATE NOWAIT or WAIT [n], you can optionally decide not to wait for an enqueue lock if your session would be blocked, but if you do block and wait, you will wait in a queue.

---

As such, an enqueue is not as fast as a latch can be, but it does provide functionality over and above what a latch can offer. Enqueues may be obtained at various levels, so you can have many share locks and locks with various degrees of shareability.

# Latch "Spinning"

One thing I'd like to drive home with regard to latches is this: latches are a type of lock, locks are serialization devices, and serialization devices inhibit scalability. If your goal is to construct an application that scales well in an Oracle environment, you must look for approaches and solutions that minimize the amount of latching you need to perform.

Even seemingly simple activities, such as parsing a SQL statement, acquire and release hundreds or thousands of latches on the library cache and related structures in the shared pool. If we have a latch, then someone else might be waiting for it. When we go to get a latch, we may well have to wait for it ourselves.

Waiting for a latch can be an expensive operation. If the latch is not available immediately and we are willing to wait for it, as we likely are most of the time, then on a multi-CPU machine our session will spin, trying over and over, in a loop, to get the latch. The reasoning behind this is that context switching (i.e., getting kicked off the CPU and having to get back on the CPU) is expensive. So, if the process cannot get a latch immediately, we'll stay on the CPU and try again immediately rather than just going to sleep, giving up the CPU, and trying later when we'll have to get scheduled back on the CPU. The hope is that the holder of the latch is busy processing on the other CPU (and since latches are designed to be held for very short periods of time, this is likely) and will give it up soon. If after spinning and constantly trying to get the latch, we still fail to obtain it, only then will our process sleep, or take itself off of the CPU, and let some other work take place. This sleep action is usually the result of many sessions concurrently requesting the same latch; it is not that a single session is holding it for a long time, but rather that so many sessions want it at the same time and each holds it for a short duration. If you do something short (fast) often enough, it adds up! The pseudocode for a latch get might look like this:

```
Loop
        for i in 1 .. 2000
        loop
                try to get latch
                if got latch, return
                if i = 1 then misses=misses+1
        end loop
        INCREMENT WAIT COUNT
        sleep
        Add WAIT TIME
End loop;
```

The logic is to try to get the latch and, failing that, to increment the miss count, a statistic we can see in a Statspack report or by querying the V$LATCH view directly. Once the process misses, it will loop some number of times (an undocumented parameter controls the number of times and is typically set to 2,000), attempting to get the latch over and over. If one of these get attempts succeeds, then it returns and we continue processing. If they all fail, the process will go to sleep for a short duration of time, after incrementing the sleep count for that latch. Upon waking up, the process begins all over again. This implies that the cost of getting a latch is not just the "test and set"-type operation that takes place, but also a considerable amount of CPU while we try to get the latch. Our system will appear to be very busy (with much CPU being consumed), but not much work is getting done.

## Measuring the Cost of Latching a Shared Resource

As an example, we'll study the cost of latching the shared pool. We'll compare a well-written program (one that uses bind variables) and a program that is not so well written (it uses literal SQL, or unique SQL for each statement). To do this, we'll use a very small PL/SQL program that simply logs into Oracle and executes 25,000 unique INSERT statements in a loop. We'll perform two sets of tests: our program will not use bind variables in the first set, and in the second set it will.

To evaluate these programs and their behavior in a multiuser environment, I opted to use Statspack to gather the metrics, as follows:

1. Execute a Statspack snapshot to gather the current state of the system.

2. Run N copies of the program, having each program INSERT into its own database table so as to avoid the contention associated with having all programs trying to insert into a single table.

3. Take another snapshot immediately after the last copy of the program finishes.

Then, it is a simple matter of printing out the Statspack report and finding out how long it took N copies of the program to complete, how much CPU was used, what major wait events occurred, and so on.

**Note**    Why not use AWR (Automatic Workload Repository) to perform this analysis? The answer to that is because everyone has access to Statspack, everyone. It might have to be installed by your DBA, but every Oracle customer has access to it. I want to present results that are reproducible by everyone.

These tests were performed on a multiple CPU machine. Given that there were multiple physical CPUs, you might expect very linear scaling here—that is, if one user uses 1 unit of CPU to process her inserts, then you might expect that two users would require 2 units of CPU. You'll discover that this premise, while sounding plausible, may well be inaccurate (just how inaccurate depends on your programming technique, as you'll see). It would be correct if the processing we were performing needed no shared resource, but our process will use a shared resource, namely, the shared pool. We need to latch the shared pool to parse SQL statements, and we need to latch the shared pool because it is a shared data structure, and we cannot modify it while others are reading it and we cannot read it while it is being modified.

**Note**    I've performed these tests using Java, PL/SQL, Pro*C, and other languages. The end results are very much the same every time. This demonstration and discussion applies to all languages and all interfaces to the database.

## Setting Up for the Test

In order to test, we'll need a schema (set of tables) to work with. We'll be testing with multiple users and want to measure the contention due to latching most of all, meaning that we're not interested in measuring the contention you might observe due to multiple sessions inserting into the same database table. So, we'll want a table per user to be created and we'll name these tables T1 ... T10, for example:

```
SQL> begin
        for i in 1 .. 10
        loop
            for x in (select * from user_tables where table_name = 'T'||i )
```

```
        loop
                execute immediate 'drop table ' || x.table_name;
            end loop;
            execute immediate 'create table t' || i || ' ( x int )';
        end loop;
    end;
  /

PL/SQL procedure successfully completed.
```

---

**Note**    Statspack must be installed to run the examples in this section. Ensure that you review the material in the "Setting Up Your Environment" section of the "Introduction" of this book. It contains instructions for installing Statspack.

---

We'll run this script before each iteration of the test to follow in order to reset our schema and to force hard parsing to take place if we run a test more than once. During our testing, we'll follow these steps:

1. Run `statspack.snap`.

2. Immediately start N of our PL/SQL code, where N will vary from 1 to 10, representing 1 to 10 concurrent users.

3. Wait for all N to complete.

4. Run `statspack.snap`.

5. Generate the Statspack report for the last two Statspack IDs.

The numbers presented for the following test runs were collected using this technique.

## Without Bind Variables

In the first instance, our PL/SQL code will not use bind variables, but rather will use string concatenation to insert data:

```
declare
begin
    for i in 1 .. 25000 loop
      begin
        execute immediate
          'insert into t' || &1 || ' values(' || i || ')';
      exception
        when no_data_found then null;
      end;
    end loop;
end;
/
```

To automate this, the prior code was placed in a text file named nb.sql. Then, the next bit of SQL automatically generates a shell script to call the prior PL/SQL as well as the call to Statspack:

```
define NumUsers=&1
-- create the temp.sh shell script to run the parallel sessions
set echo off
set verify off
set feedback off
set serverout on
spool temp.sh
begin
  dbms_output.put_line( 'echo exec statspack.snap | sqlplus / as sysdba' );
  for i in 1 .. &NumUsers
  loop
    dbms_output.put_line( 'sqlplus yoda/foo@localhost:1521/orcl @nb.sql '
    || i ||' ' || chr(38) );
  end loop;
  dbms_output.put_line( 'wait' );
  dbms_output.put_line( 'echo exec statspack.snap | sqlplus / as sysdba' );
end;
/
spool off
```

The contents of the generated shell script contain this (varies depending on the number of variables you pass to the prior code):

```
echo exec statspack.snap | sqlplus / as sysdba
sqlplus yoda/foo@localhost:1521/orcl @nb.sql 1 &
wait
echo exec statspack.snap | sqlplus / as sysdba
```

The shell script is then executed from the SQL*Plus from the same session that generated the script:

```
host /bin/bash temp.sh
```

You can download the script that encapsulates the logic and code for this example from the Apress website for this book. The script with this code is named nobind.sql and is executed as follows:

```
sqlplus yoda/foo@localhost:1521/orcl
SQL> @nobind.sql 1
```

I ran the test in single-user mode with just one session for the first test (i.e., by itself with no other active database sessions). The Statspack report came back with this information:

```
    Elapsed:      0.23 (mins) Av Act Sess:      0.7
    DB time:      0.16 (mins)     DB CPU:      0.16 (mins)

Cache Sizes                 Begin        End
~~~~~~~~~~~           ----------  ----------
    Buffer Cache:       5,920M            Std Block Size:        8K
    Shared Pool:        1,168M               Log Buffer:     7,344K

Load Profile          Per Second   Per Transaction   Per Exec    Per Call
~~~~~~~~~~~~         -------------  ----------------- ----------  -----------
...
        Parses:         1,825.2          12,776.5
   Hard parses:         1,796.9          12,578.0
...
```

| Event | Waits | Time (s) | Avg wait (ms) | %Total Call Time |
|---|---|---|---|---|
| Top 5 Timed Events | | | | |
| pman timer | 5 | 15 | 3000 | 60.6 |
| CPU time | | 9 | | 38.3 |
| log file parallel write | 45 | 0 | 2 | .3 |
| direct path sync | 8 | 0 | 7 | .2 |
| buffer busy waits | 1 | 0 | 38 | .2 |

I included the SGA configuration for reference, but the relevant statistics are as follows:

- Elapsed (DB time) time of approximately 10 seconds (0.16 of a minute)

- 1,796.9 hard parses per second

- 9 CPU seconds used

Now, if we were to run two of these programs simultaneously, we might expect the hard parsing to jump to about 3,600 per second (we have multiple CPUs available, after all) and the CPU time to double to perhaps 22 CPU seconds. Let's take a look:

```
sqlplus yoda/foo@localhost:1521/orcl
SQL> @nobind.sql 2

   Elapsed:      0.20 (mins) Av Act Sess:      1.8
   DB time:      0.36 (mins)    DB CPU:      0.35 (mins)
...
Load Profile           Per Second    Per Transaction    Per Exec    Per Call
~~~~~~~~~~~~           -------------- ------------------ ----------- -----------
...
        Parses:         4,178.3          16,713.0
   Hard parses:         4,167.7          16,670.7
...
```

```
Top 5 Timed Events                                            Avg %Total
~~~~~~~~~~~~~~~~~~~~                                          wait   Call
Event                              Waits   Time (s)   (ms)    Time
--------------------------------- ----------- ----------- ------ ------
CPU time                                          21           61.8
pman timer                             4          12   3000    35.6
latch: shared pool                17,586           1      0     2.0
log file parallel write               19           0      4      .2
library cache: dependency mutex X      2           0     19      .1
```

What we discover is that the hard parsing goes up a little bit, but the CPU time more than doubles. How could that be? The answer lies in Oracle's implementation of latching. On this multi-CPU machine, when we could not immediately get a latch, we spun. The act of spinning itself consumes CPU. Process 1 attempted many times to get a latch onto the shared pool only to discover that process 2 held that latch, so process 1 had to spin and wait for it (consuming CPU). The converse would be true for process 2; many times it would find that process 1 was holding the latch to the resource it needed. So, much of our processing time was spent not doing real work, but waiting for a resource to become available. If we page down through the Statspack report to the "Latch Sleep Breakdown" report, we discover the following:

```
Latch Name                Requests         Misses        Sleeps          Gets
------------------- ---------------- ------------ ----------- -----------
shared pool             2,151,856        131,050       17,789       113,513
```

Note how the number 17,789 appears in the SLEEPS column here? That number corresponds very closely to the number of WAITS reported in the preceding "Top 5 Timed Events" report.

---

**Note**    The number of sleeps corresponds *closely* to the number of waits; this might raise an eyebrow. Why not *exactly*? The reason is that the act of taking a snapshot is not atomic; a series of queries are executed gathering statistics into tables during a Statspack snapshot, and each query is *as* of a slightly different point in time. So, the wait event metrics were gathered at a time slightly before the latching details were.

---

Our "Latch Sleep breakdown" report shows us the number of times we tried to get a latch and failed in the spin loop. That means the Top 5 report is showing us only the tip of the iceberg with regard to latching issues—the 131,050 misses (which means we spun trying to get the latch) are not revealed in the Top 5 report for us. After examination of the Top 5 report, we might not be inclined to think we have a hard parse problem here, even though we have a very serious one. To perform 2 units of work, we needed to use more than 2 units of CPU. This was due entirely to the fact that we need that shared resource, the shared pool. Such is the nature of latching.

You can see that it can be very hard to diagnose a latching-related issue, unless you understand the mechanics of how they are implemented. A quick glance at a Statspack report, using the Top 5 section, might cause us to miss the fact that we have a fairly bad scaling issue on our hands. Only by deeper investigation in the latching section of the Statspack report will we see the problem at hand.

Additionally, it is not normally possible to determine how much of the CPU time used by the system is due to this spinning—all we know in looking at the two-user test is that we used 21 seconds of CPU time and that we missed getting a latch on the shared pool 131,050 times. We don't know how many times we spun trying to get the latch each time we missed, so we have no real way of gauging how much of the CPU time was spent spinning and how much was spent processing. We need multiple data points to derive that information.

In our tests, because we have the single-user example for comparison, we can conclude that about 3 CPU seconds or so was spent spinning on the latch, waiting for that resource. We can come to this conclusion because we know that a single user needs only 9 seconds of CPU time so two single users would need 18 seconds, and 21 (total CPU seconds) minus 18 is 3.

## With Bind Variables

Now I'd like to look at the same situation as presented in the previous section, but this time using a program that uses significantly less latches during its processing. We'll take that PL/SQL program and code it using bind variables. To accomplish this, we'll simply replace the hard coded variable with a bind variable:

```
sqlplus yoda/foo@localhost:1521/orcl
SQL> @bind.sql 1
```

```
declare
begin
   for i in 1 .. 25000 loop
     begin
       execute immediate
         'insert into t1 values(:i)' using i;
     exception
       when no_data_found then null;
     end;
   end loop;
end;
/
```

Let's look at the single- and dual-user Statspack reports, as we did for the no bind variable example. We'll see dramatic differences here. Here is the single-user report:

```
      Elapsed:     0.03 (mins) Av Act Sess:       0.5
      DB time:     0.02 (mins)    DB CPU:      0.02 (mins)

Load Profile            Per Second    Per Transaction    Per Exec    Per Call
~~~~~~~~~~~~            ------------   ----------------   --------    --------
...
          Parses:         46.0              46.0
     Hard parses:          1.5               1.5
...
```

| Top 5 Timed Events | | | Avg | %Total |
|---|---|---|---|---|
| ~~~~~~~~~~~~~~~~~~~ | | | wait | Call |
| Event | Waits | Time (s) | (ms) | Time |
| ------------------------------------- | ----------- | ----------- | ------ | ------ |
| pman timer | 1 | 3 | 3000 | 74.2 |
| CPU time | | 1 | | 24.0 |
| log file parallel write | 14 | 0 | 3 | 1.0 |
| LGWR worker group ordering | 3 | 0 | 5 | .4 |
| log file sync | 4 | 0 | 3 | .3 |

The difference between nobinding and binding is quite dramatic! We went from 11 CPU seconds in the no bind variable example to 1 CPU second here. From 1,796 hard parses per second to about 1.5 per second (and based on my knowledge of how Statspack works, most of those were from running Statspack). Even the elapsed time was dramatically reduced from about 0.23 minutes (14 seconds) down to 0.03 minutes (2 seconds). When not using bind variables, we spent much of our CPU time parsing SQL. This was not entirely latch related, as much of the CPU time incurred without bind variables was spent parsing and optimizing the SQL. Parsing SQL is very CPU intensive, but to expend most of our CPU doing something (parsing) that doesn't really do useful work for us—work we didn't need to perform—is pretty expensive.

When we get to the two-user test, the results continue to look much better for the test using bind variables:

```
sqlplus yoda/foo@localhost:1521/orcl
SQL> @bind.sql 2

   Elapsed:       0.03 (mins) Av Act Sess:      0.7
   DB time:       0.02 (mins)    DB CPU:        0.02 (mins)
...
Load Profile           Per Second    Per Transaction   Per Exec    Per Call
~~~~~~~~~~~~~~         ------------   ----------------  ----------  -----------
...
         Parses:          53.0              35.3
    Hard parses:           1.0               0.7
...
```

| Top 5 Timed Events | | | Avg | %Total |
| ~~~~~~~~~~~~~~~~~~~~~~~ | | | wait | Call |
| Event | Waits | Time (s) | (ms) | Time |
| --- | --- | --- | --- | --- |
| pman timer | 1 | 3 | 3000 | 66.7 |
| CPU time | | 1 | | 29.3 |
| log file parallel write | 18 | 0 | 4 | 1.6 |
| buffer busy waits | 2,101 | 0 | 0 | .6 |
| library cache lock | 2 | 0 | 10 | .5 |

The amount of CPU time is about the same as reported by the single-user test case.

**Note**   Due to rounding, the 1 CPU seconds is really anywhere from 0 to 2, and the 3 is really anywhere from 2 to 4 seconds.

Further, the amount of CPU used by two users with bind variables is *far* less than half the amount of CPU a single user not using bind variables required! When I looked at the latch report in this Statspack report, I found there was so little contention for the shared pool and library cache that it was not even worth reporting. In fact, digging deeper turned up the fact that the shared pool latch doesn't even register shared pool requests, whereas the no-bind two-user test logged well over 2.2 million requests.

## Performance/Scalability Comparison

Table 3-1 summarizes the CPU usage by each implementation, as well as the latching results as we increase the number of users beyond two. As you can see, the solution using fewer latches (binds) will scale much better as the user load goes up.

***Table 3-1.***  *CPU Usage Comparison with and Without Bind Variables*

| Users | CPU (sec)/DB Time (min.) | | Shared Pool Latch Requests | |
|-------|--------------------------|--------|----------------------------|-------|
|       | No Binds | Binds | No Binds | Binds |
| 1 | 11/0.22 | 1.0/0.02 | 0 | 0 |
| 2 | 21/0.21 | 1.0/0.02 | 2.2 million | 0 |
| 5 | 60/2.9 | 3.0/0.05 | 5.3 million | 0 |
| 10 | 130/9.52 | 4.0/0.19 | 10 million | 1,179 |

The 10 user test without bind variables took 130 CPU seconds, whereas with using bind variables took only 4 CPU seconds! The interesting observation is that 10 users using bind variables (and very few latch requests as a result) use about the same amount of hardware resources (CPU) as 1 user that does not use bind variables (i.e., that overuse a latch or process more than they need to). It's quite dramatic when you examine the results for 10 users. You see that nonuse of bind variables uses orders of magnitude more hardware resources than when compared with the use of bind variables. The more users are added over time, the longer each user spends waiting for these latches. However, the bind variable implementation avoided overuse of the latch and suffered no ill effects as it scaled up.

As a developer, the results of this test really drive home the impact of using bind variables. Nonuse of bind variables in your code can cripple application performance. As a DBA, you need to be aware of how to spot the nonuse of bind variables and work with application teams to ensure bind variables are always used.

# Mutexes

A *mutex* is a serialization device much like a latch is; in fact, the name mutex stands for *mutual exclusion*. It is another serialization tool used by the database; it was introduced in Oracle 10g Release 1 and is used in place of traditional latches in many places in the server. A mutex differs from a latch in that it is even more lightweight in its implementation. It requires less code to implement, approximately one-fifth of the instructions (which results in less CPU to request in general), and it requires less memory, approximately one-seventh of the size, to implement. A mutex, in addition to being lighter weight, is a little less functional in some respects. Just like an enqueue lock is much heavier than a latch, a latch is heavier than a mutex. But, like the enqueue to latch comparison, the latch can do more than a mutex in some cases (like an enqueue can do more than a latch in some cases). This means that not every latch will be, or should be, replaced by a mutex, just as every enqueue lock will not be, or should not be, replaced by a latch.

When reading about mutexes in various reports, just remember that they are lighter-weight serialization devices. They enable possibly more scalability than a latch (just as latches are more scalable than enqueues), but they are still *a serialization device.* If you can avoid doing something that requires a mutex, in general, you should, for the same reason you would avoid requesting a latch if possible.

# Manual Locking and User-Defined Locks

So far, we have looked mostly at locks that Oracle places for us transparently. When we update a table, Oracle places a TM lock on it to prevent other sessions from dropping that table (or performing most DDL, in fact). We have TX locks that are left on the various blocks we modify so others can tell what data we own. The database employs DDL locks to protect objects from change while we ourselves are changing them. It uses latches and locks internally to protect its own structure.

Next, let's take a look at how we can get involved in some of this locking action. Our options are as follows:

- Manually lock data via a SQL statement.

- Create our own locks via the DBMS_LOCK package.

The following sections briefly discuss why you might want to do each of these.

## Manual Locking

We have, in fact, already seen a couple of cases where we might want to use manual locking. The SELECT...FOR UPDATE statement is the predominant method of manually locking data. We used it in previous examples to avoid the lost update issue whereby one session would overwrite another session's changes. We've seen it used as a method to serialize access to detail records to enforce business rules.

We can also manually lock data using the LOCK TABLE statement. This statement is used rarely, because of the coarseness of the lock. It simply locks the table, not the rows in the table. If you start modifying the rows, they will be locked as normal. So, this is not a method to save on resources (as it might be in other RDBMSs). You might use the LOCK TABLE IN EXCLUSIVE MODE statement if you were writing a large batch update that would affect most of the rows in a given table and you wanted to be sure that no one would block you. By locking the table in this manner, you can be assured that your update will be able to do all of its work without getting blocked by other transactions. It would be the rare application, however, that has a LOCK TABLE statement in it.

## Creating Your Own Locks

Oracle actually exposes to developers the enqueue lock mechanism that it uses internally, via the DBMS_LOCK package. You might be wondering why you would want to create your own locks. The answer is typically application specific. For example, you might use this package to serialize access to some resource external to Oracle. Say you are using the UTL_FILE routine that allows you to write to a file on the server's file system. You might have developed a common message routine that every application calls to record messages. Since the file is external, Oracle won't coordinate the many users trying to modify it simultaneously. In comes the DBMS_LOCK package. Now, before you open, write, and close the file, you will request a lock named after the file in exclusive mode, and after you close the file, you will manually release the lock. In this fashion, only one person at a time will be able to write a message to this file. Everyone else will queue up. The DBMS_LOCK package allows you to manually release a lock when you are done with it, or to give it up automatically when you commit, or even to keep it as long as you are logged in.

# Summary

In this chapter, we looked at how Oracle manages concurrency through locks on rows, objects, and memory structures. Oracle uses TX locks to ensure that only one transaction is modifying a row at a given time. Oracle uses DM locks to ensure that the structure of an object isn't changed while its contents are being modified. We examined helpful queries that show the transaction details and identify sessions holding the lock and also show the sessions blocked from obtaining a lock.

We also discussed latches, which are lightweight serialization devices used to coordinate multiuser access to shared data structures, objects, and files. Latches are locks designed to be held for very short amount of time. They are used to protect memory structures in the block buffer cache, library cache, and the shared pool. We also talked about a mutex, which is a serialization device similar to a latch. A mutex is a much more efficient serialization device and is used in place of traditional latches in many places in the server (starting with Oracle 10g and above).

Lastly, we briefly looked at manual locking methods. The most common manual locking method is the SELECT...FOR UPDATE statement. Other than that, for the most part you'll never need to implement manual locking methods (such as LOCK TABLE).

In the next chapter, we'll investigate multiversioning (Oracle's ability to simultaneously materialize multiple versions of the data). This is the mechanism by which Oracle provides read-consistent views of data. We'll also take a detailed look at how Oracle implements multiversioning in regard to transaction isolation levels.

# CHAPTER 4

# Concurrency and Multiversioning

As stated in the previous chapter, one of the key challenges in developing multiuser, database-driven applications is to maximize concurrent access but, at the same time, ensure that each user is able to read and modify the data in a consistent fashion. In this chapter, we're going to take a detailed look at how Oracle achieves *multiversion read consistency* and what that means to you, the developer. I will also introduce a new term, *write consistency*, and use it to describe how Oracle works not only in a read environment with read consistency but also in a mixed read and write environment.

## What Are Concurrency Controls?

*Concurrency controls* are the collection of functions that the database provides to allow many people to access and modify data simultaneously. As noted in the previous two chapters, the *lock* is one of the core mechanisms by which Oracle regulates concurrent access to shared database resources and prevents interference between concurrent database transactions. To briefly summarize, Oracle uses a variety of locks, including the following:

- *TX (transaction) locks*: These locks are acquired for the duration of a data-modifying transaction.

- *TM (DML enqueue) and DDL locks*: These locks ensure that the structure of an object is not altered while you are modifying its contents (TM lock) or the object itself (DDL lock).

- *Latches and mutexes*: These are internal locks that Oracle employs to mediate access to its shared data structures. We'll refer to both as latches in this chapter, although they might be implemented by a mutex on your operating system, depending on the Oracle version.

© Darl Kuhn and Thomas Kyte 2021
D. Kuhn and T. Kyte, *Oracle Database Transactions and Locking Revealed*,
https://doi.org/10.1007/978-1-4842-6425-6_4

In each case, there is minimal overhead associated with lock acquisition. TX transaction locks are extremely scalable both in terms of performance and cardinality. TM and DDL locks are applied in the least restrictive mode whenever possible. Latches and enqueues are both very lightweight and fast (enqueues are slightly the heavier of the two, though more feature-rich). Problems only arise from poorly designed applications that hold locks for *longer than necessary* and cause blocking in the database. If you design your code well, Oracle's locking mechanisms will allow for scalable, highly concurrent applications.

---

**Note**   I used the phrase "longer than necessary." That does not mean you should attempt to commit (end your transaction) as soon as possible. Transactions should be exactly as long as they need to be—and no longer than that. That is, your transaction is your unit of work; it is all or nothing. You should commit when your unit of work is complete and not before—and not any later either!

---

But Oracle's support for concurrency goes beyond efficient locking. It implements a *multiversioning* architecture that provides controlled yet highly concurrent access to data. Multiversioning describes Oracle's ability to simultaneously materialize multiple versions of the data and is the mechanism by which Oracle provides read-consistent views of data (i.e., consistent results with respect to a point in time). A rather pleasant side effect of multiversioning is that a reader of data will never be blocked by a writer of data. In other words, writes do not block reads. This is one of the fundamental differences between Oracle and other databases. A query that only reads information in Oracle will never be blocked; it will never deadlock with another session, and it will never get an answer that didn't exist in the database.

---

**Note**   There is a short period of time during the processing of a distributed *Two-Phase Commit* where Oracle will prevent read access to information. As this processing is somewhat rare and exceptional (the problem applies only to queries that start between the prepare and the commit phases and try to read the data before the commit arrives), I will not cover it in detail.

---

Oracle's multiversioning model for read consistency is applied by default at the *statement level* (for each and every query) and can also be applied at the *transaction level*. This means that each and every SQL statement submitted to the database sees a read-consistent view of the database, at least—and if you would like this read-consistent view of the database to be at the level of a transaction (a set of SQL statements), you may do that as well, as we'll see in the "SERIALIZABLE" section in this chapter.

The basic purpose of a transaction in the database is to take the database from one consistent state to the next. The ISO SQL standard specifies various *transaction isolation levels*, which define how *sensitive* one transaction is to changes made by another. The greater the level of sensitivity, the greater the degree of isolation the database must provide between transactions executed by your application. In the following section, we'll look at how, via its multiversioning architecture and with absolutely minimal locking, Oracle can support each of the defined isolation levels.

# Transaction Isolation Levels

The ANSI/ISO SQL standard defines four levels of transaction isolation, with different possible outcomes for the same transaction scenario. That is, the same work performed in the same fashion with the same inputs may result in different answers, depending on your isolation level. These isolation levels are defined in terms of three "phenomena" that are either permitted or not at a given isolation level:

- *Dirty read*: The meaning of this term is as bad as it sounds. You are permitted to read uncommitted, or *dirty*, data. You would achieve this effect by just opening an OS file that someone else is writing and reading whatever data happens to be there. Data integrity is compromised, foreign keys are violated, and unique constraints are ignored.

- *Nonrepeatable read*: This simply means that if you read a row at time T1 and attempt to reread that row at time T2, the row may have changed, or it may have disappeared, or it may have been updated, and so on.

- *Phantom read*: This means that if you execute a query at time T1 and reexecute it at time T2, additional rows may have been added to the database, which will affect your results. This differs from the nonrepeatable read in that with a phantom read, data you already read has not been changed, but rather that *more* data satisfies your query criteria than before.

> **Note**   The ANSI/ISO SQL standard defines *transaction*-level characteristics, not just individual statement-by-statement–level characteristics. In the following pages, we'll examine transaction-level isolation, not just statement-level isolation.

The SQL isolation levels are defined based on whether or not they allow each of the preceding phenomena. I find it interesting to note that the SQL standard does not impose a specific locking scheme or mandate particular behaviors, but rather describes these isolation levels in terms of these phenomena, allowing for many different locking/concurrency mechanisms to exist (see Table 4-1).

**Table 4-1.**  *ANSI Isolation Levels*

| Isolation Level | Dirty Read | Nonrepeatable Read | Phantom Read |
|---|---|---|---|
| READ UNCOMMITTED | Permitted | Permitted | Permitted |
| READ COMMITTED | -- | Permitted | Permitted |
| REPEATABLE READ | -- | -- | Permitted |
| SERIALIZABLE | -- | -- | -- |

Oracle explicitly supports the READ COMMITTED and SERIALIZABLE isolation levels as they are defined in the standard. However, this doesn't tell the whole story. The SQL standard was attempting to set up isolation levels that would permit various degrees of consistency for queries performed in each level. REPEATABLE READ is the isolation level that the SQL standard claims will guarantee a read-consistent result from a query. In their definition, READ COMMITTED does not give you consistent results, and READ UNCOMMITTED is the level to use to get nonblocking reads.

However, in Oracle, READ COMMITTED has all of the attributes required to achieve read-consistent queries. In many other databases, READ COMMITTED queries can and will return answers that never existed in the database at any point in time. Moreover, Oracle also supports the *spirit* of READ UNCOMMITTED. The goal of providing a dirty read is to supply a nonblocking read, whereby queries are not blocked by, and do not block, updates of the same data. However, Oracle does not need dirty reads to achieve this goal, nor does it support them. Dirty reads are an implementation other databases must use in order to provide nonblocking reads.

In addition to the four defined SQL isolation levels, Oracle provides another level, namely, READ ONLY. A READ ONLY transaction is equivalent to a REPEATABLE READ or SERIALIZABLE transaction that can't perform any modifications in SQL. A transaction using a READ ONLY isolation level only sees those changes that were committed *at the time the transaction began*, but inserts, updates, and deletes are not permitted in this mode (other sessions may update data, but not the READ ONLY transaction). Using this mode, you can achieve REPEATABLE READ and SERIALIZABLE levels of isolation.

Let's now move on to discuss exactly how multiversioning and read consistency fit into the isolation scheme and how databases that do not support multiversioning achieve the same results. This information is instructive for anyone who has used another database and believes she understands how the isolation levels must work. It is also interesting to see how a standard that was supposed to remove the differences between the databases, ANSI/ISO SQL, actually allows for them. The standard, while very detailed, can be implemented in very different ways.

# READ UNCOMMITTED

The READ UNCOMMITTED isolation level allows dirty reads. Oracle does not make use of dirty reads, nor does it even allow for them. The basic goal of a READ UNCOMMITTED isolation level is to provide a standards-based definition that caters for nonblocking reads. As we have seen, Oracle provides for nonblocking reads by default. You would be hard-pressed to make a SELECT query block in the database (as noted earlier, there is the special case of a distributed transaction). Every single query, be it a SELECT, INSERT, UPDATE, MERGE, or DELETE, executes in a read-consistent fashion. It might seem funny to refer to an UPDATE statement as a query, but it is. UPDATE statements have two components: a read component as defined by the WHERE clause and a write component as defined by the SET clause. UPDATE statements read and write to the database; all DML statements have this ability. The case of a single-row INSERT using the VALUES clause is the only exception, as such statements have no read component, just the write component.

In Chapter 1, Oracle's method of obtaining read consistency was demonstrated by way of a simple single table query that retrieved rows that were deleted *after* the cursor was opened. We're now going to explore a real-world example to see what happens in Oracle using multiversioning, as well as what happens in any number of other databases.

Let's start with a basic table and query:

```
create table accounts
( account_number number primary key,
  account_balance number not null
);
```

```
select sum(account_balance) from accounts;
```

Before the query begins, assume we have the data shown in Table 4-2.

**Table 4-2.** *ACCOUNTS Table Before Modifications*

| Row | Account Number | Account Balance |
|-----|----------------|-----------------|
| 1 | 123 | $500.00 |
| 2 | 456 | $240.25 |
| ... | ... | ... |
| 342,023 | 987 | $100.00 |

Now, our select statement starts executing and reads row 1, row 2, and so on.

**Note**   I do not mean to imply that rows have any sort of physical ordering on disk in this example. There really is not a first row, second row, or last row in a table. There is just a set of rows. We are assuming here that row 1 really means "the first row we happened to read" and row 2 is the second row we happened to read and so on.

At some point while we are in the middle of the query, a transaction moves $400.00 from account 123 to account 987. This transaction does the two updates but does not commit. The table now looks as shown in Table 4-3.

**Table 4-3.** *ACCOUNTS Table During Modifications*

| Row | Account Number | Account Balance | Locked? |
| --- | --- | --- | --- |
| 1 | 123 | ($500.00) changed to $100.00 | X |
| 2 | 456 | $240.25 | -- |
| ... | ... | ... | -- |
| 342,023 | 987 | ($100.00) changed to $500.00 | X |

So, two of those rows are locked. If anyone tried to update them, that user would be blocked. So far, the behavior we are seeing is more or less consistent across all databases. The difference will be in what happens when the query gets to the locked data.

When the query we are executing gets to the block containing the locked row (row 342,023) at the bottom of the table, it will notice that the data in it has changed since the time at which it started execution. To provide a consistent (correct) answer, Oracle will at this point create a copy of the block containing this row *as it existed when the query began*. That is, it will read a value of $100.00, the value that existed at the time the query began. Effectively, Oracle takes a detour around the modified data; it reads around it, reconstructing it from the undo segment (also known as a *rollback segment*). A consistent and correct answer comes back without waiting for the transaction to commit.

Now, a database that allowed a dirty read would simply return the value it saw in account 987 at the time it read it, in this case $500.00. The query would count the transferred $400 twice. Therefore, not only does it return the wrong answer, but also it returns a total that never existed in the table at any committed point in time. In a multiuser database, a dirty read can be a dangerous feature and, personally, I have never seen the usefulness of it. Say that, rather than transferring, the transaction was actually just depositing $400.00 in account 987. The dirty read would count the $400.00 and get the "right" answer, wouldn't it? Well, suppose the uncommitted transaction was rolled back. We have just counted $400.00 that was never actually in the database.

The point here is that dirty read is not a feature; rather, it is a liability. In Oracle, it is just not needed. You get all of the advantages of a dirty read (no blocking) without any of the incorrect results.

# READ COMMITTED

The READ COMMITTED isolation level states that a transaction may only read data that has been committed in the database. There are no dirty reads. There may be nonrepeatable reads (i.e., rereads of the same row may return a different answer in the same transaction) and phantom reads (i.e., newly inserted and committed rows become visible to a query that were not visible earlier in the transaction). READ COMMITTED is perhaps the most commonly used isolation level in database applications everywhere, and it is the default mode for Oracle databases; it is rare to see a different isolation level used.

However, achieving READ COMMITTED isolation is not as cut and dried as it sounds. If you look at Table 4-1, it looks straightforward. Obviously, given the earlier rules, a query executed in any database using the READ COMMITTED isolation will behave in the same way, will it not? *It will not.* If you query multiple rows in a single statement, in almost every other database, READ COMMITTED isolation can be as bad as a dirty read, depending on the implementation.

In Oracle, using multiversioning and read-consistent queries, the answer we get from the ACCOUNTS query is the same in READ COMMITTED as it was in the READ UNCOMMITTED example. Oracle will reconstruct the modified data as it appeared when the query began, returning the answer that was in the database when the query started.

Let's now take a look at how our previous example might work in READ COMMITTED mode in other databases—you might find the answer surprising. We'll pick up our example at the point described in the previous table:

- We are in the middle of the table. We have read and summed the first N rows.

- The other transaction has moved $400.00 from account 123 to account 987.

- The transaction has not yet committed, so rows containing the information for accounts 123 and 987 are locked.

We know what happens in Oracle when it gets to account 987—it will read around the modified data, find out it should be $100.00, and complete. Table 4-4 shows how another database, running in some default READ COMMITTED mode, might arrive at the answer.

***Table 4-4.*** *Timeline in a Non-Oracle Database Using READ COMMITTED Isolation*

| Time | Query | Account Transfer Transaction |
|------|-------|------------------------------|
| T1 | Reads row 1, account 123, value=$500. Sum=$500.00 so far. | -- |
| T2 | Reads row 2, account 456, value=$240.25. Sum=$740.25 so far. | -- |
| T3 | -- | Updates row 1 (account 123) and puts an exclusive lock on row 1, preventing other updates and reads. Row 1 had $500.00, now it has $100.00. |
| T4 | Reads row N. Sum = … | -- |
| T5 | -- | Updates row 342,023 (account 987) and puts an exclusive lock on this row. This row had $100, now it has $500.00. |
| T6 | Tries to read row 342,023, account 987. Discovers that it is locked. This session will block and wait for this row's block to become available. *All processing on this query stops.* | -- |
| T7 | -- | Commits transaction. |
| T8 | Reads row 342,023, account 987, sees $500.00, and presents a final answer that includes the $400.00 double-counted. | -- |

The first thing to notice is that this other database, upon getting to account 987, will block our query. This session must wait on that row until the transaction holding the exclusive lock commits. This is one reason why many people have a bad habit of committing every statement, instead of processing well-formed transactions consisting of all of the statements needed to take the database from one consistent state to the next. *Updates interfere with reads in most other databases.* The really bad news in this scenario is that we are making the end user wait for the *wrong* answer. We still receive an answer that never existed in the committed database state at any point in time, as with the dirty read, but this time we made the user wait for the wrong answer. In the next section, we'll look at what these other databases need to do to achieve read-consistent, correct results.

The important lesson here is that various databases executing in the same, apparently safe isolation level can and will return very different answers under the exact same circumstances. It is important to understand that, in Oracle, nonblocking reads are not had at the expense of correct answers. You can have your cake and eat it too, sometimes.

# REPEATABLE READ

The goal of REPEATABLE READ is to provide an isolation level that gives consistent, correct answers and prevents lost updates. We'll take a look at examples of both, see what we have to do in Oracle to achieve these goals, and examine what happens in other systems.

## Getting a Consistent Answer

If we have a REPEATABLE READ isolation, the results from a given query must be consistent with respect to some point in time. Most databases (not Oracle) achieve repeatable reads via the use of row-level shared read locks. A shared read lock prevents other sessions from modifying data that we have read. This, of course, decreases concurrency. Oracle opted for the more concurrent, multiversioning model to provide read-consistent answers.

In Oracle, using multiversioning, we get an answer that is consistent with respect to the point in time the query began execution. In other databases, using shared read locks, we get an answer that is consistent with respect to the point in time the query completes—that is, when we can get the answer at all (more on this in a moment).

In a system that employs a shared read lock to provide repeatable reads, we would observe rows in a table getting locked as the query processed them. So, using the earlier example, as our query reads the ACCOUNTS table, it would leave shared read locks on each row, as shown in Table 4-5.

***Table 4-5.*** *Timeline 1 in Non-Oracle Database Using READ REPEATABLE Isolation*

| Time | Query | Account Transfer Transaction |
|------|-------|------------------------------|
| T1 | Reads row 1. Sum=$500.00 so far. Row 1 has a shared read lock on it. | -- |
| T2 | Reads row 2. Sum=$740.25 so far. Row 2 has a shared read lock on it. | -- |
| T3 | -- | Attempts to update row 1 but is blocked. Transaction is suspended until it can obtain an exclusive lock. |
| T4 | Reads row N. Sum = ... | -- |
| T5 | Reads row 342,023, sees $100.00, and presents final answer. | -- |
| T6 | Commits transaction. | -- |
| T7 | -- | Updates row 1 and puts an exclusive lock on this row. Row now has $100.00. |
| T8 | -- | Updates row 342,023 and puts an exclusive lock on this row. Row now has $500.00. Commits transaction. |

Table 4-5 shows that we now get the correct answer, but at the cost of physically blocking one transaction and executing the two transactions sequentially. This is one of the side effects of shared read locks for consistent answers: *readers of data will block writers of data*. This is in addition to the fact that, in these systems, writers of data will block readers of data. Imagine if automatic teller machines (ATMs) worked this way in real life.

So, you can see how shared read locks would inhibit concurrency, but they can also cause spurious errors to occur. In Table 4-6, we start with our original table, but this time with the goal of transferring $50.00 from account 987 to account 123.

***Table 4-6.*** *Timeline 2 in Non-Oracle Database Using READ REPEATABLE Isolation*

| Time | Query | Account Transfer Transaction |
|---|---|---|
| T1 | Reads row 1. Sum=$500.00 so far. Row 1 has a shared read lock on it. | -- |
| T2 | Reads row 2. Sum=$740.25 so far. Row 2 has a shared read lock on it. | -- |
| T3 | -- | Updates row 342,023 and puts an exclusive lock on row 342,023, preventing other updates and shared read locks. This row now has $50.00. |
| T4 | Reads row N. Sum = ... | -- |
| T5 | -- | Attempts to update row 1 but is blocked. Transaction is suspended until it can obtain an exclusive lock. |
| T6 | Attempts to read row 342,023 but can't as an exclusive lock is already in place. | -- |

We have just reached the classic deadlock condition. Our query holds resources the update needs and vice versa. Our query has just deadlocked with our update transaction. One of them will be chosen as the victim and will be killed. We just spent a long time and a lot of resources only to fail and get rolled back at the end. This is the second side effect of shared read locks: *readers and writers of data can and frequently will deadlock each other.*

In Oracle, we have statement-level read consistency without reads blocking writes or deadlocks. Oracle never uses shared read locks—*ever.* Oracle has chosen the harder-to-implement but infinitely more concurrent multiversioning scheme.

# Lost Updates: Another Portability Issue

A common use of REPEATABLE READ in databases that employ the shared read locks could be for lost update prevention.

> **Note**   Lost update detection and solutions to the lost update problem are discussed in Chapter 2.

If we have REPEATABLE READ enabled in a database *that employs shared read locks* (and not multiversioning), lost update errors can't happen. The reason lost updates will not happen in those databases is because the simple act of selecting the data *leaves a lock on it, and once read by our transaction, that data cannot be modified by any other transaction.* Now, if your application assumes that REPEATABLE READ implies "lost updates can't happen," you are in for a painful surprise when you move your application to a database that does not use shared read locks as an underlying concurrency control mechanism.

> **Note**   In a stateless environment, such as a web-based application, lost updates would likely be a cause for concern—even in REPEATABLE READ isolation. This is because a single database session is used by many clients via a connection pool and locks are not held across calls. REPEATABLE READ isolation only prevents lost updates in a stateful environment, such as that observed with a client/server application.

While this sounds good, you must remember that leaving the shared read locks behind on all data as it is read will, of course, severely limit concurrent reads and modifications. So, while this isolation level in those databases provides for lost update prevention, it does so by removing the ability to perform concurrent operations! You can't always have your cake and eat it too.

# SERIALIZABLE

This is generally considered the most restrictive level of transaction isolation, but it provides the highest degree of isolation. A SERIALIZABLE transaction operates in an environment that makes it appear as if there are no other users modifying data in the database. Any row we read is assured to be the same upon a reread, and any query we execute is guaranteed to return the same results for the life of a transaction. For example, if we execute the following, the answers returned from T would be the same, even though we just slept for 24 hours (or we might get an ORA-01555, snapshot too old error, which is discussed in Chapter 8):

```
Select * from T;
Begin dbms_lock.sleep( 60*60*24 ); end;
Select * from T;
```

The isolation level SERIALIZABLE assures us these two queries will always return the same results. Side effects (changes) made by other transactions are not visible to the query regardless of how long it has been running.

In Oracle, a SERIALIZABLE transaction is implemented so that the read consistency we normally get at the statement level is extended to the transaction.

---

**Note**    As noted earlier, there is also an isolation level in Oracle denoted READ ONLY. It has all of the qualities of the SERIALIZABLE isolation level, but it prohibits modifications. It should be noted that the SYS user (or users connected with the SYSDBA privilege) *can't* have a READ ONLY or SERIALIZABLE transaction. SYS is special in this regard.

---

Instead of results being consistent with respect to the start of a statement, they are preordained at the time you begin the transaction. In other words, Oracle uses the undo segments to reconstruct the data as it existed when our transaction began, instead of just when our statement began.

That's a pretty deep thought there: the database already knows the answer to any question you might ask it, before you ask it.

This degree of isolation comes with a price, and that price is the following possible error:

```
ERROR at line 1:
ORA-08177: can't serialize access for this transaction
```

You will get this message whenever you attempt to update a row that has changed since your transaction began.

---

**Note**    Oracle attempts to do this purely at the row level, but you may receive an ORA-08177 error even when the row you are interested in modifying has not been modified. The ORA-08177 error may happen due to some other row(s) being modified on the block that contains your row.

---

Oracle takes an optimistic approach to serialization—it gambles on the fact that the data your transaction wants to update won't be updated by any other transaction. This is typically the way it happens, and usually the gamble pays off, especially in quick-transaction, OLTP-type systems. If no one else updates your data during your transaction, this isolation level, which will generally decrease concurrency in other systems, will provide the same degree of concurrency as it would without `SERIALIZABLE` transactions. The downside to this is that you may get the `ORA-08177` error if the gamble doesn't pay off. If you think about it, however, it's worth the risk. If you're using `SERIALIZABLE` transactions, you shouldn't expect to update the same information as other transactions. If you do, you should use the `SELECT ... FOR UPDATE` as described in Chapter 2, and this will serialize the access. So, using an isolation level of `SERIALIZABLE` will be achievable and effective if you

- Have a high probability of no one else modifying the same data

- Need transaction-level read consistency

- Will be doing short transactions (to help make the first bullet point a reality)

Oracle finds this method scalable enough to run all of their TPC-Cs (an industry-standard OLTP benchmark; see `www.tpc.org` for details). In many other implementations, you will find this being achieved with shared read locks and their corresponding deadlocks and blocking. In Oracle, we do not get any blocking, but we will get the `ORA-08177` error if other sessions change the data we want to change as well. However, we will not get the error as frequently as we will get deadlocks and blocks in the other systems.

But—there is always a "but"—you must take care to understand these different isolation levels and their implications. Remember, with isolation set to `SERIALIZABLE`, you will not see any changes made in the database after the start of your transaction, until you commit. Applications that attempt to enforce their own data integrity constraints must take extra care in this regard. Using `SERIALIZABLE`, you will not see the uncommitted changes; furthermore, you will not see the committed changes made after the transaction began.

As a final point, be aware that `SERIALIZABLE` *does not* mean that all transactions executed by users will behave as if they were executed one right after another in a serial fashion. It does not imply that there is some serial ordering of the transactions that will result in the same outcome. The phenomena previously described by the SQL standard do not make this happen. This last point is a frequently misunderstood concept, and a small demonstration will clear it up. The following table represents two sessions performing work over time. The database tables A and B start out empty and are created as follows:

```
SQL> create table a ( x int );
Table created.

SQL> create table b ( x int );
Table created.
```

Now, we have the series of events shown in Table 4-7.

***Table 4-7.*** *SERIALIZABLE Transaction Example*

| Time | Session 1 Executes | Session 2 Executes |
|------|--------------------|--------------------|
| T1 | Alter session set isolation_ level=serializable; | -- |
| T2 | -- | Alter session set isolation_ level=serializable; |
| T3 | Insert into a select count(*) from b; | -- |
| T4 | -- | Insert into b select count(*) from a; |
| T5 | Commit; | -- |
| T6 | -- | Commit; |

Now, when this is all said and done, tables A and B will each have a row with the value 0 in it. If there were some serial ordering of the transactions, we could not possibly have both tables containing the value 0 in them. If session 1 executed *in its entirety* before session 2, then table B would have a row with the value 1 in it. If session 2 executed *in its entirety* before session 1, then table A would have a row with the value 1 in it. As executed here, however, both tables will have rows with a value of *0*. They just executed as if they were the only transaction in the database at that point in time. No matter how many times session 1 queries table B and no matter the committed state of session 2, the count will be the count that was committed in the database at time T1. Likewise, no matter how many times session 2 queries table A, the count will be the same as it was at time T2.

# READ ONLY

READ ONLY transactions are very similar to SERIALIZABLE transactions, the only difference being that they do not allow modifications, so they are not susceptible to the ORA-08177 error. READ ONLY transactions are intended to support reporting needs where the contents of the report need to be consistent with respect to a single point in time. In other systems, you would use REPEATABLE READ and suffer the associated effects of the shared read lock. In Oracle, you will use the READ ONLY transaction. In this mode, the output you produce in a report that uses 50 SELECT statements to gather the data will be consistent with respect to a single point in time—the time the transaction began. You will be able to do this without locking a single piece of data anywhere.

This aim is achieved by using the same multiversioning as used for individual statements. The data is reconstructed as needed from the undo segments and presented to you as it existed when the report began. READ ONLY transactions are not trouble-free, however. Whereas you might see an ORA-08177 error in a SERIALIZABLE transaction, you expect to see an ORA-01555 snapshot too old error with READ ONLY transactions. This will happen on a system where other people are actively modifying the information you are reading. The changes (undo) made to this information are recorded in the undo segments. But undo segments are used in a circular fashion in much the same manner as redo logs. The longer the report takes to run, the better the chance that some undo you need to reconstruct your data won't be there anymore. The undo segment will have wrapped around, and the portion of it you need would be reused by some other transaction. At this point, you will receive the ORA-01555 error and have to start over again.

The only solution to this sticky issue is to have the undo tablespace sized correctly for your system. Time and time again, I see people trying to save a few megabytes of disk space by having the smallest possible undo tablespace ("Why 'waste' space on something I don't really need?" is the thought). The problem is that the undo tablespace is a key component of the way the database works, and unless it is sized correctly, you will hit this error. In many years of using Oracle 6, 7, 8, 9, 10, 11, and 12, I can say I have never hit an ORA-01555 error outside of a testing or development system. In such a case, you know you have not sized the undo tablespace correctly and you fix it. We will revisit this issue in Chapter 8.

# Implications of Multiversion Read Consistency

So far, we've seen how multiversioning provides us with nonblocking reads, and I have stressed that this is a good thing: consistent (correct) answers with a high degree of concurrency. What could be wrong with that? Well, unless you understand that it exists and what it implies, then you are probably doing some of your transactions incorrectly. But can it affect us in other ways? The answer to that is definitely yes. We'll go into the specifics in the sections that follow.

# A Common Data Warehousing Technique That Fails

A common data warehousing technique I've seen people employ goes like this:

1. They use a trigger to maintain a LAST_UPDATED column in the source table, much like the method described in the Chapter 2 in the "Optimistic Locking" section.

2. To initially populate a data warehouse table, they remember what time it is *right now* by selecting out SYSDATE on the source system. For example, suppose it is exactly 9:00 a.m. right now.

3. They then pull all of the rows from the transactional system—a full SELECT * FROM TABLE—to get the data warehouse initially populated.

4. To refresh the data warehouse, they remember what time it is *right now* again. For example, suppose an hour has gone by—it is now 10:00 a.m. on the source system. They will remember that fact. They then pull all changed records since 9:00 a.m. (the moment before they started the first pull) and merge them in.

---

**Note**   This technique may *pull* the same record twice in two consecutive refreshes. This is unavoidable due to the granularity of the clock. A MERGE operation will not be affected by this (i.e., update existing record in the data warehouse or insert a new record).

---

They believe that they now have all of the records in the data warehouse that were modified since they did the initial pull. They may actually have all of the records, but just as likely they may not. This technique does work on some other databases—ones that employ a locking system whereby reads are blocked by writes and vice versa. But in a system where you have nonblocking reads, the logic is flawed.

To see the flaw in this example, all we need to do is assume that at 9:00 a.m. there was at least one open, uncommitted transaction. At 8:59:30 a.m., it had updated a row in the table we were to copy. At 9:00 a.m., when we started pulling the data and thus reading the data in this table, we would not see the modifications to that row; we would see the last committed version of it. If it was locked when we got to it in our query, we would read around the lock. If it was committed by the time we got to it, we would still read around it since read consistency permits us to read only data that was committed in the database when our statement began. We would *not* read that new version of the row during the 9:00 a.m. initial pull, nor would we read the modified row during the 10:00 a.m. refresh. The reason? The 10:00 a.m. refresh would only pull records modified since 9:00 a.m. that morning, but this record was modified at 8:59:30 a.m. We would never pull this changed record.

In many other databases where reads are blocked by writes and a committed but inconsistent read is implemented, this refresh process would work perfectly. If at 9:00 a.m., when we did the initial pull of data, we hit that row and it was locked, we would have blocked and waited for it and read the committed version. If it were not locked, we would just read whatever was there, committed.

So, does this mean the preceding logic just cannot be used? No, it means that we need to get the "right now" time a little differently. We need to query V$TRANSACTION and find out which is the earliest of the current time and the time recorded in START_TIME column of this view. We will need to pull all records changed since the start time of the oldest transaction (or the current SYSDATE value if there are no active transactions):

```
select nvl( min(to_date(start_time,'mm/dd/rr hh24:mi:ss')),sysdate)
  from v$transaction;
```

---

**Note**    The preceding query works regardless of the presence of any data in V$TRANSACTION. That is, even if V$TRANSACTION is empty (because there are no transactions currently), this query returns a record. A query that has an aggregate with no WHERE clause always returns *at least* one row and *at most* one row.

---

In this example, that would be 8:59:30 a.m. when the transaction that modified the row started. When we go to refresh the data at 10:00 a.m., we pull all of the changes that had occurred since that time; when we merge these into the data warehouse, we'll have everything we need.

# An Explanation for Higher Than Expected I/O on Hot Tables

Another situation where it is vital that you understand read consistency and multiversioning is when you are faced with a query that in production, under a heavy load, uses many more I/Os than you observe in your test or development systems, and you have no way to account for it. You review the I/O performed by the query and note that it is much higher than you have ever seen—much higher than seems possible. You restore the production instance on test and discover that the I/O is way down. But in production, it is still very high (but seems to vary: sometimes it is high, sometimes it is low, and sometimes it is in the middle). The reason, as we'll see, is that in your test system, in isolation, you do not have to undo other transactions' changes. In production, however, when you read a given block, you might have to undo (roll back) the changes of many transactions, and each rollback could involve I/O to retrieve the undo and apply it.

This is probably a query against a table that has many concurrent modifications taking place; you are seeing the reads to the undo segment taking place, the work that Oracle is performing to restore the block back the way it was when your query began. You can see the effects of this easily in a single session, just to understand what is happening. We'll start with a very small table:

```
SQL> create table t ( x int );
Table created.

SQL> insert into t values ( 1 );
1 row created.

SQL> exec dbms_stats.gather_table_stats( user, 'T' );
PL/SQL procedure successfully completed.

SQL> select * from t;

        X
----------
        1
```

Now, we'll set our session to use the SERIALIZABLE isolation level, so that no matter how many times we run a query in our session, the results will be "as of" that transaction's start time:

```
SQL> alter session set isolation_level=serializable;
Session altered.
```

Now, we'll query that small table and observe the amount of I/O performed:

```
SQL> set autotrace on statistics
SQL> select * from t;

        X
----------
        1

Statistics
----------------------------------------------------------
        0  recursive calls
        0  db block gets
        7  consistent gets
...
```

So, that query took seven I/Os (consistent gets) in order to complete. In *another session*, we'll modify this table repeatedly:

```
SQL> begin
    for i in 1 .. 10000
    loop
    update t set x = x+1;
    commit;
    end loop;
    end;
    /
PL/SQL procedure successfully completed.
```

And returning to our SERIALIZABLE session, we'll rerun the same query:

```
SQL> select * from t;
```

```
          X
- - - - - - - - - -
          1
```

Statistics

```
- - - - - - - - - - - - - - - - - - - - - - - - - - - - - - - - - - - - - - - -
          0   recursive calls
          0   db block gets
      10004   consistent gets
```

...

It did 10,004 I/Os that time—a marked difference. So, where did all of the I/O come from? That was Oracle rolling back the changes made to that database block. When we ran the second query, Oracle knew that all of the blocks retrieved and processed by that query had to be "as of" the start time of the transaction. When we got to the buffer cache, we discovered that the block in the cache was simply "too new"—the other session had modified it some 10,000 times. Our query could not see those changes, so it started walking the undo information and undid the last change. It discovered this rolled-back block was still too new and did another rollback of the block. It did this repeatedly until finally it found the version of the block that was committed in the database when our transaction began. That was the block we may use—and did use.

---

**Note**    Interestingly, if you were to rerun the SELECT * FROM T, you would likely see the I/O go back down to 7 or so again; it would not be 10,004. The reason? Oracle has the ability to store multiple versions of the same block in the buffer cache. When you undid the changes to this block for the query that did 10,004 I/Os, you left that version in the cache, and subsequent executions of your query are able to access it.

---

So, do we only encounter this problem when using the SERIALIZABLE isolation level? No, not at all. Consider a query that runs for five minutes. During the five minutes the query is running, it is retrieving blocks from the buffer cache. Every time it retrieves a block from the buffer cache, it will perform this check: "Is the block too new? If so, roll it back." And remember, the longer the query runs, the higher the chance that a block it needs has been modified over time.

Now, the database is expecting this check to happen (i.e., to see if a block is "too new" and the subsequent rolling back of the changes), and for just such a reason, the buffer cache may actually contain multiple versions of the same block in memory. In that fashion, chances are that a version you require will be there, ready and waiting to go, instead of having to be materialized using the undo information. A query such as the following may be used to view these blocks:

```
select file#, block#, count(*)
from v$bh
group by file#, block#
having count(*) > 3
order by 3
/
```

In general, you will find no more than about six versions of a block in the cache at any point in time, but these versions can be used by any query that needs them.

It is generally these small *hot* tables that run into the issue of inflated I/Os due to read consistency. Other queries most often affected by this issue are long-running queries against volatile tables. The longer they run, the longer they run, because over time they may have to perform more work to retrieve a block from the buffer cache.

# Write Consistency

So far, we've looked at read consistency: Oracle's ability to use undo information to provide nonblocking query and consistent (correct) reads. We understand that as Oracle reads blocks for queries out of the buffer cache, it will ensure that the version of the block is "old" enough to be seen by that query.

But that begs the following questions: What about writes/modifications? What happens when you run an UPDATE statement, as follows, and while that statement is running, someone updates a row it has yet to read from Y=5 to Y=6 and commits?

```
Update t Set x = 2 Where y = 5;
```

That is, when your UPDATE began, some row had the value Y=5. As your UPDATE reads the table using consistent reads, it sees that the row was Y=5 when the UPDATE began. But, the current value for Y is now 6 (it's not 5 anymore), and before updating the value of X, Oracle will check to see that Y is still 5. Now what happens? How are the updates affected by this?

Obviously, we can't modify an old version of a block; when we go to modify a row, we must modify the current version of that block. Additionally, Oracle can't just simply skip this row, as that would be an inconsistent read and unpredictable. What we'll discover is that in such cases, Oracle will restart the write modification from scratch.

# Consistent Reads and Current Reads

Oracle does do two types of block gets when processing a modification statement. It performs

- *Consistent reads*: When "finding" the rows to modify

- *Current reads*: When getting the block to actually update the row of interest

We can see this easily using TKPROF. Consider this small one row example, which reads and updates the single row in table T from earlier:

```
SQL> exec dbms_monitor.session_trace_enable
PL/SQL procedure successfully completed.

SQL> select * from t;

         X
----------
     10001

SQL> update t t1 set x = x+1;
1 row updated.

SQL> update t t2 set x = x+1;
1 row updated.
```

Next, we navigate to the trace file directory, locate the trace file we just generated, and process it with the TKPROF utility:

```
tkprof orclcdb_ora_24586.trc trc.out
```

If you're unsure of how to find the trace file directory, you can view it via this query:

```
SQL>  select value from v$diag_info where name='Diag Trace';
```

After we run TKPROF and examine the results, we'll see something like this (note that I removed the ELAPSED, CPU, and DISK columns from this report):

```
select * from t

call       count   query   current        rows
-------    ------  ------  ----------    ----------
Parse         1      0         0             0
Execute       1      0         0             0
Fetch         2      7         0             1
-------    ------  ------  ----------    ----------
total         4      7         0             1

update t t1 set x = x+1

call       count   query   current        rows
-------    ------  ------  ----------    ----------
Parse         1      0         0             0
Execute       1      7         3             1
Fetch         0      0         0             0
-------    ------  ------  ----------    ----------
total         2      7         3             1

update t t2 set x = x+1

call       count   query   current        rows
-------    ------  ------  ----------    ----------
Parse         1      0         0             0
Execute       1      7         1             1
Fetch         0      0         0             0
-------    ------  ------  ----------    ----------
total         2      7         1             1
```

So, during just a normal query, we incur seven *query (consistent) mode gets*. During the first UPDATE, we incur the same seven I/Os (the search component of the update involves finding all of the rows that are in the table when the update began, in this case) and three *current mode gets* as well. The current mode gets are performed in order to retrieve the *table block* as it exists right now, the one with the row on it, to get an *undo segment block* to begin our transaction, and an *undo block*. The second update has exactly one current mode get; since we did not have to do the undo work again, we had only the one current get on the block with the row we want to update. The very presence of the current mode gets tells us that a modification of some sort took place. Before Oracle will modify a block with new information, it must get the most current copy of it.

So, how does read consistency affect a modification? Well, imagine you were executing the following UPDATE statement against some database table:

```
Update t Set x = x+1 Where y = 5;
```

We understand that the WHERE Y=5 component, the read-consistent phase of the query, will be processed using a consistent read (query mode gets in the TKPROF report). The set of WHERE Y=5 records that were committed in the table at the beginning of the statement's execution are the records it will see (assuming READ COMMITTED isolation; if the isolation is SERIALIZABLE, it would be the set of WHERE Y=5 records that existed when the transaction began). This means if that UPDATE statement were to take five minutes to process from start to finish, and someone added and committed a new record to the table with a value of 5 in the Y column, then that UPDATE would not see it because the consistent read would not see it. This is expected and normal. But, the question is, what happens if two sessions execute the following statements in order:

```
Update t Set y = 10 Where y = 5;
Update t Set x = x+1 Where y = 5;
```

Table 4-8 demonstrates the timeline.

**Table 4-8.** *Sequence of Updates*

| Time | Session 1 | Session 2 | Comment |
|------|-----------|-----------|---------|
| T1 | Update t Set y=10 Where y=5; | | This updates the one row that matches the criteria. |
| T2 | | Update t Set x=x+1 Where y=5; | Using consistent reads, this will find the record session 1 modified, but it won't be able to update it since session 1 has it locked. Session 2 will block and wait for this row. |
| T3 | Commit; | | This releases session 2; session 2 becomes unblocked. It can finally do the current read on the block containing this row, where Y was equal to 5 when session 1 began its update. The current read will show that Y is now equal to 10, not 5 anymore. |

So the record that was Y=5 when you began the UPDATE is no longer Y=5. The consistent read component of the UPDATE says, "You want to update this record because Y was 5 when we began," but the current version of the block makes you think, "Oh, no, I can't update this row because Y isn't 5 anymore. It would be wrong."

If we just skipped this record at this point and ignored it, then we would have a nondeterministic update. It would be throwing data consistency and integrity out the window. The outcome of the update (how many and which rows were modified) would depend on the order in which rows got hit in the table and what other activity just happened to be going on. You could take the same exact set of rows and in two different databases, each one running the transactions in exactly the same mix, and you could observe different results, just because the rows were in different places on the disk.

In this case, Oracle will choose to *restart* the update. When the row that was Y=5 when you started is found to contain the value Y=10, Oracle will silently roll back your update (just the update, not any other part of the transaction) and restart it, assuming you are using READ COMMITTED isolation. If you are using SERIALIZABLE isolation, then at this point you would receive an ORA-08177: can't serialize access for this transaction error. In READ COMMITTED mode, after the transaction rolls back your update, the database will restart the update (i.e., change the point in time at which the

update is "as of"), and instead of updating the data again, it will go into SELECT FOR
UPDATE mode and attempt to lock all of the rows WHERE Y=5 for your session. Once it does
this, it will run the UPDATE against that locked set of data, thus ensuring this time that it
can complete without restarting.

But to continue on with the "but what happens if…" train of thought, what happens
if, after restarting the update and going into SELECT FOR UPDATE mode (which has the
same read-consistent and read-current block gets going on as an update does), a row
that was Y=5 when you started the SELECT FOR UPDATE is found to be Y=11 when you
go to get the current version of it? That SELECT FOR UDPDATE will restart and the cycle
begins again.

This raises several interesting questions. Can we observe this? Can we see this
actually happen? And if so, so what? What does this mean to us as developers? We'll
address these questions in turn now.

# Seeing a Restart

It is easier to see a restart than you might, at first, think. We'll be able to observe one, in
fact, using a simple one-row table. This is the table we'll use to test with:

```
SQL> create table t ( x int, y int );
Table created.

SQL> insert into t values ( 1, 1 );
1 row created.

SQL> commit;
Commit complete.
```

To observe the restart, all we need is a trigger to print out some information. We'll
use a BEFORE UPDATE FOR EACH ROW trigger to print out the before-and-after image of
the row as the result of an update:

```
SQL> create or replace trigger t_buffer
    before update on t for each row
    begin
        dbms_output.put_line
        ( 'old.x = ' || :old.x ||
          ', old.y = ' || :old.y );
```

```
        dbms_output.put_line
        ( 'new.x = ' || :new.x ||
          ', new.y = ' || :new.y );
    end;
  /
Trigger created.
```

Now, we'll update that row:

```
SQL> set serveroutput on
SQL> update t set x = x+1;
old.x = 1, old.y = 1
new.x = 2, new.y = 1
1 row updated.
```

So far, everything is as we expect: the trigger fired once, and we see the old and new values. Note that we have not yet committed, however—the row is still locked. In another session, we'll execute this update:

```
SQL> set serveroutput on
SQL> update t set x = x+1 where x > 0;
```

This will immediately block, of course, since the first session has that row locked. If we now go back to the first session and commit, we'll see this output (the update is repeated for clarity) in the second session:

```
SQL> update t set x = x+1 where x > 0;
old.x = 1, old.y = 1
new.x = 2, new.y = 1
old.x = 2, old.y = 1
new.x = 3, new.y = 1
1 row updated.
```

As you can see, that row trigger saw two versions of that row here. The row trigger was fired two times: once with the original version of the row and what we tried to modify that original version to, and again with the final row that was actually updated. Since this was a BEFORE FOR EACH ROW trigger, Oracle saw the read-consistent version of the record and the modifications we would like to have made to it. However, Oracle

retrieved the block in current mode to actually perform the update *after* the BEFORE
FOR EACH ROW trigger fired. It waits until after this trigger fires to get the block in current
mode, because the trigger can modify the :NEW values. So Oracle can't modify the block
until *after* this trigger executes, and the trigger could take a very long time to execute.
Since only one session at a time can hold a block in current mode, Oracle needs to limit
the time we have it in that mode.

After this trigger fired, Oracle retrieved the block in current mode and noticed that
the column used to find this row, X, had been modified. Since X was used to locate this
record and X was modified, the database decided to restart our query. Notice that the
update of X from 1 to 2 did not put this row out of scope; we'll still be updating it with
this UPDATE statement. Rather, it is the fact that X was used to locate the row, and the
consistent read value of X (1 in this case) differs from the current mode read of X (2).
Now, upon restart, the trigger sees the value of X=2 (following modification by the other
session) as the :OLD value and X=3 as the :NEW value.

So, this shows that these restarts happen. It takes a trigger to see them in action;
otherwise, they are generally *undetectable*. That does not mean you can't see other
symptoms—such as a large UPDATE statement rolling back work after updating
many rows and then discovering a row that causes it to restart—just that it is hard to
definitively say, "This symptom is caused by a restart."

An interesting observation is that triggers themselves may cause restarts to occur
even when the statement itself doesn't warrant them. Normally, the columns referenced
in the WHERE clause of the UPDATE or DELETE statement are used to determine whether or
not the modification needs to restart. Oracle will perform a consistent read using these
columns, and upon retrieving the block in current mode, it will restart the statement if it
detects that any of them have changed. Normally, the other columns in the row are not
inspected. For example, let's simply rerun the previous example and use WHERE Y>0 to
find the rows in both sessions; the output we'll see in the first session (the one that gets
blocked) would be

```
SQL> update t set x = x+1 where y > 0;
old.x = 1, old.y = 1
new.x = 2, new.y = 1
old.x = 2, old.y = 1
new.x = 3, new.y = 1
1 row updated.
```

So why did Oracle fire the trigger twice when it was looking at the Y value? Does it examine the whole row? As you can see from the output, the update was, in fact, restarted and the trigger again fired twice, even though we were searching on Y>0 and did not modify Y at all. But, if we re-create the trigger to simply print out the fact that it fired, rather than reference the :OLD and :NEW values, as follows, and go into that second session again and run the update, we observe it gets blocked (of course):

```
SQL> create or replace trigger t_bufer
     before update on t for each row
     begin
             dbms_output.put_line( 'fired' );
     end;
   /
Trigger created.

SQL> update t set x = x+1;
fired
1 row updated.
```

After committing the blocking session, we'll see the following:

```
SQL> update t set x = x+1 where y > 0;
fired
1 row updated.
```

The trigger fired just once this time, not twice. Thus, the :NEW and :OLD column values, when referenced in the trigger, are also used by Oracle to do the restart checking. When we referenced :NEW.X and :OLD.X in the trigger, X's consistent read and current read values were compared and found to be different. A restart ensued. When we removed the reference to that column from the trigger, there was no restart.

So the rule is that the set of columns used in the WHERE clause to find the rows plus the columns referenced in the row triggers will be compared. The consistent read version of the row will be compared to the current read version of the row; if any of them are different, the modification will restart.

> **Note**    You can use this bit of information to further understand why using an AFTER FOR EACH ROW trigger is more efficient than using a BEFORE FOR EACH ROW. The AFTER trigger won't have the same effect—we've already retrieved the block in current mode by then.

This leads us to the "Why do we care?" question.

## Why Is a Restart Important to Us?

The first thing that pops out should be "Our trigger fired twice!" We had a one-row table with a BEFORE FOR EACH ROW trigger on it. We updated one row, yet the trigger fired two times.

Think of the potential implications of this. If you have a trigger that does anything nontransactional, this could be a fairly serious issue. For example, consider a trigger that sends an update where the body of the email is "This is what the data used to look like. It has been modified to look like this now." If you sent the email directly from the trigger (e.g., UTL_MAIL), then the user would receive two emails, with one of them reporting an update that never actually happened.

Anything you do in a trigger that is nontransactional will be impacted by a restart. Consider the following implications:

- Consider a trigger that maintains some PL/SQL global variables, such as for the number of rows processed. When a statement that restarts rolls back, the modifications to PL/SQL variables won't roll back.

- Virtually any function that starts with UTL_ (UTL_FILE, UTL_HTTP, UTL_ SMTP, and so on) should be considered susceptible to a statement restart. When the statement restarts, UTL_FILE won't *unwrite* to the file it was writing to.

- Any trigger that is part of an autonomous transaction must be suspect. When the statement restarts and rolls back, the autonomous transaction can't be rolled back.

All of these consequences must be handled with care in the belief that they may be fired more than once per row or be fired for a row that won't be updated by the statement after all.

The second reason you should care about potential restarts is performance related. We have been using a single-row example, but what happens if you start a large batch update and it is restarted after processing the first 100,000 records? It will roll back the 100,000 row changes, restart in SELECT FOR UPDATE mode, and do the 100,000 row changes again after that.

You might notice, after putting in that simple audit trail trigger (the one that reads the :NEW and :OLD values), that performance is much worse than you can explain, even though nothing else has changed except the new triggers. It could be that you are restarting queries you never used in the past. Or the addition of a tiny program that updates just a single row here and there makes a batch process that used to run in an hour suddenly run in many hours due to restarts that never used to take place.

This is not a new feature of Oracle—it has been in the database since version 4.0, when read consistency was introduced. I myself was not totally aware of how it worked until the summer of 2003, and after I discovered what it implied, I was able to answer a lot of "How could that have happened?" questions from my own past. It has made me swear off using autonomous transactions in triggers almost entirely, and it has made me rethink the way some of my applications have been implemented. For example, I'll never send email from a trigger directly; rather, I'll always use DBMS_JOB or something similar to send the email after my transaction commits. This makes the sending of the email *transactional*; that is, if the statement that caused the trigger to fire and send the email is restarted, the rollback it performs will roll back the DBMS_JOB request. Most everything nontransactional that I did in triggers was modified to be done in a job after the fact, making it all transactionally consistent.

# Summary

In this chapter, we covered a lot of material that, at times, might not have been obvious. However, it is vital that you understand these issues. For example, if you were not aware of the statement-level restart, you might not be able to figure out how a certain set of circumstances could have taken place. That is, you would not be able to explain some of the daily empirical observations you make. In fact, if you were not aware of the restarts, you might wrongly suspect the actual fault to be due to the circumstances or end-user error. It would be one of those unreproducible issues, as it takes many things happening in a specific order to observe.

We took a look at the meaning of the isolation levels set out in the SQL standard and at how Oracle implements them; at times, we contrasted Oracle's implementation with that of other databases. We saw that in other implementations (i.e., ones that employ read locks to provide consistent data), there is a huge trade-off between concurrency and consistency. To get highly concurrent access to data, you would have to decrease your need for consistent answers. To get consistent, correct answers, you would need to live with decreased concurrency. In Oracle, that is not the case, due to its multiversioning feature.

Table 4-9 sums up what you might expect in a database that employs read locking vs. Oracle's multiversioning approach.

**Table 4-9.** *A Comparison of Transaction Isolation Levels and Locking Behavior in Oracle vs. Databases That Employ Read Locking*

| Isolation Level | Implementation | Writes Block Reads | Reads Block Writes | Deadlock-Sensitive Reads | Incorrect Query Results | Lost Updates | Lock Escalation or Limits |
|---|---|---|---|---|---|---|---|
| READ UNCOMMITTED | Not Oracle | No | No | No | Yes | Yes | Yes |
| READ COMMITTED | Not Oracle | Yes | No | No | Yes | Yes | Yes |
| READ COMMITTED | Oracle | No | No | No | No | No* | No |
| REPEATABLE READ | Not Oracle | Yes | Yes | Yes | No | No | Yes |
| SERIALIZABLE | Not Oracle | Yes | Yes | Yes | No | No | Yes |
| SERIALIZABLE | Oracle | No | No | No | No | No | No |

*With SELECT FOR UPDATE NOWAIT.

Concurrency controls and how the database implements them are definitely things you want to understand. I've been singing the praises of multiversioning and read consistency, but like everything else in the world, they are double-edged swords. If you don't understand that multiversioning is there and how it works, you will make errors in application design. Unless you know how multiversioning works, you will write programs that corrupt data. It is that simple.

# CHAPTER 5

# Transactions

Transactions are one of the features that set databases apart from file systems. In a file system, if you are in the middle of writing a file and the operating system crashes, that file will probably be corrupted, though there are "journaled" file systems and the like that may be able to recover your file to some point in time. However, if you need to keep two files synchronized, such a system won't help—if you update one file and the system fails before you finish updating the second, your files won't be synchronized.

This is the main purpose of *transactions*—they take the database from one consistent state to the next. That is their function. When you commit work in the database, you are assured that either all of your changes, or none of them, have been saved. Furthermore, you are assured that the various rules and checks that protect data integrity were implemented.

In the previous chapter, we discussed transactions in terms of concurrency control and how, as a result of Oracle's multiversioning, read-consistent model, Oracle transactions can provide consistent data every time, under highly concurrent data access conditions. Transactions in Oracle exhibit all of the required ACID characteristics:

- *Atomicity*: Either all of a transaction happens or none of it happens.

- *Consistency*: A transaction takes the database from one consistent state to the next.

- *Isolation*: The effects of a transaction may not be visible to other transactions until the transaction has committed.

- *Durability*: Once the transaction is committed, it is permanent.

In particular, we discussed how Oracle obtains *consistency* and *isolation* in the previous chapter. Here, we'll focus most of our attention on the concept of *atomicity* and how that is applied in Oracle.

© Darl Kuhn and Thomas Kyte 2021
D. Kuhn and T. Kyte, *Oracle Database Transactions and Locking Revealed*,
https://doi.org/10.1007/978-1-4842-6425-6_5

In this chapter, we'll discuss the implications of atomicity and how it affects statements in Oracle. We'll cover transaction control statements such as COMMIT, SAVEPOINT, and ROLLBACK, and we'll discuss how integrity constraints are enforced in a transaction. We'll also look at why you may have some bad transaction habits if you've been developing in other databases. We'll look at distributed transactions and the two-phase commit (2PC). Lastly, we'll examine autonomous transactions, what they are, and the role they play.

# Transaction Control Statements

You don't need a "begin transaction" statement in Oracle. A transaction implicitly begins with the first statement that modifies data (the first statement that gets a TX lock). You can explicitly begin a transaction using SET TRANSACTION or the DBMS_TRANSACTION package, but it is not a necessary step, unlike in some other databases. Issuing either a COMMIT or ROLLBACK statement explicitly ends a transaction.

**Note**   Not all ROLLBACK statements are created equal. It should be noted that a ROLLBACK TO SAVEPOINT command will not end a transaction! Only a full, proper ROLLBACK will.

You should always explicitly terminate your transactions with a COMMIT or ROLLBACK; otherwise, the tool or environment you're using will pick one or the other for you. If you exit your SQL*Plus session normally, without committing or rolling back, SQL*Plus assumes you wish to commit your work and it does so. If you just exit from a Pro*C program, on the other hand, an implicit rollback takes place. Never rely on implicit behavior, as it could change in the future. Always explicitly COMMIT or ROLLBACK your transactions.

**Note**   As an example of something changing in the future, SQL*Plus in Oracle 11*g* Release 2 and above contains a setting, "exitcommit." This setting controls whether SQL*Plus issues a COMMIT or ROLLBACK upon exit. So when you use 11*g* Release 2, the default behavior that has been in place since SQL*Plus was invented may well be different!

Transactions are *atomic* in Oracle, meaning that either every statement that comprises the transaction is committed (made permanent) or all of the statements are rolled back. This protection is extended to individual statements as well. Either a statement entirely succeeds, or the statement is entirely rolled back. Note that I said the "statement" is rolled back. The failure of one statement does not cause previously executed statements to be automatically rolled back. Their work is preserved and must either be committed or rolled back by you. Before we get into the details of exactly what it means for a statement and transaction to be atomic, let's take a look at the various transaction control statements available to us:

- COMMIT: To use this statement's simplest form, you just issue COMMIT. You could be more verbose and say COMMIT WORK, but the two are equivalent. A COMMIT ends your transaction and makes any changes permanent (durable). There are extensions to the COMMIT statement used in distributed transactions that allow you to label a COMMIT (label a transaction) with some meaningful comment and force the commit of an in-doubt distributed transaction. There are also extensions that allow you to perform an asynchronous commit—a commit that actually breaks the *durability* concept. We'll take a look at this in a bit and see when it might be appropriate to use.

- ROLLBACK: To use this statement's simplest form, you just issue ROLLBACK. Again, you could be more verbose and say ROLLBACK WORK, but the two are equivalent. A rollback ends your transaction and undoes any uncommitted changes. It does this by reading information stored in the rollback/undo segments (going forward I'll refer to these exclusively as *undo segments*, the favored terminology for Oracle 10*g* and later) and restoring the database blocks to the state they were before your transaction began.

- SAVEPOINT: A SAVEPOINT allows you to create a marked point within a transaction. You may have multiple SAVEPOINTs within a single transaction.

- ROLLBACK TO <SAVEPOINT>: This statement is used with the SAVEPOINT command. You can roll back your transaction to that marked point without rolling back any of the work that preceded it. So, you could issue two UPDATE statements, followed by a SAVEPOINT and then two DELETE statements. If an error or some sort of exceptional condition occurs during execution of the DELETE statements, and you catch that exception and issue the ROLLBACK TO SAVEPOINT command, the transaction will roll back to the named SAVEPOINT, undoing any work performed by the DELETEs but leaving the work performed by the UPDATE statements intact.

- SET TRANSACTION: This statement allows you to set various transaction attributes, such as the transaction's isolation level and whether it is read-only or read-write. You can also use this statement to instruct the transaction to use a specific undo segment when using manual undo management, but this is not recommended. We'll discuss manual and automatic undo management in more detail in Chapter 8.

That's it—there are no other transaction control statements. The most frequently used control statements are COMMIT and ROLLBACK. The SAVEPOINT statement has a somewhat special purpose. Internally, Oracle uses it frequently; in fact, Oracle uses it every time you execute any SQL or PL/SQL statement, and you may find some use for it in your applications as well.

# Atomicity

Now, we're ready to see what's meant by statement, procedure, and transaction atomicity.

## Statement-Level Atomicity

Consider the following statement:

```
Insert into t values ( 1 );
```

It seems fairly clear that if the statement were to fail due to a constraint violation, the row would not be inserted. However, consider the following example, where an INSERT or DELETE on table T fires a trigger that adjusts the CNT column in table T2 appropriately:

```
SQL> create table t2 ( cnt int );
Table created.

SQL> insert into t2 values ( 0 );
1 row created.

SQL> commit;
Commit complete.

SQL> create table t ( x int check ( x>0 ) );
Table created.

SQL> create trigger t_trigger
     before insert or delete on t for each row
     begin
        if ( inserting ) then
             update t2 set cnt = cnt +1;
        else
             update t2 set cnt = cnt -1;
        end if;
        dbms_output.put_line( 'I fired and updated '  ||
                                   sql%rowcount || ' rows' );
   end;
 /
Trigger created.
```

In this situation, it is less clear what should happen. If the error occurs *after* the trigger has fired, should the effects of the trigger persist, or not? That is, if the trigger fired and updated T2, but the row was not inserted into T, what should the outcome be? Clearly the answer is that we don't want the CNT column in T2 to be incremented if a row is not actually inserted into T. Fortunately in Oracle, the original statement from the client—INSERT INTO T, in this case—either entirely succeeds or entirely fails. This statement is atomic. We can confirm this, as follows:

```
SQL> set serveroutput on
SQL> insert into t values (1);
I fired and updated 1 rows

1 row created.
```

```
SQL> insert into t values(-1);
```
**I fired and updated 1 rows**
```
insert into t values(-1)
*
ERROR at line 1:
ORA-02290: check constraint (YODA.SYS_C0013023) violated

SQL> select * from t2;

       CNT
----------
         1
```

So, one row was successfully inserted into T and we duly received the message I fired and updated 1 rows. The next INSERT statement violates the integrity constraint we have on T. The DBMS_OUTPUT message appeared—the trigger on T in fact did fire and we have evidence of that. The trigger performed its updates of T2 successfully. We might expect T2 to have a value of 2 now, but we see it has a value of 1. Oracle made the *original* INSERT atomic—the original INSERT INTO T is the statement, and any side effects of that original INSERT INTO T are considered part of that statement.

Oracle achieves this statement-level atomicity by silently wrapping a SAVEPOINT around each of our calls to the database. The preceding two INSERTs were really treated like this:

```
Savepoint statement1;
    Insert into t values ( 1 );
If error then rollback to statement1;
Savepoint statement2;
    Insert into t values ( -1 );
If error then rollback to statement2;
```

For programmers used to Sybase or SQL Server, this may be confusing at first. In those databases, *exactly the opposite is true*. The triggers in those systems execute independently of the firing statement. If they encounter an error, the triggers must explicitly roll back their own work and then raise another error to roll back the triggering statement. Otherwise, the work done by a trigger could persist even if the triggering statement, or some other part of the statement, ultimately fails.

In Oracle, this statement-level atomicity extends as deep as it needs to. In the preceding example, if the INSERT INTO T fires a trigger that updates another table, and that table has a trigger that deletes from another table (and so on, and so on), either *all* of the work succeeds or *none* of it does. You don't need to code anything special to ensure this; it's just the way it works.

## Procedure-Level Atomicity

It is interesting to note that Oracle considers PL/SQL blocks to be statements as well. Consider the following stored procedure and reset of the example tables:

```
SQL> create or replace procedure p
    as
    begin
            insert into t values ( 1 );
            insert into t values (-1 );
    end;
  /
Procedure created.

SQL> delete from t;
0 rows deleted.

SQL> update t2 set cnt = 0;
1 row updated.

SQL> commit;
Commit complete.

SQL> select * from t;
no rows selected

SQL> select * from t2;

       CNT
----------
         0
```

So, we have a procedure we know will fail, and the second INSERT will always fail in this case. Let's see what happens if we run that stored procedure:

```
SQL> begin
          p;
       end;
  /
I fired and updated 1 rows
I fired and updated 1 rows
begin
*
ERROR at line 1:
ORA-02290: check constraint (YODA.SYS_C0013025) violated
ORA-06512: at "YODA.P", line 5

SQL> select * from t;
no rows selected

SQL> select * from t2;


       CNT
----------
         0
```

As you can see, Oracle treated the stored procedure call as an atomic statement. The client submitted a block of code—BEGIN P; END;—and Oracle wrapped a SAVEPOINT around it. Since P failed, Oracle restored the database back to the point right before it was called.

---

**Note**  The preceding behavior—statement-level atomicity—relies on the PL/SQL routine not performing any commits or rollbacks. It is my opinion that COMMIT and ROLLBACK should not be used in general in PL/SQL; the invoker of the PL/SQL stored procedure is the only one that knows when a transaction is complete. It is a bad programming practice to issue a COMMIT or ROLLBACK in your developed PL/SQL routines.

---

Now, if we submit a slightly different block, we will get entirely different results:

```
SQL> begin
        p;
    exception
        when others then
            dbms_output.put_line( 'Error!!!! ' || sqlerrm );
    end;
  /
```

**I fired and updated 1 rows**
**Error!!!! ORA-02290: check constraint (YODA.SYS_C0013025) violated**

**PL/SQL procedure successfully completed.**

```
SQL> select * from t;

        X
----------
        1

SQL> select * from t2;

      CNT
----------
        1

SQL> rollback;
Rollback complete.
```

Here, we ran a block of code that ignored any and all errors, and the difference in outcome is huge. Whereas the first call to P effected no changes, this time the first INSERT succeeds and the CNT column in T2 is incremented accordingly.

Oracle considered the "statement" to be the block that the client submitted. This statement succeeded by catching and ignoring the error itself, so the If error then rollback... didn't come into effect and Oracle didn't roll back to the SAVEPOINT after execution. Hence, the partial work performed by P was preserved. The reason this partial work is preserved in the first place is that we have statement-level atomicity within P: each statement in P is atomic. P becomes the client of Oracle when it submits its two

INSERT statements. Each INSERT either succeeds or fails entirely. This is evidenced by the fact that we can see that the trigger on T fired twice and updated T2 twice, yet the count in T2 reflects only one UPDATE. The second INSERT executed in P had an implicit SAVEPOINT wrapped around it.

---

## THE "WHEN OTHERS" CLAUSE

I consider virtually all code that contains a WHEN OTHERS exception handler that does not also include a RAISE or RAISE_APPLICATION_ERROR to reraise the exception to be a bug. It silently ignores the error and it changes the transaction semantics. Catching WHEN OTHERS and translating the exception into an old-fashioned return code changes the way the database is supposed to behave.

In fact, when Oracle 11*g* Release 1 was still on the drawing board, I was permitted to submit three requests for new features in PL/SQL. I jumped at the chance, and my first suggestion was simply "remove the WHEN OTHERS clause from the language." My reasoning was simple: the most common cause of developer-introduced bugs I see—*the most common cause*—is a WHEN OTHERS not followed by a RAISE or RAISE_APPLICATION_ERROR. I felt the world would be a safer place without this language feature. The PL/SQL implementation team could not do this, of course, but they did the next best thing. They made it so that PL/SQL will generate a compiler warning if you have a WHEN OTHERS that is not followed by a RAISE or RAISE_APPLICATION_ERROR call, for example:

```
SQL> alter session set
     PLSQL_Warnings = 'enable:all'
     /
Session altered.

SQL> create or replace procedure some_proc( p_str in varchar2 )
     as
     begin
             dbms_output.put_line( p_str );
     exception
       when others
       then
         -- call some log_error() routine
         null;
     end;
```

```
     /
SP2-0804: Procedure created with compilation warnings

SQL> show errors procedure some_proc
Errors for PROCEDURE P:

LINE/COL ERROR
-------- ------------------------------------------------------------------
1/1      PLW-05018: unit SOME_PROC omitted optional AUTHID clause; default
         value DEFINER used

6/10     PLW-06009: procedure "SOME_PROC" OTHERS handler does not end in
         RAISE or RAISE_APPLICATION_ERROR
```

So, if you include WHEN OTHERS in your code and it is not followed by a RAISE or RAISE_
APPLICATION_ERROR, be aware that you are *almost certainly* looking at a bug in your
developed code, a bug placed there by you.

The difference between the two blocks of code, one with a WHEN OTHERS exception
block and one without, is subtle, and something you must consider in your applications.
Adding an exception handler to a block of PL/SQL code can radically change its
behavior. A different way to code this—one that restores the statement-level atomicity to
the entire PL/SQL block—is as follows:

```
SQL> begin
        savepoint sp;
        p;
    exception
        when others then
            rollback to sp;
            dbms_output.put_line( 'Error!!!! ' || sqlerrm );
    end;
    /
I fired and updated 1 rows
I fired and updated 1 rows
Error!!!! ORA-02290: check constraint (YODA.SYS_C0013025) violated
PL/SQL procedure successfully completed.
```

```
SQL> select * from t;
no rows selected

SQL> select * from t2;

        CNT
----------
          0
```

> **Caution**    The preceding code represents an exceedingly bad practice. In general, you should neither catch a WHEN OTHERS nor explicitly code what Oracle already provides as far as transaction semantics is concerned.

Here, by mimicking the work Oracle normally does for us with the SAVEPOINT, we are able to restore the original behavior while still catching and "ignoring" the error. I provide this example for illustration only; this is an exceedingly bad coding practice.

# Transaction-Level Atomicity

The entire goal of a transaction, a set of SQL statements executed together as a unit of work, is to take the database from one consistent state to another consistent state. To accomplish this goal, transactions are atomic as well—the entire set of successful work performed by a transaction is either entirely committed and made permanent or rolled back and undone. Just like a statement, the transaction is an atomic unit of work. Upon receipt of "success" from the database after committing a transaction, you know that all of the work performed by the transaction has been made persistent.

# DDL and Atomicity

It is worth noting that there is a certain class of statements in Oracle that are atomic—but only at the statement level. Data Definition Language (DDL) statements are implemented in a manner such that

1. They begin by committing any outstanding work, ending any transaction you might already have in place

2. They perform the DDL operation, such as a CREATE TABLE

3. They commit the DDL operation if it was successful, or roll back the DDL operation otherwise

This means that any time you issue a DDL statement such as CREATE, ALTER, and so on, you must expect your existing transaction to be immediately committed and the subsequent DDL command to be performed and either committed and made durable or rolled back in the event of any error. DDL does not break the ACID concepts in any way, but the fact that it commits is something you definitely need to be aware of.

# Durability

Normally, when a transaction is committed, its changes are permanent; you can rely on those changes being in the database, even if the database crashed the instant after the commit completed. This is not true, however, in two specific cases:

- You use the WRITE extensions (available in Oracle 10g Release 2 and above) available in the COMMIT statement.

- You issue COMMITs in a nondistributed (accesses only a single database, no database links) PL/SQL block of code.

We'll look at each in turn.

# WRITE Extensions to COMMIT

Starting with Oracle 10g Release 2 and above, you may add a WRITE clause to your COMMIT statements. The WRITE clause allows the commit to either WAIT for the redo you generated to be written to disk (the default) or NOWAIT—to not wait—for the redo to be written. The NOWAIT option is the capability—a capability that must be used carefully, with forethought and with understanding of exactly what it means.

Normally, a COMMIT is a synchronous process. Your application invokes COMMIT and then your application *waits* for the entire COMMIT processing to be complete. This is the behavior of COMMIT in all the database releases before Oracle 10g Release 2 and is the default behavior in Oracle 10g Release 2 and above.

In current releases of the database, instead of waiting for the commit to complete, which may take measurable time since a commit involves a physical write—a physical I/O—to the redo log files stored on disk, you may have the commit performed in the background, without waiting for it. That comes with the side effect that *your commit is no longer assured to be durable*. That is, your application may get a response back from the database that the asynchronous commit you submitted was received; other sessions may be able to see your changes but later find that the transaction you thought was committed was not. This situation will occur only in very rare cases and will always involve a serious failure of the hardware or software. It requires the database to be shut down abnormally in order for an asynchronous commit to not be durable, meaning the database instance or computer the database instance is running on would have to suffer a complete failure.

So, if transactions are meant to be durable, what is the potential use of a feature that might make them possibly not durable? Raw performance. When you issue a COMMIT in your application, you are asking the LGWR process to take the redo you've generated and ensure that it is written to the online redo log files. Performing physical I/O, which this process involves, is measurably slow; it takes a long time, relatively speaking, to write data to disk. So, a COMMIT may well take longer than the DML statements in the transaction itself! If you make the COMMIT asynchronous, you remove the need to wait for that physical I/O in the client application, perhaps making the client application appear faster—especially if it does lots of COMMITs.

This might suggest that you'd want to use this COMMIT WRITE NOWAIT all of the time—after all isn't performance the most important thing in the world? No, it is not. Most of the time, you need the durability achieved by default with COMMIT. When you COMMIT and report back to an end user "we have committed," you need to be sure that the change is permanent. It will be recorded in the database even if the database/hardware failed right after the COMMIT. If you report to an end user that "Order 12352 has been placed," you need to make sure that Order 12352 was truly placed and persistent. So, for most every application, the default COMMIT WRITE WAIT is the only correct option (note that you only need say COMMIT—the default setting is WRITE WAIT).

When would you want to use this capability to commit without waiting then? Three scenarios come to mind:

- *A custom data load program*: It must be custom, since it will have additional logic to deal with the fact that a commit might not persist a system failure.

- *An application that processes a live data feed of some sort, say a stock quote feed from the stock markets that inserts massive amounts of time-sensitive information into the database*: If the database goes offline, the data stream keeps on going and the data generated during the system failure will never be processed. (Nasdaq does not shut down because your database crashed, after all!) That this data is not processed is OK, because the stock data is so time-sensitive, after a few seconds it would be overwritten by new data anyway.

- *An application that implements its own "queuing" mechanism, for example, one that has data in a table with a PROCESSED_FLAG column*: As new data arrives, it is inserted with a value of PROCESSED_FLAG='N' (unprocessed). Another routine is tasked with reading the PROCESSED_FLAG='N' records, performing some small, fast transaction and updating the PROCESSED_FLAG='N' to 'Y'. If it commits but that commit is later undone (by a system failure), it is OK because the application that processes these records will just process the record again—it is "restartable."

If you look at these application categories, you'll notice that all three of them are background, noninteractive applications. They do not interact with a human being directly. Any application that does interact with a person—that reports to the person "Commit complete"—should use the synchronous commit. Asynchronous commits are not a tuning device for your online customer-facing applications. Asynchronous commits are applicable only to batch-oriented applications, those that are automatically restartable upon failure. Interactive applications are not restartable automatically upon failure—a human being must redo the transaction. Therefore, you have another flag that tells you whether this capability can be considered—do you have a batch application or an interactive one? Unless it is batch-oriented, synchronous commit is the way to go.

So, outside of those three categories of batch applications, this capability—COMMIT WRITE NOWAIT—should probably not be used. If you do use it, you need to ask yourself what would happen if your application is told *commit processed*, but later, the commit is undone. You need to be able to answer that question and come to the conclusion that it will be OK if that happens. If you can't answer that question, or if a committed change being lost would have serious repercussions, you should not use the asynchronous commit capability.

# COMMITS in a Nondistributed PL/SQL Block

Since PL/SQL was first introduced in version 6 of Oracle, it has been transparently using an asynchronous commit. That approach has worked because all PL/SQL is like a batch program in a way—the end user does not know the outcome of the procedure until it is completely finished. That's also why this asynchronous commit is used only in nondistributed PL/SQL blocks of code; if we involve more than one database, then there are two things—two databases—relying on the commit being durable. When two databases are relying on the commit being durable, we have to utilize synchronous protocols or a change might be committed in one database but not the other.

> **Note**   Of course, pipelined PL/SQL functions deviate from "normal" PL/SQL functions. In normal PL/SQL functions, the outcome is not known until the end of the stored procedure call. Pipelined functions in general are able to return data to a client long before they complete (they return "chunks" of data to the client, a bit at a time). But since pipelined functions are called from SELECT statements and would not be committing anyway, they do not come into play in this discussion.

Therefore, PL/SQL was developed to utilize an asynchronous commit, allowing the COMMIT statement in PL/SQL to not have to wait for the physical I/O to complete (avoiding the "log file sync" wait). That does not mean that you can't rely on a PL/SQL routine that commits and returns control to your application to not be durable with respect to its changes—PL/SQL will wait for the redo it generated to be written to disk before returning to the client application—but it will only wait once, right before it returns.

> **Note**   The following example demonstrates a bad practice—one that I call "slow-by-slow processing" or "row-by-row processing," as row-by-row is synonymous with slow-by-slow in a relational database. It is meant just to illustrate how PL/SQL processes a COMMIT statement.

First, let's create table T:

```
SQL> create table t
     as
     select *
```

```
      from all_objects
    where 1=0
  /
Table created.
```

Now, consider this PL/SQL procedure:

```
SQL> create or replace procedure p
    as
    begin
        for x in ( select * from all_objects )
        loop
            insert into t values X;
            commit;
        end loop;
    end;
  /

Procedure created.
```

That PL/SQL code reads a record at a time from ALL_OBJECTS, inserts the record into table T, and commits each record as it is inserted. Logically, that code is the same as this:

```
SQL> create or replace procedure p
    as
    begin
        for x in ( select * from all_objects )
        loop
            insert into t values X;
            commit write NOWAIT;
        end loop;

        -- make internal call here to ensure
        -- redo was written by LGWR
    end;
  /

Procedure created.
```

So, the commits performed in the routine are done with WRITE NOWAIT, and before the PL/SQL block of code returns to the client application, PL/SQL makes sure that the last bit of redo it generated was safely recorded to disk—making the PL/SQL block of code and its changes durable.

# Integrity Constraints and Transactions

It is interesting to note exactly when integrity constraints are checked. By default, integrity constraints are checked after the entire SQL statement has been processed. There are also deferrable constraints that permit the validation of integrity constraints to be postponed until either the application requests they be validated by issuing a SET CONSTRAINTS ALL IMMEDIATE command or upon issuing a COMMIT.

## IMMEDIATE Constraints

For the first part of this discussion, we'll assume that constraints are in IMMEDIATE mode, which is the norm. In this case, the integrity constraints are checked immediately after the entire SQL statement has been processed. Note that I used the term "SQL statement," not just "statement." If I have many SQL statements in a PL/SQL stored procedure, each SQL statement will have its integrity constraints validated immediately after its individual execution, not after the stored procedure completes.

So, why are constraints validated *after* the SQL statement executes? Why not *during*? This is because it is very natural for a single statement to make individual rows in a table momentarily inconsistent. Taking a look at the partial work by a statement would result in Oracle rejecting the results, even if the end result would be OK. For example, suppose we have a table like this:

```
SQL> create table t ( x int unique );
Table created.

SQL> insert into t values ( 1 );
1 row created.

SQL> insert into t values ( 2 );
1 row created.

SQL> commit;
Commit complete.
```

And we want to execute a multiple-row UPDATE:

```
SQL> update t set x=x-1;
2 rows updated.
```

If Oracle checked the constraint after each row was updated, on any given day we would stand a 50-50 chance of having the UPDATE fail. The rows in T are accessed in *some* order, and if Oracle updated the X=1 row first, we would momentarily have a duplicate value for X and it would reject the UPDATE. Since Oracle waits patiently until the end of the statement, the statement succeeds because by the time it is done, there are no duplicates.

## DEFERRABLE Constraints and Cascading Updates

In Oracle we also have the ability to *defer* constraint checking, which can be quite advantageous for various operations. The one that immediately jumps to mind is the requirement to cascade an UPDATE of a primary key to the child keys. Many people claim you should never need to do this—that primary keys are immutable (I am one of those people), but many others persist in their desire to have a cascading UPDATE. Deferrable constraints make this possible.

---

**Note**   It is considered an extremely bad practice to perform update cascades to modify a primary key. It violates the intent of the primary key. If you have to do it once to correct bad information, that's one thing, but if you find you are constantly doing it as part of your application, you will want to go back and rethink that process—you have chosen the wrong attributes to be the key!

---

In early releases of Oracle, it was possible to do a CASCADE UPDATE, but doing so involved a tremendous amount of work and had certain limitations. With deferrable constraints, it becomes almost trivial. The code could look like this:

```
SQL> create table parent
     ( pk  int primary key )
     /
Table created.
```

```
SQL> create table child
     ( fk  constraint child_fk_parent
           references parent(pk)
           deferrable
           initially immediate
     )
     /
Table created.

SQL> insert into parent values ( 1 );
1 row created.

SQL> insert into child values ( 1 );
1 row created.
```

We have a parent table, PARENT, and a child table, CHILD. Table CHILD references table PARENT, and the constraint used to enforce that rule is called CHILD_FK_PARENT (child foreign key to parent). This constraint was created as DEFERRABLE, but it is set to INITIALLY IMMEDIATE. This means we can defer that constraint until COMMIT or to some other time. By default, however, it will be validated at the statement level. This is the most common use of the deferrable constraints. Most existing applications won't check for constraint violations on a COMMIT statement, and it is best not to surprise them with that. As defined, table CHILD behaves in the fashion tables always have, but it gives us the ability to explicitly change its behavior. Now, let's try some DML on the tables and see what happens:

```
SQL> update parent set pk = 2;
update parent set pk = 2
*
ERROR at line 1:
ORA-02292: integrity constraint (YODA.CHILD_FK_PARENT) violated - child
record
found
```

Since the constraint is in IMMEDIATE mode, this UPDATE fails. We'll change the mode and try again:

```
SQL> set constraint child_fk_parent deferred;
Constraint set.

SQL> update parent set pk = 2;
1 row updated.
```

Now it succeeds. For illustration purposes, I'll show how to check a deferred constraint explicitly before committing, to see if the modifications we made are in agreement with the business rules (in other words, to check that the constraint isn't currently being violated). It's a good idea to do this before committing or releasing control to some other part of the program (which may not be expecting the deferred constraints):

```
SQL> set constraint child_fk_parent immediate;
set constraint child_fk_parent immediate
*
ERROR at line 1:
ORA-02291: integrity constraint (YODA.CHILD_FK_PARENT) violated - parent
key
not found
```

It fails and returns an error immediately as expected, since we knew that the constraint had been violated. The UPDATE to PARENT was not rolled back (that would violate the statement-level atomicity); it is still outstanding. Also note that our transaction is still working with the CHILD_FK_PARENT constraint deferred because the SET CONSTRAINT command failed. Let's continue now by cascading the UPDATE to CHILD:

```
SQL> update child set fk = 2;
1 row updated.

SQL> set constraint child_fk_parent immediate;
Constraint set.

SQL> commit;
Commit complete.
```

And that's the way it works. Note that to defer a constraint, you must create it that way—you have to drop and re-create the constraint to change it from nondeferrable to deferrable. That might lead you to believe that you should create all of your constraints as "deferrable initially immediate," just in case you wanted to defer them at some point. In general, that is *not* true. You want to allow constraints to be deferred only if you have a real need to do so. By creating deferred constraints, you introduce differences in the physical implementation (in the structure of your data) that might not be obvious. For example, if you create a deferrable UNIQUE or PRIMARY KEY constraint, the index that Oracle creates to support the enforcement of that constraint will be a nonunique index. Normally, you expect a unique index to enforce a unique constraint, but since you have specified that the constraint could temporarily be ignored, it can't use that unique index. Other subtle changes will be observed, for example, with NOT NULL constraints. If you allow your NOT NULL constraints to be deferrable, the optimizer will start treating the column as if it supports NULLs—because it in fact *does* support NULLs during your transaction. For example, suppose you have a table with the following columns and data:

```
SQL> create table t
     ( x int constraint x_not_null not null deferrable,
       y int constraint y_not_null not null,
       z varchar2(30)
     );
Table created.

SQL> insert into t(x,y,z)
     select rownum, rownum, rpad('x',30,'x')
       from all_users;
61 rows created.

SQL> exec dbms_stats.gather_table_stats( user, 'T' );
PL/SQL procedure successfully completed.
```

In this example, column X is created such that when you COMMIT, X will not be null. However, during your transaction, X is allowed to be null since the constraint is deferrable. Column Y, on the other hand, is always NOT NULL. Let's say you were to index column Y:

```
SQL> create index t_idx on t(y);
Index created.
```

And you then ran a query that could make use of this index on Y—but only if Y is NOT NULL, as in the following query:

```
SQL> explain plan for select count(*) from t;
Explained.

SQL> select * from table(dbms_xplan.display(null,null,'BASIC'));

----------------------------------
| Id  | Operation      | Name  |
----------------------------------
|   0 | SELECT STATEMENT |       |
|   1 |   SORT AGGREGATE  |       |
|   2 |    INDEX FULL SCAN| T_IDX |
----------------------------------
```

You would be happy to see the optimizer chose to use the small index on Y to count the rows rather than to full-scan the entire table T. However, let's say that you drop that index and index column X instead:

```
SQL> drop index t_idx;
Index dropped.

SQL> create index t_idx on t(x);
Index created.
```

And you then ran the query to count the rows once more; you would discover that the database does not, in fact cannot, use your index:

```
SQL> explain plan for select count(*) from t;
Explained.

SQL> select * from table(dbms_xplan.display(null,null,'BASIC'));

----------------------------------
| Id  | Operation       | Name  |
----------------------------------
|   0 | SELECT STATEMENT  |       |
|   1 |   SORT AGGREGATE   |       |
|   2 |    TABLE ACCESS FULL| T    |
----------------------------------
```

It full-scanned the table. It had to full-scan the table in order to count the rows. This is due to the fact that in an Oracle B*Tree index, index key entries that are entirely null are not made. That is, the index will not contain an entry for any row in the table T, such that all of the columns in the index are null. Since X is allowed to be null *temporarily,* the optimizer has to assume that X might be null and therefore would not be in the index on X. Hence, a count returned from the index might be different (wrong) from a count against the table.

We can see that if X had a nondeferrable constraint placed on it, this limitation is removed; that is, column X is in fact as good as column Y *if* the NOT NULL constraint is not deferrable:

```
SQL> alter table t drop constraint x_not_null;
Table altered.

SQL> alter table t modify x constraint x_not_null not null;
Table altered.

SQL> explain plan for select count(*) from t;
Explained.

SQL> select * from table(dbms_xplan.display(null,null,'BASIC'));
-----------------------------------
| Id | Operation       | Name  |
-----------------------------------
|  0 | SELECT STATEMENT |       |
|  1 |  SORT AGGREGATE |       |
|  2 |   INDEX FULL SCAN| T_IDX |
-----------------------------------
```

So, the bottom line is, only use deferrable constraints where you have an identified need to use them. They introduce subtle side effects that could cause differences in your physical implementation (nonunique vs. unique indexes) or in your query plans—as just demonstrated!

# Bad Transaction Habits

Many developers have some bad habits when it comes to transactions. I see this frequently with developers who have worked with a database that "supports" but does not "promote" the use of transactions. For example, in Informix (by default), Sybase, and SQL Server, you must explicitly `BEGIN` a transaction; otherwise, each individual statement is a transaction all by itself. In a similar manner to the way in which Oracle wraps a `SAVEPOINT` around discrete statements, these databases wrap a `BEGIN WORK/COMMIT` or `ROLLBACK` around each statement. This is because, in these databases, locks are precious resources, and readers block writers and vice versa. In an attempt to increase concurrency, these databases want you to make the transaction as short as possible—sometimes at the expense of data integrity.

Oracle takes the opposite approach. Transactions are always implicit, and there is no way to have an "autocommit" unless an application implements it (see the "Using Autocommit" section later in this chapter for more details). In Oracle, every transaction should be committed when it must and never before. Transactions should be as large as they need to be. Issues such as locks, blocking, and so on should not really be considered the driving forces behind transaction size—data integrity is *the driving* force behind the size of your transaction. Locks are not a scarce resource, and there are no contention issues between concurrent readers and writers of data. This allows you to have robust transactions in the database. These transactions do not have to be short in duration— they should be exactly as long as they need to be (but no longer). Transactions are not for the convenience of the computer and its software; they are to protect your data.

## Committing in a Loop

Faced with the task of updating many rows, most programmers will try to figure out some procedural way to do it in a loop, so that they can commit every so many rows. I've heard two *(false!)* reasons for doing it this way:

- It is faster and more efficient to frequently commit lots of small transactions than it is to process and commit one big transaction.

- We don't have enough undo space.

Both of these reasons are misguided. Furthermore, committing too frequently leaves you prone to the danger of leaving your database in an "unknown" state should your update fail halfway through. It requires complex logic to write a process that is smoothly restartable in the event of failure. By far, the best option is to commit only as frequently as your business processes dictate and to size your undo segments accordingly.

Let's take a look at these issues in more detail.

# Performance Implications

It is generally not faster to commit frequently—it is almost always faster to do the work in a single SQL statement. By way of a small example, say we have a table, T, with lots of rows, and we want to update a column value for every row in that table. We'll use this to set up such a table (run these four setup steps before each of the following three cases):

```
SQL> drop table t;
Table dropped.

SQL> create table t as select * from all_objects;
Table created.

SQL> exec dbms_stats.gather_table_stats( user, 'T' );
PL/SQL procedure successfully completed.

SQL> variable n number
```

Well, when we go to update, we could simply do it in a single UPDATE statement, like this:

```
SQL> exec :n := dbms_utility.get_cpu_time;
PL/SQL procedure successfully completed.

SQL> update t set object_name = lower(object_name);
72614 rows updated.

SQL> set serverout on;
SQL> exec dbms_output.put_line((dbms_utility.get_cpu_time-:n)||
' cpu hsecs...' );
117 cpu hsecs...
```

Many people, for whatever reason, feel compelled to do it like this—slow-by-slow/row-by-row—in order to have a commit every N records:

```
SQL> exec :n := dbms_utility.get_cpu_time;
PL/SQL procedure successfully completed.

SQL> begin
        for x in ( select rowid rid, object_name, rownum r
                        from t )
        loop
            update t
                set object_name = lower(x.object_name)
             where rowid = x.rid;
             if ( mod(x.r,100) = 0 ) then
                 commit;
             end if;
        end loop;
        commit;
    end;
  /
PL/SQL procedure successfully completed.

SQL> exec dbms_output.put_line((dbms_utility.get_cpu_time-:n)||' cpu hsecs...' );
323 cpu hsecs...
```

In this simple example, it is many times *slower* to loop in order to commit frequently. If you can do it in a *single* SQL statement, do it that way, as it is almost certainly faster. Even if we "optimize" the procedural code, using bulk processing for the updates (as follows), it is in fact much faster, but still much slower than it could be.

```
SQL> exec :n := dbms_utility.get_cpu_time;
PL/SQL procedure successfully completed.

SQL> declare
        type ridArray is table of rowid;
        type vcArray is table of t.object_name%type;
```

```
        l_rids   ridArray;
        l_names vcArray;

        cursor c is select rowid, object_name from t;
    begin
       open c;
       loop
           fetch c bulk collect into l_rids, l_names LIMIT 100;
           forall i in 1 .. l_rids.count
               update t
                  set object_name = lower(l_names(i))
                where rowid = l_rids(i);
           commit;
           exit when c%notfound;
       end loop;
       close c;
    end;
  /

PL/SQL procedure successfully completed.

SQL> exec dbms_output.put_line((dbms_utility.get_cpu_time-:n)||'
cpu hsecs...' );
```
**67 cpu hsecs...**

```
PL/SQL procedure successfully completed.
```

Not only that, but you should notice that the code is getting more and more complex. From the sheer simplicity of a single UPDATE statement, to procedural code, to even more complex procedural code—we are going in the wrong direction! Furthermore (yes, there is more to complain about), the preceding procedural code is not done yet. It doesn't deal with "what happens when we fail" (not *if we* but rather *when we*). What happens if this code gets halfway done and then the system fails? How do you restart the procedural code with a commit? You'd have to add yet more code so you knew where to pick up and continue processing. With the single UPDATE statement, we just reissue the UPDATE. We know that it will entirely succeed or entirely fail; there will not be partial work to worry about. We visit this point more in the section "Restartable Processes Require Complex Logic."

Now, just to supply a counterpoint to this discussion, recall in Chapter 4 when we discussed the concept of write consistency and how an UPDATE statement, for example, could be made to restart. In the event that the preceding UPDATE statement was to be performed against a subset of the rows (it had a WHERE clause, and other users were modifying the columns this UPDATE was using in the WHERE clause), then there would be a case either for using a series of smaller transactions rather than one large transaction or for locking the table prior to performing the mass update. The goal here would be to reduce the opportunity for restarts to occur.

If we were to UPDATE the vast majority of the rows in the table, that would lead us toward using the LOCK TABLE command. In my experience, however, these sorts of large mass updates or mass deletes (the only statement types really that would be subject to the restart) are done in isolation. That large, one-time bulk update or the purge of old data generally is not done during a period of high activity. Indeed, the purge of data should not be affected by this at all, since you would typically use some date field to locate the information to purge, and other applications would not modify this data.

## Snapshot Too Old Error

Let's now look at the second reason developers are tempted to commit updates in a procedural loop, which arises from their (misguided) attempts to use a "limited resource" (undo segments) sparingly. This is a configuration issue; you *need* to ensure that you have enough undo space to size your transactions correctly. Committing in a loop, apart from generally being slower, is also the most common cause of the dreaded ORA-01555 error. Let's look at this in more detail.

As you will appreciate after reading Chapter 4, Oracle's multiversioning model uses undo segment data to reconstruct blocks as they appeared at the beginning of your statement or transaction (depending on the isolation mode). If the necessary undo information no longer exists, you will receive an ORA-01555: snapshot too old error message and your query will not complete. So, if you are modifying the table that you are reading (as in the previous example), you are generating undo information required for your query. Your UPDATE generates undo information that your query will probably be making use of to get the read-consistent view of the data it needs to update. If you commit, you are allowing the system to reuse the undo segment space you just filled up. If it does reuse the undo, wiping out old undo data that your query subsequently needs, you are in big trouble. Your SELECT will fail and your UPDATE will stop partway through. You have a partly finished logical transaction and probably no good way to restart it (more about this in a moment).

Let's see this concept in action with a small demonstration. In a small test database, we set up a table:

```
SQL> create table t as select * from all_objects;
Table created.

SQL> create index t_idx on t(object_name);
Index created.

SQL> exec dbms_stats.gather_table_stats( user, 'T', cascade=>true );
PL/SQL procedure successfully completed.
```

I then created a very small undo tablespace and altered the system to use it. Note that by setting AUTOEXTEND off, I have limited the size of all UNDO to be 10MB or less in this system:

```
SQL> create undo tablespace undo_small
        datafile '/tmp/undo_small.dbf'
        size 10m reuse
        autoextend off
    /

Tablespace created.
SQL> alter system set undo_tablespace = undo_small;
System altered.
```

Now, with only the small undo tablespace in use, I ran this block of code to do the UPDATE:

```
SQL> begin
        for x in ( select /*+ INDEX(t t_idx) */ rowid rid, object_name,
        rownum r
                    from t
                  where object_name > ' ' )
        loop
            update t
              set object_name = lower(x.object_name)
             where rowid = x.rid;
            if ( mod(x.r,100) = 0 ) then
```

144

```
            commit;
         end if;
      end loop;
      commit;
   end;
 /
begin
*
ERROR at line 1:
ORA-01555: snapshot too old: rollback segment number  with name "" too small
ORA-06512: at line 2
```

I get the error. I should point out that I added an index hint to the query and a WHERE clause to make sure I was reading the table randomly (together, they caused the cost-based optimizer to read the table "sorted" by the index key). When we process a table via an index, we tend to read a block for a single row, and then the next row we want will be on a different block. Ultimately, we will process all of the rows on block 1, just not all at the same time. Block 1 might hold, say, the data for all rows with OBJECT_NAMEs starting with the letters A, M, N, Q, and Z. So we would hit the block many times, since we are reading the data sorted by OBJECT_NAME and presumably many OBJECT_NAMEs start with letters between A and M. Since we are committing frequently and reusing undo space, we eventually revisit a block where we can simply no longer roll back to the point our query began, and at that point, we get the error.

This was a very artificial example just to show how it happens in a reliable manner. My UPDATE statement was generating undo. I had a very small undo tablespace to play with (10MB). I wrapped around in my undo segments many times, since they are used in a circular fashion. Every time I committed, I allowed Oracle to overwrite the undo data I generated. Eventually, I needed some piece of data I had generated, but it no longer existed and I received the ORA-01555 error.

You would be right to point out that in this case, if I had not committed on line 10, I would have received the following error:

```
begin
*
ERROR at line 1:
ORA-30036: unable to extend segment by 8 in undo tablespace 'UNDO_SMALL'
ORA-06512: at line 6
```

The major differences between the two errors are as follows:

- The ORA-01555 example *left my update in a totally unknown state.* Some of the work had been done; some had not.

- There is absolutely *nothing I can do to avoid the* ORA-01555 error, given that I committed in the cursor FOR loop.

- *The* ORA-30036 *error can be avoided* by allocating appropriate resources in the system. This error is avoidable by correct sizing; the first error is not. Further, even if I don't avoid this error, at least the update is rolled back and the database is left in a known, consistent state—not halfway through some large update.

The bottom line here is that you can't "save" on undo space by committing frequently—you need that undo. I was in a single-user system when I received the ORA-01555 error. It takes only one session to cause that error, and many times even in real life, it is a single session causing its own ORA-01555 errors. Developers and DBAs need to work together to size these segments adequately for the jobs that need to be done. There can be no short-changing here. You must discover, through analysis of your system, what your biggest transactions are and size appropriately for them. The dynamic performance view V$UNDOSTAT can be very useful to monitor the amount of undo you are generating and the duration of your longest running queries. Many people consider things like temp, undo, and redo as overhead—things to allocate as little storage to as possible. This is reminiscent of a problem the computer industry had on January 1, 2000, which was all caused by trying to save 2 bytes in a date field. These components of the database are not overhead, but rather are key components of the system. They must be sized appropriately (not too big and not too small).

Speaking of UNDO segments being too small, make sure to set your undo tablespace back to your regular one after running these tests, for example:

```
SQL> alter system set undo_tablespace=undotbs2;
SQL> drop tablespace undo_small including contents and datafiles;
```

If you don't set your undo tablespace back to a normally sized one, you'll be hitting ORA-30036 errors for the rest of the book!

# Restartable Processes Require Complex Logic

The most serious problem with the "commit before the logical transaction is over" approach is the fact that it frequently leaves your database in an unknown state if the UPDATE fails halfway through. Unless you planned for this ahead of time, it is very hard to restart the failed process, allowing it to pick up where it left off. For example, say we were not applying the LOWER() function to the column, as in the previous example, but rather some other function of the column, such as this:

```
last_ddl_time = last_ddl_time + 1;
```

If we halted the UPDATE loop partway through, how would we restart it? We could not just rerun it, as we would end up adding 2 to some dates, and 1 to others. If we fail again, we would add 3 to some, 2 to others, 1 to the rest, and so on. We need yet more complex logic—some way to "partition" the data. For example, we could process every OBJECT_NAME that starts with A, and then B, and so on:

```
SQL> create table to_do
     as
     select distinct substr( object_name, 1,1 ) first_char
       from T
     /
Table created.

SQL> set serverout on
SQL> begin
             for x in ( select * from to_do )
             loop
                 update t set last_ddl_time = last_ddl_time+1
                   where object_name like x.first_char || '%';

                 dbms_output.put_line( sql%rowcount || ' rows updated' );
                 delete from to_do where first_char = x.first_char;

               commit;
           end loop;
    end;
```

```
    /
238 rows updated
5730 rows updated
1428 rows updated
...
262 rows updated
1687 rows updated
PL/SQL procedure successfully completed.
```

Now, we could restart this process if it fails, since we would not process any object name that had already been processed successfully. The problem with this approach, however, is that unless we have some attribute that evenly partitions the data, we will end up having a very wide distribution of rows. The second UPDATE did more work than all of the others combined. Additionally, if other sessions are accessing this table and modifying the data, they might update the OBJECT_NAME field as well. Suppose that some other session updates the object named Z to be A, *after* we already processed the As. We would miss that record. Furthermore, this is a very inefficient process compared to UPDATE T SET LAST_DDL_TIME = LAST_DDL_TIME+1. We are probably using an index to read every row in the table, or we are full-scanning it *n* times, both of which are undesirable. There are so many bad things to be said about this approach.

The best approach is to do it simply. If it can be done in SQL, do it in SQL. What can't be done in SQL, do in PL/SQL. Do it using the least amount of code you can. Have sufficient resources allocated. Always think about what happens in the event of an error. So many times, I've seen people code update loops that worked great on the test data but then failed halfway through when applied to the real data. Then, they are really stuck, as they have no idea where the loop stopped processing. It's a lot easier to size undo correctly than to write a restartable program. If you have truly large tables that need to be updated, you should be using partitions, which you can update each individually. You can even use parallel DML to perform the update or, in Oracle11g Release 2 and above, the DBMS_PARALLEL_EXECUTE package.

# Using Autocommit

My final words on bad transaction habits concern the one that arises from using the popular programming APIs ODBC and JDBC. These APIs "autocommit" by default. Consider the following statements, which transfer $1,000 from a checking account to a savings account:

```
update accounts set balance = balance - 1000 where account_id = 123;
update accounts set balance = balance + 1000 where account_id = 456;
```

If your program is using ODBC or JDBC when you submit these statements, they (silently) inject a commit after *each* UPDATE. Consider the impact of this if the system fails after the first UPDATE and before the second. You've just lost $1,000!

I can sort of understand why ODBC does this. The developers of SQL Server designed ODBC, and this database demands that you use very short transactions due to its concurrency model (writes block reads, reads block writes, and locks are a scarce resource). What I can't understand is how this got carried over into JDBC, an API that is supposed to support "the enterprise." It is my belief that the very next line of code after opening a connection in JDBC should always be this:

```
Connection conn = DriverManager.getConnection
            ("jdbc:oracle:oci:@database","scott","tiger");

conn.setAutoCommit (false);
```

This returns control over the transaction back to you, the developer, which is where it belongs. You can then safely code your account transfer transaction and commit it after both statements have succeeded. Lack of knowledge of your API can be deadly in this case. I've seen more than one developer unaware of this autocommit "feature" get into big trouble with his application when an error occurred.

# Distributed Transactions

One of the really nice features of Oracle is its ability to transparently handle distributed transactions. I can update data in many different databases in the scope of a single transaction. When I commit, either I commit the updates in all of the instances or I commit none of them (they will all be rolled back). I need no extra code to achieve this; I simply "commit."

A key to distributed transactions in Oracle is the *database link*. A database link is a database object that describes how to log into another instance from your instance. However, the purpose of this section is not to cover the syntax of the database link command (it is fully documented in the *Oracle Database SQL Language Reference* manual), but rather to expose you to its very existence. Once you have a database link set up, accessing remote objects is as easy as this:

```
select * from T@another_database;
```

This would select from the table T in the database instance defined by the database link ANOTHER_DATABASE. Typically, you would "hide" the fact that T is a remote table by creating a view of it, or a synonym. For example, I can issue the following and then access T as if it were a local table:

```
create synonym T for T@another_database;
```

Now that I have this database link set up and can read some tables, I am also able to modify them (assuming I have the appropriate privileges, of course). Performing a distributed transaction is now no different from a local transaction. All I would do is this:

```
update local_table set x = 5;
update remote_table@another_database set y = 10;
commit;
```

That's it. Oracle will commit either in both databases or in neither. It uses a two-phase commit protocol (2PC) to do this. 2PC is a distributed protocol that allows for a modification that affects many disparate databases to be committed atomically. It attempts to close the window for distributed failure as much as possible before committing. In a 2PC between many databases, one of the databases—typically the one the client is logged into initially—will be the coordinator for the distributed transaction. This one site will ask the other sites if they are ready to commit. In effect, this site will go to the other sites and ask them to be prepared to commit. Each of the other sites reports back its "prepared state" as YES or NO. If any one of the sites votes NO, the entire transaction is rolled back. If all sites vote YES, the site coordinator broadcasts a message to make the commit permanent on each of the sites.

This limits the window in which a serious error could occur. Prior to the "voting" on the 2PC, any distributed error would result in all of the sites rolling back. There would be no doubt as to the outcome of the transaction. After the order to commit or roll back, there again is no doubt as to the outcome of the distributed transaction. It is only during the very short window when the coordinator is collecting the votes that the outcome might be in doubt, after a failure.

Assume, for example, we have three sites participating in the transaction with Site 1 being the coordinator. Site 1 has asked Site 2 to prepare to commit, and Site 2 has done so. Site 1 then asks Site 3 to prepare to commit, and it does so. At this point, Site 1 is the only site that knows the outcome of the transaction, and it is now responsible for broadcasting the outcome to the other sites. If an error occurs right now—the network fails, Site 1 loses power, whatever—Sites 2 and 3 will be left hanging. They will have what is known as an *in-doubt distributed transaction*. The 2PC protocol attempts to close the window of error as much as possible, but it can't close it entirely. Sites 2 and 3 must keep that transaction open, awaiting notification of the outcome from Site 1.

It is the function of the RECO background process to resolve this issue. This is also where COMMIT and ROLLBACK with the FORCE option come into play. If the cause of the problem was a network failure between Sites 1, 2, and 3, then the DBAs at Sites 2 and 3 could actually call the DBA at Site 1, ask him for the outcome, and apply the commit or roll back manually, as appropriate.

There are some, but not many, limitations to what you can do in a distributed transaction, and they are reasonable (to me, anyway, they seem reasonable). The big ones are as follows:

- You can't issue a COMMIT over a database link. That is, you can't issue a COMMIT@remote_site. You may commit only from the site that initiated the transaction.

- You can't do DDL over a database link. This is a direct result of the preceding issue. DDL commits. You can't commit from any site other than the initiating site; hence, you can't do DDL over a database link.

- You can't issue a SAVEPOINT over a database link. In short, you can't issue any transaction control statements over a database link. All transaction control is inherited from the session that opened the database link in the first place; you can't have different transaction controls in place in the distributed instances in your transaction.

The lack of transaction control over a database link is reasonable, since the initiating site is the only one that has a list of everyone involved in the transaction. If in our three-site configuration, Site 2 attempted to commit, it would have no way of knowing that Site 3 was involved. In Oracle, only Site 1 can issue the commit command. At that point, it is permissible for Site 1 to delegate responsibility for distributed transaction control to another site.

We can influence which site will be the actual commit site by setting the COMMIT_POINT_STRENGTH (a parameter) of the site. A COMMIT_POINT_STRENGTH associates a relative level of importance to a server in a distributed transaction. The more important the server (the more available the data needs to be), the more probable that it will coordinate the distributed transaction. You might want to do this if you need to perform a distributed transaction between your production machine and a test machine. Since the transaction coordinator is *never* in doubt as to the outcome of a transaction, it's best if the production machine coordinated the distributed transaction. You don't care so much if your test machine has some open transactions and locked resources. You certainly do care if your production machine does.

The inability to do DDL over a database link is actually not so bad at all. First, DDL is rare. You do it once at installation or during an upgrade. Production systems don't do DDL (well, they *shouldn't* do DDL). Second, there is a method to do DDL over a database link, in a fashion, using the job queue facility, DBMS_JOB or, in Oracle 10*g* and higher, the scheduler package, DBMS_SCHEDULER. Instead of trying to do DDL over the link, you use the link to schedule a remote job to be executed as soon as you commit. In that fashion, the job runs on the remote machine, is not a distributed transaction, and can do the DDL. In fact, this is the method by which the Oracle Replication Services perform distributed DDL to do schema replication.

# Autonomous Transactions

Autonomous transactions allow you to create a "transaction within a transaction" that will commit or roll back changes independently of its parent transaction. They allow you to suspend the currently executing transaction, start a new one, do some work, and commit or roll back—all without affecting the currently executing transaction state. Autonomous transactions provide a new method of controlling transactions in PL/SQL and may be used in

- Top-level anonymous blocks

- Local (a procedure in a procedure), stand-alone, or packaged functions and procedures

- Methods of object types

- Database triggers

Before we take a look at how autonomous transactions work, I'd like to emphasize that this type of transaction is a powerful and therefore dangerous tool when used improperly. The true need for an autonomous transaction is very rare indeed. I would be very suspicious of any code that makes use of them—that code would get extra examination. It is far too easy to accidentally introduce logical data integrity issues into a system using them. In the sections that follow, we'll discuss when they may safely be used after seeing how they work.

# How Autonomous Transactions Work

The best way to demonstrate the actions and consequences of an autonomous transaction is by example. We'll create a simple table to hold a message:

```
SQL> create table t ( msg varchar2(25) );
Table created.
```

Next, we'll create two procedures, each of which simply INSERTs its name into the message table and commits. However, one of these procedures is a normal procedure and the other is coded as an autonomous transaction. We'll use these objects to show what work persists (is committed) in the database under various circumstances.

First, here's the AUTONOMOUS_INSERT procedure:

```
SQL> create or replace procedure Autonomous_Insert
    as
            pragma autonomous_transaction;
    begin
            insert into t values ( 'Autonomous Insert' );
            commit;
    end;
    /
Procedure created.
```

Note the use of the pragma AUTONOMOUS_TRANSACTION. This directive tells the database that this procedure, when executed, is to be executed as a new autonomous transaction, independent from its parent transaction.

---

**Note**   A *pragma* is simply a compiler directive, a method to instruct the compiler to perform some compilation option. Other pragmas are available. Refer to the *Oracle Database PL/SQL Language Reference* manual; you'll find a list of them in its index.

---

And here's the "normal" NONAUTONOMOUS_INSERT procedure:

```
SQL> create or replace procedure NonAutonomous_Insert
     as
     begin
             insert into t values ( 'NonAutonomous Insert' );
             commit;
     end;
     /
Procedure created.
```

Now, let's observe the behavior of the *nonautonomous* transaction in an anonymous block of PL/SQL code:

```
SQL> begin
             insert into t values ( 'Anonymous Block' );
             NonAutonomous_Insert;
             rollback;
     end;
     /
PL/SQL procedure successfully completed.

SQL> select * from t;

MSG
-------------------------
Anonymous Block
NonAutonomous Insert
```

As you can see, the work performed by the anonymous block, its INSERT, was *committed* by the NONAUTONOMOUS_INSERT procedure. Both rows of data were committed, so the ROLLBACK command had nothing to roll back. Compare this to the behavior of the autonomous transaction procedure:

```
SQL> delete from t;
2 rows deleted.

SQL> commit;
Commit complete.

SQL> begin
            insert into t values ( 'Anonymous Block' );
            Autonomous_Insert;
            rollback;
    end;
    /
PL/SQL procedure successfully completed.

SQL> select * from t;

MSG
-------------------------
Autonomous Insert
```

Here, only the work done by and committed in the autonomous transaction persists. The INSERT done in the anonymous block was rolled back by the ROLLBACK statement on line 4. The autonomous transaction procedure's COMMIT has no effect on the parent transaction started in the anonymous block. In a nutshell, this captures the essence of autonomous transactions and what they do.

To summarize, if you COMMIT inside a "normal" procedure, it will make durable not only its own work but also any outstanding work performed in that session. However, a COMMIT performed in a procedure with an autonomous transaction will make durable only that procedure's work.

# When to Use Autonomous Transactions

The Oracle database has supported autonomous transactions internally for quite a while. We see them all of the time in the form of recursive SQL. For example, a recursive transaction may be performed when selecting from a sequence, in order for you to increment the sequence immediately in the SYS.SEQ$ table. The update of the SYS.SEQ$ table in support of your sequence is immediately committed and visible to other transactions, but your transaction is not yet committed. Additionally, if you roll back your transaction, the increment to the sequence remains in place; it is not rolled back with your transaction, as it has already been committed. Space management, auditing, and other internal operations are performed in a similar recursive fashion.

This feature has now been exposed for all to use. However, I have found that the legitimate real-world use of autonomous transactions *is very limited*. Time after time, I see them used as a workaround to such problems as a mutating table constraint in a trigger. This almost always leads to data integrity issues, however, since the cause of the mutating table is an attempt to read the table upon which the trigger is firing. Well, by using an autonomous transaction, you can query the table, but you are querying the table now without being able to see your changes (which is what the mutating table constraint was trying to do in the first place; the table is in the middle of a modification, so query results would be inconsistent). Any decisions you make based on a query from that trigger would be questionable—you are reading "old" data at that point in time.

A potentially valid use for an autonomous transaction is in custom auditing, but I stress the words "potentially valid." There are more efficient ways to audit information in the database than via a custom-written trigger. For example, you can use the DBMS_FGA package or just the AUDIT command itself.

A question that application developers often pose to me is, "How can I log errors in my PL/SQL routines in a manner that will persist, even when my PL/SQL routines' work is rolled back?" Earlier, we described how PL/SQL statements are *atomic*—they either completely succeed or completely fail. If we logged an error in our PL/SQL routines, by default, our logged error information would roll back when Oracle rolled back our statement. Autonomous transactions allow us to change that behavior, to have our error logging information persist even while the rest of the partial work is rolled back.

Let's start by setting up a simple error logging table to use; we'll record the timestamp of the error, the error message, and the PL/SQL error stack (for pinpointing where the error emanated from):

```
SQL> create table error_log
    ( ts   timestamp,
      err1 clob,
      err2 clob )
    /
Table created.
```

Now, we need the PL/SQL routine to log errors into this table. We can use this small example:

```
SQL> create or replace
    procedure log_error
    ( p_err1 in varchar2, p_err2 in varchar2 )
    as
        pragma autonomous_transaction;
    begin
        insert into error_log( ts, err1, err2 )
        values ( systimestamp, p_err1, p_err2 );
        commit;
    end;
  /
Procedure created.
```

The "magic" of this routine is on line 5 where we used the `pragma autonomous_transaction` directive to inform PL/SQL that we want this subroutine to start a new transaction, perform some work in it, and commit it—without affecting any other transaction currently in process. The `COMMIT` on line 9 can affect only the SQL performed by this `LOG_ERROR` procedure.

Now, let's test it out. To make it interesting, we'll create a couple of procedures that will call each other:

```
SQL> create table t ( x int check (x>0) );
Table created.
```

```
SQL> create or replace procedure p1( p_n in number )
     as
     begin
         -- some code here
         insert into t (x) values ( p_n );
     end;
     /
Procedure created.

SQL> create or replace procedure p2( p_n in number )
     as
     begin
         -- code
         -- code
         p1(p_n);
     end;
     /
Procedure created.
```

And then we'll invoke those routines from an anonymous block:

```
SQL> begin
         p2( 1 );
         p2( 2 );
         p2( -1);
     exception
         when others
         then
             log_error( sqlerrm, dbms_utility.format_error_backtrace );
             RAISE;
     end;
  /
begin
*
```

```
ERROR at line 1:
ORA-02290: check constraint (YODA.SYS_C0013043) violated
ORA-06512: at line 9
```

Now, we can see the code failed (you want that error returned, hence the RAISE on line 9). We can verify that Oracle undid our work (we know that the first two calls to procedure P2 succeeded; the values 1 and 2 are successfully inserted into our table T):

```
SQL> select * from t;
no rows selected
```

But we can also verify that our error log information has persisted and in fact is committed:

```
SQL> rollback;
Rollback complete.

SQL> select * from error_log;

TS
-------------------------------------------------------------------------------
ERR1
-------------------------------------------------------------------------------
ERR2
-------------------------------------------------------------------------------
30-MAY-20 02.59.41.969061 PM
ORA-02290: check constraint (YODA.SYS_C0013043) violated
ORA-06512: at "YODA.P1", line 5
ORA-06512: at "YODA.P2", line 6
```

In my experience, that is the only truly valid use of an autonomous transaction—to log errors or informational messages in a manner that can be committed independently of the parent transaction.

# Summary

In this chapter, we looked at many aspects of transaction management in Oracle. Transactions are among the major features that set a database apart from a file system. Understanding how they work and how to use them is necessary to implement applications correctly in any database. Understanding that in Oracle all statements are atomic (including their side effects) and that this atomicity is extended to stored procedures is crucial. We saw how the placement of a WHEN OTHERS exception handler in a PL/SQL block could radically affect what changes took place in the database. As database developers, having a good understanding of how transactions work is crucial.

We took a look at the somewhat complex interaction between integrity constraints (unique keys, check constraints, and the like) and transactions in Oracle. We discussed how Oracle typically processes integrity constraints immediately after a statement executes, but that we can defer this constraint validation until the end of the transaction if we wish. This feature is key in implementing complex multitable updates when the tables being modified are all dependent on each other—the cascading update is an example of that.

We moved on to consider some of the bad transaction habits that people tend to pick up from working with databases that "support" rather than "promote" the use of transactions. We looked at the cardinal rule of transactions: they should be as short as they can be but as long as they need to be. *Data integrity drives the transaction size*—that is a key concept to take away from this chapter. The only things that should drive the size of your transactions are the business rules that govern your system. Not undo space, not locks—business rules.

We covered distributed transactions and how they differ from single database transactions. We explored the limitations imposed upon us in a distributed transaction and discussed why they exist. Before you build a distributed system, you need to understand these limitations. What works in a single instance might not work in a distributed database.

The chapter closed with a look at autonomous transactions and covered what they are and, more important, when they should and should not be used. I would like to emphasize once again that the legitimate real-world use of autonomous transactions is exceedingly rare. If you find them to be a feature you are using constantly, you'll want to take a long, hard look at why.

# CHAPTER 6

# Redo and Undo

This chapter introduces you to two of the most important pieces of data in an Oracle database: redo and undo. *Redo* is the information Oracle records in online (and archived) redo log files in order to "replay" your transaction in the event of a failure. *Undo* is the information Oracle records in the undo segments in order to reverse, or roll back, your transaction.

In this chapter, we will discuss topics such as how redo and undo (rollback) are generated, and how they fit into transactions. We'll also discuss the performance implications of `COMMIT` and `ROLLBACK` statements. I will present the pseudocode for these mechanisms in Oracle and a conceptual explanation of what actually takes place. I will not cover every internal detail of what files get updated with what bytes of data. What actually takes place is a little more involved, but having a good understanding of the flow of how it works is valuable and will help you to understand the ramifications of your actions.

Time and time again, I get questions regarding the exact bits and bytes of redo and undo. People seem to want to have a very detailed specification of exactly, precisely, what is in there. I never answer those questions. Instead, I focus on the intent of redo and undo, the concepts behind redo and undo. I focus on the use of redo and undo—not on the bits and bytes. I myself do not "dump" redo log files or undo segments. I do use the supplied tools, such as LogMiner, to read redo and flashback transaction history to read undo, but that presents the information to me in a human-readable format. So, we won't be doing internals in this chapter but rather building a strong foundation.

## What Is Redo?

Redo log files are crucial to the Oracle database. These are the transaction logs for the database. Oracle maintains two types of redo log files: *online* and *archived*. They are used for recovery purposes; their main purpose in life is to be used in the event of an instance or media failure.

© Darl Kuhn and Thomas Kyte 2021
D. Kuhn and T. Kyte, *Oracle Database Transactions and Locking Revealed*,
https://doi.org/10.1007/978-1-4842-6425-6_6

If the power goes off on your database machine, causing an instance failure, Oracle will use the online redo logs to restore the system to exactly the committed point it was at immediately prior to the power outage. If your disk drive fails (a media failure), Oracle will use both archived redo logs and online redo logs to recover a backup of the data that was on that drive to the correct point in time. Moreover, if you "accidentally" truncate a table or remove some critical information and commit the operation, you can restore a backup of the affected data and recover it to the point in time immediately prior to the "accident" using online and archived redo log files.

I should point out that modern versions of Oracle (e.g., 10g and above) also have flashback technology. This allows us to perform flashback queries (query the data as of some point in time in the past), un-drop a database table, put a table back the way it was some time ago, and so on. As a result, the number of occasions in which we need to perform a conventional recovery (using database backups and archived redo logs) has decreased. However, the ability to perform a recovery is the DBA's most important job.

---

**Note**   Database restore and recovery is the one thing a DBA is not allowed to get wrong.

---

Archived redo log files are simply copies of old, full online redo log files. As the system fills up log files, the Oracle archiver (ARCn) process makes a copy of the online redo log file in another location and optionally puts several other copies into local and remote locations as well. These archived redo log files are used to perform media recovery when a failure is caused by a disk drive going bad or some other physical fault. Oracle can take these archived redo log files and apply them to backups of the data files to catch them up to the rest of the database. They are the transaction history of the database.

Every Oracle database has at least two online redo log groups with at least a single member (redo log file) in each group. These online redo log groups are written to in a circular fashion by the log writer (LGWR) background process. Oracle will write to the log files in group 1, and when it gets to the end of the files in group 1, it will switch to log file group 2 and begin writing to that one. When it has filled log file group 2, it will switch back to log file group 1 (assuming you have only two redo log file groups; if you have three, Oracle would, of course, proceed to the third group).

Redo logs, or transaction logs, are one of the major features that make a database a database. They are perhaps its most important recovery structure, although without the other pieces such as undo segments, distributed transaction recovery, and so on, nothing works. They are a major component of what sets a database apart from a conventional file system. The online redo logs allow us to effectively recover from a power outage—one that might happen while Oracle's database writer (DBWR) background process is in the middle of writing to disk. The archived redo logs let us recover from media failures when, for instance, the hard disk goes bad or human error causes data loss. Without redo logs, the database would not offer any more protection than a file system.

There's one additional item I want to mention regarding redo. In an Oracle RAC environment, you typically have two or more instances. RAC configurations have one common set of data files (meaning each instance transacts against a common set of data files). However, each instance participating in a RAC cluster has its own memory structures and background processes (e.g., log writer and archiver). Also, each instance will have its own redo stream (or often called a thread of redo). And it follows that each instance will also have its own undo segments. This is important because you may find yourself troubleshooting performing issues with redo and it's critical to pinpoint which instance or instances may be having redo bottleneck issues.

# What Is Undo?

Undo is conceptually the opposite of redo. Undo information is generated by the database as you make modifications to data so that the data can be put back the way it was before the modifications took place. This might be done in support of multiversioning, or in the event the transaction or statement you are executing fails for any reason, or if we request it with a ROLLBACK statement. Whereas redo is used to replay a transaction in the event of failure—to recover the transaction—undo is used to reverse the effects of a statement or set of statements. Undo, unlike redo, is stored internally in the database in a special set of segments known as undo segments.

---

**Note**    "Rollback segment" and "undo segment" are considered synonymous terms.

---

It is a common misconception that undo is used to restore the database *physically* to the way it was before the statement or transaction executed, but this is not so. The database is *logically* restored to the way it was—any changes are logically undone—but the data structures, the database blocks themselves, may well be different after a rollback. The reason for this lies in the fact that, in any multiuser system, there will be tens or hundreds or thousands of concurrent transactions. One of the primary functions of a database is to mediate concurrent access to its data. The blocks that our transaction modifies are, in general, being modified by many other transactions as well. Therefore, we can't just put a block back exactly the way it was at the start of our transaction—that could undo someone else's work!

For example, suppose our transaction executed an INSERT statement that caused the allocation of a new extent (i.e., it caused the table to grow). Our INSERT would cause us to get a new block, format it for use, and put some data into it. At that point, some other transaction might come along and insert data into this block. If we roll back our transaction, obviously we can't unformat and unallocate this block. Therefore, when Oracle rolls back, it is really doing the logical equivalent of the opposite of what we did in the first place. For every INSERT, Oracle will do a DELETE. For every DELETE, Oracle will do an INSERT. For every UPDATE, Oracle will do an "anti-UPDATE," or an UPDATE that puts the row back the way it was prior to our modification.

---

**Note**    This undo generation is not true for direct-path operations, which have the ability to bypass undo generation on the table. We'll discuss these operations in more detail shortly.

---

How can we see this in action? Perhaps the easiest way is to follow these steps:

1.  Create an empty table.

2.  Full-scan the table and observe the amount of I/O performed to read it.

3.  Fill the table with many rows (no commit).

4.  Roll back that work and undo it.

5.  Full-scan the table a second time and observe the amount of I/O performed.

So, let's create an empty table:

```
SQL> create table t
     as
     select *
       from all_objects
      where 1=0;
Table created.
```

And now we'll query it, with AUTOTRACE enabled in SQL*Plus to measure the I/O.

---

**Note**    In this example, we will full-scan the table twice each time. The goal is to only measure the I/O performed the second time in each case. This avoids counting additional I/Os performed by the optimizer during any parsing and optimization that may occur.

---

The query initially takes *no* I/Os to full-scan the table:

```
SQL> select * from t;
no rows selected

SQL> set autotrace traceonly statistics
SQL> select * from t;
no rows selected

Statistics
-----------------------------------------------------------
          0   recursive calls
          0   db block gets
          0   consistent gets
          0   physical reads

SQL> set autotrace off
```

Now, that might surprise you at first—especially if you are an Oracle user dating back to versions before Oracle 11*g* Release 2—that there are *zero* I/Os against the table. This is due to a new Oracle 11*g* Release 2 feature—deferred segment creation.

---

**Note**  The deferred segment creation feature is available only with the Enterprise Edition of Oracle. This feature is enabled by default in Oracle 11g Release 2 and higher. You can override this default behavior when creating the table.

---

If you run this example in older releases, you'll likely see three or so I/Os performed. We'll discuss that in a moment, but for now let's continue this example. Next, we'll add lots of data to the table. We'll make it "grow" and then roll it all back:

```
SQL> insert into t select * from all_objects;
72516 rows created.

SQL> rollback;
Rollback complete.
```

Now, if we query the table again, we'll discover that it takes considerably more I/Os to read the table this time:

```
SQL> select * from t;
no rows selected

SQL> set autotrace traceonly statistics
SQL> select * from t;
no rows selected

Statistics
----------------------------------------------------------
          0  recursive calls
          0  db block gets
       1451  consistent gets
          0  physical reads

SQL> set autotrace off
```

The blocks that our INSERT caused to be added under the table's high-water mark (HWM) are still there—formatted, but empty. Our full scan had to read them to see if they contained any rows. Moreover, the first time we ran the query, we observed *zero* I/Os. That was due to the default mode of table creation in Oracle 11g Release 2—using deferred segment creation. When we issued that CREATE TABLE, no storage, not a single extent, was allocated. The segment creation was deferred until the INSERT took place, and when we rolled back, the segment persisted. You can see this easily with a smaller example; I'll explicitly request deferred segment creation this time although it is enabled by default in 11*g* Release 2 and higher:

```
SQL> drop table t purge;
Table dropped.

SQL> create table t ( x int ) segment creation deferred;
Table created.

SQL> select extent_id, bytes, blocks
       from user_extents
     where segment_name = 'T'
     order by extent_id;
no rows selected

SQL> insert into t(x) values (1);
1 row created.

SQL> rollback;
Rollback complete.

SQL> select extent_id, bytes, blocks
       from user_extents
     where segment_name = 'T'
     order by extent_id;

 EXTENT_ID       BYTES      BLOCKS
---------- ----------- -----------
         0       65536           8
```

As you can see, after the table was initially created, there was no allocated storage—no extents were used by this table. Upon performing an INSERT, followed immediately by ROLLBACK, we can see the INSERT allocated storage—but the ROLLBACK does not "release" it.

Those two things together—that the segment was actually created by the INSERT but not "uncreated" by the ROLLBACK, and that the new formatted blocks created by the INSERT were scanned the second time around—show that a rollback is a logical "put the database back the way it was" operation. The database will not be exactly the way it was, just logically the same.

# How Redo and Undo Work Together

Now let's take a look at how redo and undo work together in various scenarios. We will discuss, for example, what happens during the processing of an INSERT with regard to redo and undo generation, and how Oracle uses this information in the event of failures at various points in time.

An interesting point to note is that undo information, stored in undo tablespaces or undo segments, is protected by redo as well. In other words, undo data is treated just like table data or index data—changes to undo generate some redo, which is logged (to the log buffer and then the redo log file). Why this is so will become clear in a moment when we discuss what happens when a system crashes. Undo data is added to the undo segment and is cached in the buffer cache, just like any other piece of data would be.

## Example INSERT-UPDATE-DELETE-COMMIT Scenario

For this example, assume we've created a table with an index as follows:

```
create table t(x int, y int);
create index ti on t(x);
```

And then we will investigate what might happen with a set of statements like this:

```
insert into t (x,y) values  (1,1);
update t set x = x+1 where x = 1;
delete from t where x = 2;
```

We will follow this transaction down different paths and discover the answers to the following questions:

- What happens if the system fails at various points in the processing of these statements?

- What happens if the buffer cache fills up?

- What happens if we ROLLBACK at any point?

- What happens if we succeed and COMMIT?

# The INSERT

The initial INSERT INTO T statement will generate both redo and undo. The undo generated will be enough information to make the INSERT "go away." The redo generated by the INSERT INTO T will be enough information to make the INSERT "happen again."

After the INSERT has occurred, we have the scenario illustrated in Figure 6-1.

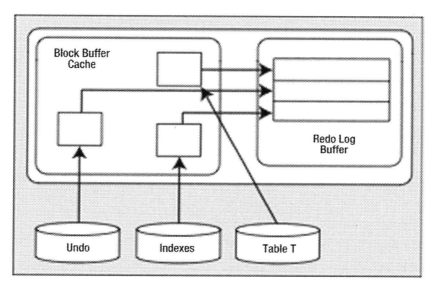

**Figure 6-1.**  *State of the system after an INSERT*

There are some cached, modified undo blocks, index blocks, and table data blocks. Each of these blocks is protected by entries in the redo log buffer.

## Hypothetical Scenario: The System Crashes Right Now

In this scenario, the system crashes before a COMMIT is issued or before the redo entries are written to disk. Everything is OK. The SGA memory area is wiped out, but we don't need anything that was in the SGA. It will be as if this transaction never happened when we restart. None of the blocks with changes got flushed to disk, and none of the redo got flushed to disk. We have no need of any of this undo or redo to recover from an instance failure.

## Hypothetical Scenario: The Buffer Cache Fills Up Right Now

The situation is such that DBWn must make room and our modified blocks are to be flushed from the cache. In this case, DBWn will start by asking LGWR to flush the redo entries that protect these database blocks. Before DBWn can write any of the blocks that are changed to disk, LGWR must flush (to disk) the redo information related to these blocks. This makes sense: if we were to flush the modified blocks for table T (but not the undo blocks associated with the modifications) without flushing the redo entries associated with the undo blocks, and the system failed, we would have a modified table T block with no undo information associated with it. We need to flush the redo log buffers before writing these blocks out so that we can redo all of the changes necessary to get the SGA back into the state it is in right now, so that a rollback can take place.

This second scenario shows some of the foresight that has gone into all of this. The set of conditions described by "If we flushed table T blocks *and* did not flush the redo for the undo blocks *and* the system failed" is starting to get complex. It only gets more complex as we add users, and more objects, and concurrent processing, and so on.

At this point, we have the situation depicted in Figure 6-1. We have generated some modified table and index blocks. These have associated undo segment blocks, and all three types of blocks have generated redo to protect them. The redo log buffer is flushed *at least* every three seconds, when it is one-third full or contains 1MB of buffered data, or whenever a COMMIT or ROLLBACK takes place. It is very possible that at some point during our processing, the redo log buffer will be flushed. In that case, the picture will look like Figure 6-2.

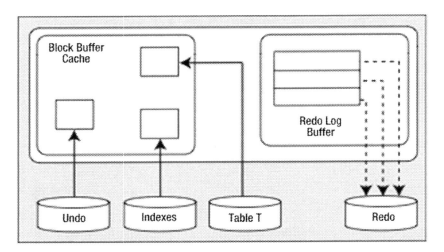

***Figure 6-2.*** *State of the system after a redo log buffer flush*

That is, we'll have modified blocks representing uncommitted changes in the buffer cache and redo for those uncommitted changes on disk. This is a very normal scenario that happens frequently.

## The UPDATE

The UPDATE will cause much of the same work as the INSERT to take place. This time, the amount of undo will be larger; we have some "before" images to save as a result of the UPDATE. Now, we have the picture shown in Figure 6-3 (the dark rectangle in the redo log file represents the redo generated by the INSERT; the redo for the UPDATE is still in the SGA and has not yet been written to disk).

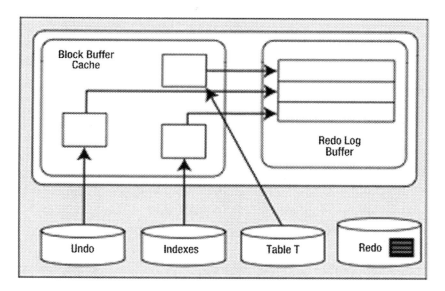

***Figure 6-3.***  *State of the system after the UPDATE*

We have more new undo segment blocks in the block buffer cache. To undo the UPDATE, if necessary, we have modified database table and index blocks in the cache. We have also generated more redo log buffer entries. Let's assume that our redo generated from the INSERT statement (discussed in the prior section) is on disk (in the redo log file) and redo generated from the UPDATE is in cache.

## Hypothetical Scenario: The System Crashes Right Now

Upon startup, Oracle would read the redo log files and find some redo log entries for our transaction. Given the state in which we left the system, we have the redo entries generated by the INSERT in the redo log files (which includes redo for undo segments associated with the INSERT). However, the redo for the UPDATE was only in the log buffer and never made it to disk (and was wiped out when the system crashed). That's okay, the transaction was never committed and the data files on disk reflect the state of the system before the UPDATE took place.

However, the redo for the INSERT was written to the redo log file. Therefore, Oracle would "roll forward" the INSERT. We would end up with a picture much like Figure 6-1, with modified undo blocks (information on how to undo the INSERT), modified table blocks (right after the INSERT), and modified index blocks (right after the INSERT). Oracle will discover that our transaction never committed and will roll it back since the system is doing crash recovery and, of course, our session is no longer connected.

To roll back the uncommitted INSERT, Oracle will use the undo it just rolled forward (from the redo and now in the buffer cache) and apply it to the data and index blocks, making them look as they did before the INSERT took place. Now, everything is back the way it was. The blocks that are on disk may or may not reflect the INSERT (it depends on whether or not our blocks got flushed before the crash). If the blocks on disk do reflect the INSERT, then the INSERT will be undone when the blocks are flushed from the buffer cache. If they do not reflect the undone INSERT, so be it—they will be overwritten later anyway.

This scenario covers the rudimentary details of a crash recovery. The system performs this as a two-step process. First, it rolls forward, bringing the system right to the point of failure, and then it proceeds to roll back everything that had not yet committed. This action will resynchronize the data files. It replays the work that was in progress and undoes anything that has not yet completed.

## Hypothetical Scenario: The Application Rolls Back the Transaction

At this point, Oracle will find the undo information for this transaction either in the cached undo segment blocks (most likely) or on disk if they have been flushed (more likely for very large transactions). It will apply the undo information to the data and index blocks in the buffer cache, or if they are no longer in the cache request, they are read from disk into the cache to have the undo applied to them. These blocks will later be flushed to the data files with their original row values restored.

This scenario is much more common than the system crash. It is useful to note that during the rollback process, the redo logs are never involved. The only time redo logs are read for recovery purposes is during recovery and archival. This is a key tuning concept: redo logs are written to. Oracle does not read them during normal processing. As long as you have sufficient devices so that when ARCn is reading a file, LGWR is writing to a different device, there is no contention for redo logs. Many other databases treat the log files as "transaction logs." They do not have this separation of redo and undo. For those systems, the act of rolling back can be disastrous—the rollback process must read the logs their log writer is trying to write to. They introduce contention into the part of the system that can least stand it. Oracle's goal is to make it so that redo logs are written sequentially, and no one ever reads them while they are being written.

## The DELETE

Again, undo is generated as a result of the DELETE, blocks are modified, and redo is sent over to the redo log buffer. This is not very different from before. In fact, it is so similar to the UPDATE that we are going to move right on to the COMMIT.

## The COMMIT

We've looked at various failure scenarios and different paths, and now we've finally made it to the COMMIT. Here, Oracle will flush the redo log buffer to disk, and the picture will look like Figure 6-4.

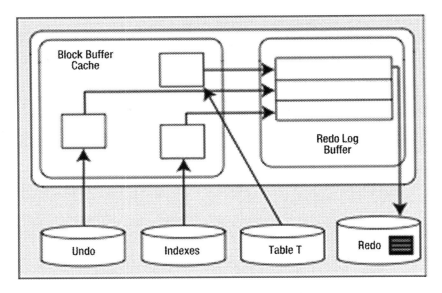

**Figure 6-4.** *State of the system after a COMMIT*

The modified blocks are in the buffer cache; maybe some of them have been flushed to disk. *All of the redo* necessary to replay this transaction is safely on disk and the changes are now permanent. If we were to read the data directly from the data files, we probably would see the blocks as they existed *before* the transaction took place, as DBWn most likely has not yet written them. That's OK—the redo log files can be used to bring those blocks up to date in the event of a failure. The undo information will hang around until the undo segment wraps around and reuses those blocks. Oracle will use that undo to provide for consistent reads of the affected objects for any session that needs them.

# Commit and Rollback Processing

It is important to understand how redo log files might impact us as developers. We will look at how the different ways we can write our code affect redo log utilization. We've already seen the mechanics of redo earlier in the chapter, and now we'll look at some specific issues. You might detect many of these scenarios, but they would be fixed by the DBA as they affect the database instance as a whole. We'll start with what happens during a COMMIT and then get into commonly asked questions and issues surrounding the online redo logs.

# What Does a COMMIT Do?

As a developer, you should have a good understanding of exactly what goes on during a COMMIT. In this section, we'll investigate what happens during the processing of the COMMIT statement in Oracle. A COMMIT is generally a very fast operation, regardless of the transaction size. You might think that the bigger a transaction (in other words, the more data it affects), the longer a COMMIT would take. This is not true. The response time of a COMMIT is generally "flat," regardless of the transaction size. This is because a COMMIT does not really have too much work to do, but what it does do is vital.

One of the reasons this is an important fact to understand and embrace is that it will lead to letting your transactions be as big as they should be. As we discussed in the previous chapter, many developers artificially constrain the size of their transactions, committing every so many rows, instead of committing when a logical unit of work has been performed. They do this in the mistaken belief that they are preserving scarce system resources, when in fact they are increasing them. If a COMMIT of one row takes X units of time, and the COMMIT of 1,000 rows takes the same X units of time, then performing work in a manner that does 1,000 one-row COMMITs will take an additional 1,000*X units of time to perform. By committing only when you have to (when the logical unit of work is complete), you will not only increase performance, you'll also reduce contention for shared resources (log files, various internal latches, and the like). A simple example demonstrates that it necessarily takes longer. We'll use a Java application, although you can expect similar results from most any client—except, in this case, PL/SQL (we'll discuss why that is after the example). To start, here is the sample table we'll be inserting into:

```
SQL> create table test
    ( id          number,
      code        varchar2(20),
      descr       varchar2(20),
      insert_user varchar2(30),
      insert_date date
    )
    /
Table created.
```

Our Java program (stored in a file named perftest.java) will accept two inputs: the number of rows to INSERT (iters) and how many rows between commits (commitCnt). It starts by connecting to the database, setting autocommit *off* (which should be done in all Java code), and then calling a doInserts() method a total of two times:

- Once just to warm up the routine (make sure all of the classes are loaded)

- A second time, with SQL Tracing on, specifying the number of rows to INSERT along with how many rows to commit at a time (i.e., commit every N rows)

It then closes the connection and exits. The main method is as follows:

```java
import java.sql.*;
import java.sql.DriverManager;
import java.sql.Connection;
import java.sql.SQLException;
import java.io.*;

public class perftest
{
  public static void main (String arr[]) throws Exception
  {
    DriverManager.registerDriver(new oracle.jdbc.OracleDriver());
    Connection con = DriverManager.getConnection
                ("jdbc:oracle:thin:@//localhost.localdomain:1521/orcl",
                 "yoda", "foo");
    Integer iters = new Integer(arr[0]);
    Integer commitCnt = new Integer(arr[1]);
    con.setAutoCommit(false);
    doInserts( con, 1, 1 );
    Statement stmt = con.createStatement ();
        stmt.execute( "begin dbms_monitor.session_trace_
        enable(waits=>true); end;" );
    doInserts( con, iters.intValue(), commitCnt.intValue() );
    con.close();
  }
```

**Note**    The SCOTT account or whatever account you use to test this with will need to have the EXECUTE privilege granted on the DBMS_MONITOR package.

Now, the method doInserts() is fairly straightforward. It starts by preparing (parsing) an INSERT statement so we can repeatedly bind/execute it over and over:

```
static void doInserts(Connection con, int count, int commitCount )
throws Exception
{
  PreparedStatement ps =
    con.prepareStatement
    ("insert into test " +
      "(id, code, descr, insert_user, insert_date)"
      + " values (?,?,?, user, sysdate)");
```

It then loops over the number of rows to insert, binding and executing the INSERT over and over. Additionally, it checks a row counter to see if it needs to COMMIT or not inside the loop:

```
int  rowcnt = 0;
int  committed = 0;
for (int i = 0; i < count; i++ )
{
  ps.setInt(1,i);
  ps.setString(2,"PS - code" + i);
  ps.setString(3,"PS - desc" + i);
  ps.executeUpdate();
  rowcnt++;
  if ( rowcnt == commitCount )
  {
    con.commit();
    rowcnt = 0;
    committed++;
  }
}
con.commit();
```

```
    System.out.println
    ("pstatement rows/commitcnt = " + count + " / " +  committed );
  }
}
```

> **Tip**  See the Oracle Database JDBC Developer's Guide for further details on how to connect to an Oracle database with Java.

Before compiling the Java code, we need to set our CLASSPATH variable (this should all go on one line, but doesn't fit within the space on the page here):

```
export CLASSPATH=$CLASSPATH:$ORACLE_HOME/jdbc/lib/ojdbc8.jar:
$ORACLE_HOME/jlib/orai18n.jar
```

Next, we compile the Java code from the OS command line:

```
javac perftest.java
```

Now, we'll run this code repeatedly with different inputs and review the resulting TKPROF file. We'll run with 100,000 row inserts—committing 1 row at a time, then 10, and so on. Here's an example of running the first test from the OS command line:

```
java perftest 100000 1
```

The prior code does the inserts and also generates a trace file. You can locate the directory the trace file is in via this query:

```
SQL> select value from v$diag_info where name='Diag Trace';

VALUE
--------------------------------------------------------------------------
/u01/app/oracle/diag/rdbms/orclcdb/orclcdb/trace
```

Look for a recently generated trace file in that directory. You can process the trace file using the TKPROF utility (this creates a human-readable output file):

```
tkprof <name of your file> output.txt sys=no
```

After running the prior command, the file output.txt has the human-readable performance output of the insert test. The resulting TKPROF files produced the results in Table 6-1.

**Table 6-1.** *Results from Inserting 100,000 Rows*

| Number of Rows to Insert | Commit Every N Rows, N= | CPU for Insert Statement (Seconds) | Wait Time for Log File Sync (Seconds) |
|---|---|---|---|
| 100,000 | 1 | 1.42 | 34.87 |
| 100,000 | 10 | 1.35 | 4.05 |
| 100,000 | 100 | 1.63 | 0.61 |
| 100,000 | 1,000 | 1.65 | 0.21 |
| 100,000 | 10,000 | 1.66 | 0.04 |
| 100,000 | 100,000 | 1.65 | 0.00 |

As you can see, the more often you commit, the longer you wait (your mileage will vary on this). And the amount of time you wait is more or less directly proportional to the number of times you commit. Remember, this is just a single-user scenario; with multiple users doing the same work, all committing too frequently, the numbers will go up rapidly.

We've heard the same story, time and time again, with similar situations. For example, we've seen how not using bind variables and performing hard parses often severely reduces concurrency due to library cache contention and excessive CPU utilization. Even when we switch to using bind variables, soft parsing too frequently—caused by closing cursors even though we are going to reuse them shortly—incurs massive overhead. We must perform operations only when we need to—a COMMIT is just another such operation. It is best to size our transactions based on business need, not based on misguided attempts to lessen resource usage on the database.

There are two factors contributing to the expense of the COMMIT in this example:

- We've obviously increased the round-trips to and from the database. If we commit every record, we are generating that much more traffic back and forth. I didn't even measure that, which would add to the overall runtime.

- Every time we commit, we must wait for our redo to be written to disk. This will result in a "wait." In this case, the wait is named "log file sync."

So, we committed after every INSERT, we waited every time for a short period of time—and if you wait a little bit of time but you wait often, it all adds up. Fully 30 seconds of our runtime was spent waiting for a COMMIT to complete when we committed 100,000 times—in other words, waiting for LGWR to write the redo to disk. In stark contrast, when we committed once, we didn't wait very long (not a measurable amount of time actually). This proves that a COMMIT is a fast operation; we expect the response time to be more or less flat, not a function of the amount of work we've done.

So, why is a COMMIT's response time fairly flat, regardless of the transaction size? It is because before we even go to COMMIT in the database, we've already done the really hard work. We've already modified the data in the database, so we've already done 99.9 percent of the work. For example, operations such as the following have already taken place:

- Undo blocks have been generated in the SGA.

- Modified data blocks have been generated in the SGA.

- Buffered redo for the preceding two items has been generated in the SGA.

- Depending on the size of the preceding three items and the amount of time spent, some combination of the previous data may be flushed onto disk already.

- All locks have been acquired.

When we COMMIT, all that is left to happen is the following:

- A System Change Number (SCN) is generated for our transaction. In case you are not familiar with it, the SCN is a simple timing mechanism Oracle uses to guarantee the ordering of transactions and to enable recovery from failure. It is also used to guarantee read consistency and checkpointing in the database. Think of the SCN as a ticker; every time someone COMMITs, the SCN is incremented by one.

- LGWR writes all of our *remaining* buffered redo log entries to disk and records the SCN in the online redo log files as well. This step is actually the COMMIT. If this step occurs, we have committed. Our transaction entry is "removed" from V$TRANSACTION—this shows that we have committed.

- All locks recorded in V$LOCK held by our session are released, and everyone who was enqueued waiting on locks we held will be woken up and allowed to proceed with their work.

- Some of the blocks our transaction modified will be visited and "cleaned out" in a fast mode if they are still in the buffer cache. *Block cleanout* refers to the lock-related information we store in the database block header. Basically, we are cleaning out our transaction information on the block, so the next person who visits the block won't have to. We are doing this in a way that need not generate redo log information, saving considerable work later (this is discussed fully in the next chapter).

As you can see, there is very little to do to process a COMMIT. The lengthiest operation is, and always will be, the activity performed by LGWR, as this is physical disk I/O. The amount of time spent by LGWR here will be greatly reduced by the fact that it has already been flushing the contents of the redo log buffer on a recurring basis. LGWR will not buffer all of the work you do for as long as you do it. Rather, it will incrementally flush the contents of the redo log buffer in the background as you are going along. This is to avoid having a COMMIT wait for a very long time in order to flush all of your redo at once.

So, even if we have a long-running transaction, much of the buffered redo log it generates would have been flushed to disk, prior to committing. On the flip side is the fact that when we COMMIT, we must typically wait until *all* buffered redo that has not been written yet is safely on disk. That is, our call to LGWR is by default a *synchronous* one. While LGWR may use asynchronous I/O to write in parallel to our log files, our transaction will normally wait for LGWR to complete all writes and receive confirmation that the data exists on disk before returning.

---

**Note**    Oracle 11*g* Release 1 and above have an asynchronous wait. However, that style of commit has limited general-purpose use. Commits in any end-user-facing application should be synchronous.

---

Now, earlier I mentioned that we were using a Java program and not PL/SQL for a reason—and that reason is a PL/SQL commit-time optimization. I said that our call to LGWR is by default a synchronous one and that we wait for it to complete its write. That is true in every version of the Oracle database for every programmatic language *except PL/SQL*. The PL/SQL engine, realizing that the client does not know whether or not a COMMIT has happened in the PL/SQL routine until the PL/SQL routine is completed, does an asynchronous commit. It does not wait for LGWR to complete; rather, it returns from the COMMIT call immediately. However, when the PL/SQL routine is completed, when we return from the database to the client, the PL/SQL routine will wait for LGWR to complete any of the outstanding COMMITs. So, if you commit 100 times in PL/SQL and then return to the client, you will likely find you waited for LGWR once—not 100 times—due to this optimization. Does this imply that committing frequently in PL/SQL is a good or OK idea? No, not at all—just that it is not *as bad an idea* as it is in other languages. The guiding rule is to commit when your logical unit of work is complete—not before.

---

**Note**    This commit-time optimization in PL/SQL may be suspended when you are performing distributed transactions or Data Guard in maximum availability mode. Since there are two participants, PL/SQL must wait for the commit to actually be complete before continuing. Also, it can be suspended by directly invoking COMMIT WORK WRITE WAIT in PL/SQL with database version Oracle 11*g* Release 1 and above.

---

To demonstrate that a COMMIT is a "flat response time" operation, we'll generate varying amounts of redo and time the INSERTs and COMMITs. As we do these INSERTs and COMMITs, we'll measure the amount of redo our session generates using this small utility function:

```
SQL> create or replace function get_stat_val( p_name in varchar2 ) return
number
    as
        l_val number;
    begin
        select b.value
          into l_val
          from v$statname a, v$mystat b
```

```
            where a.statistic# = b.statistic#
                and a.name = p_name;

            return l_val;
        end;
    /
Function created.
```

---

**Note** The owner of the previous function will need to have been directly granted the SELECT privilege on the V$ views V_$STATNAME and V_$MYSTAT.

---

Drop the table T (if it exists) and create an empty table T of the same structure as BIG_TABLE:

```
SQL> drop table t purge;

SQL> create table t
        as
        select *
          from big_table
          where 1=0;
Table created.
```

---

**Note** Directions on how to create and populate the BIG_TABLE table used in many examples are in the "Setting Up Your Environment" section at the very front of this book.

---

And we'll measure the CPU and elapsed time used to commit our transaction using the DBMS_UTILITY package routines GET_CPU_TIME and GET_TIME. The actual PL/SQL block used to generate the workload and report on it is as follows:

```
SQL> set serverout on
SQL> declare
            l_redo number;
            l_cpu  number;
            l_ela  number;
```

```
begin
    dbms_output.put_line
    ( '-' || '        Rows' || '            Redo' ||
      '      CPU' || ' Elapsed' );
    for i in 1 .. 6
    loop
        l_redo := get_stat_val( 'redo size' );
        insert into t select * from big_table  where rownum <= power(10,i);
        l_cpu  := dbms_utility.get_cpu_time;
        l_ela  := dbms_utility.get_time;
        commit work write wait;
        dbms_output.put_line
        ( '-' ||
          to_char( power( 10, i ), '9,999,999') ||
          to_char( (get_stat_val('redo size')-l_redo), '999,999,999' ) ||
          to_char( (dbms_utility.get_cpu_time-l_cpu), '999,999' ) ||
          to_char( (dbms_utility.get_time-l_ela), '999,999' ) );
    end loop;
end;
/
```

| - | Rows | Redo | CPU | Elapsed |
|---|---|---|---|---|
| - | 10 | 6,552 | 2 | 17 |
| - | 100 | 10,336 | 0 | 5 |
| - | 1,000 | 114,684 | 0 | 8 |
| - | 10,000 | 1,156,452 | 0 | 25 |
| - | 100,000 | 13,184,820 | 1 | 28 |
| - | 1,000,000 | 67,356,624 | 2 | 58 |

PL/SQL procedure successfully completed.

---

**Note**  Times are in hundredths of seconds. Your results may vary depending on variables such as number of records in BIG_TABLE, size of your log buffer, size and number of redo logs, number of log writer processes, and I/O subsystem.

---

As you can see, as we generate varying amount of redo from about 6,500 bytes to 67MB, the difference in time to COMMIT is not measurable using a timer with a one hundredth of a second resolution. As we were processing and generating the redo log, LGWR was constantly flushing our buffered redo information to disk in the background. So, when we generated 67MB of redo log information, LGWR was busy flushing every 1MB, or so. When it came to the COMMIT, there wasn't much left to do—not much more than when we created ten rows of data. You should expect to see similar (but not exactly the same) results, regardless of the amount of redo generated.

## What Does a ROLLBACK Do?

By changing the COMMIT to ROLLBACK, we can expect a totally different result. The time to roll back is definitely a function of the amount of data modified. I changed the script developed in the previous section to perform a ROLLBACK instead (simply change the COMMIT to ROLLBACK) and the timings are very different. Look at the results now:

```
SQL> declare
        l_redo  number;
        l_cpu   number;
        l_ela   number;
    begin
      dbms_output.put_line
      ( '-' || '        Rows' || '           Redo' ||
        '      CPU' || ' Elapsed' );
      for i in 1 .. 6
      loop
          l_redo := get_stat_val( 'redo size' );
          insert into t select * from big_table where rownum <= power(10,i);
          l_cpu   := dbms_utility.get_cpu_time;
          l_ela   := dbms_utility.get_time;
           --commit work write wait;
           rollback;
          dbms_output.put_line
          ( '-' ||
            to_char( power( 10, i ), '9,999,999') ||
            to_char( (get_stat_val('redo size')-l_redo), '999,999,999' ) ||
```

```
                to_char( (dbms_utility.get_cpu_time-l_cpu), '999,999' ) ||
                to_char( (dbms_utility.get_time-l_ela), '999,999' ) );
        end loop;
    end;
    /
```

```
-        Rows          Redo     CPU Elapsed
-          10         6,672       0       1
-         100        10,884       1       1
-       1,000       122,840       1       0
-      10,000     1,239,080       1       2
-     100,000    14,098,264       7      92
-   1,000,000    71,917,008      36     121
```

```
PL/SQL procedure successfully completed.
```

This difference in CPU and elapsed timings is to be expected, as a ROLLBACK has to undo the work we've done. Similar to a COMMIT, a series of operations must be performed. Before we even get to the ROLLBACK, the database has already done a lot of work. To recap, the following would have happened:

- Undo segment records have been generated in the SGA.

- Modified data blocks have been generated in the SGA.

- A buffered redo log for the preceding two items has been generated in the SGA.

- Depending on the size of the preceding three items and the amount of time spent, some combination of the previous data may be flushed onto disk already.

- All locks have been acquired.

When we ROLLBACK,

- We undo all of the changes made. This is accomplished by reading the data back from the undo segment and, in effect, reversing our operation and then marking the undo entry as applied. If we inserted a row, a ROLLBACK will delete it. If we updated a row, a rollback will reverse the update. If we deleted a row, a rollback will reinsert it again.

- All locks held by our session are released, and everyone who was enqueued waiting on locks we held will be released.

A COMMIT, on the other hand, just flushes any remaining data in the redo log buffers. It does very little work compared to a ROLLBACK. The point here is that you don't want to roll back unless you have to. It is expensive since you spend a lot of time doing the work, and you'll also spend a lot of time undoing the work. Don't do work unless you're sure you are going to want to COMMIT it. This sounds like common sense—of course I wouldn't do all of the work unless I wanted to COMMIT it. However, I've often seen a developer use a "real" table as a temporary table, fill it up with data, report on it, and then roll back to get rid of the temporary data. Later, we'll talk about true temporary tables and how to avoid this issue.

# Summary

In this chapter, we explored redo and undo and took a look at what they mean to the developer. The key point to take away from this chapter is the importance of redo and undo, and the fact that they are not overhead—they are integral components of the database and are necessary and mandatory. Once you have a good understanding of how they work and what they do, you'll be able to make better use of them. Understanding that you are not "saving" anything by committing more frequently than you should (you are actually wasting resources, as it takes more CPU, more disk, and more programming) is probably the most important point of all. Be aware of what the database needs to do, and then let the database do it.

# CHAPTER 7

# Investigating Redo

As part of processing transactions, Oracle captures how the data is modified (redo) and writes that information to the log buffer memory area. Next, the log writer background process will frequently write the redo information to disk (online redo logs). If you have archiving enabled in your database, as soon as an online redo log is filled up, the archiver process will copy the online redo log to an archived redo log. The architecture of processing transactions and the subsequent redo stream is displayed in Figure 7-1.

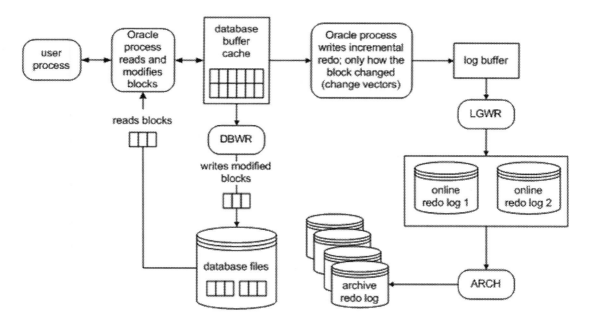

***Figure 7-1.*** *Oracle transacting data and writing redo*

© Darl Kuhn and Thomas Kyte 2021
D. Kuhn and T. Kyte, *Oracle Database Transactions and Locking Revealed*,
https://doi.org/10.1007/978-1-4842-6425-6_7

Redo management can be a point of serialization (bottleneck) within the database. This is because eventually all transactions end up at LGWR (or one of its worker processes) asking it to manage their redo and COMMIT their transaction. The amount of redo generated also influences how much work the archiver process has to process. If you have a standby database, this redo has to also be transferred and applied to the standby. The more log writer and the archiver have to do, the slower the system will be.

Therefore, as a developer, it's important to be able to measure how much redo your operations generate. The more redo you generate, the longer your operations may take, and the slower the entire system might be. You are not just affecting *your* session, but *every* session. By seeing how much redo an operation tends to generate, and testing more than one approach to a problem, you can find the best way to do things.

---

**Note**   Oracle will always start at least one LGWR background process. On multiprocessor systems, Oracle will spawn additional log writer worker processes (LG00) to help improve performance of writing redo to disk.

---

# Measuring Redo

In this first example, we'll use AUTOTRACE to observe the amount of redo generated. In subsequent examples, we'll use the GET_STAT_VAL, function introduced in Chapter 6.

---

**Note**   You will not see the exact same results when you run these examples in your environment. Your results may vary depending on variables such as number of records in BIG_TABLE, memory configuration, CPUs, and other processes running on your system.

---

Let's take a look at the difference in redo generated by conventional-path INSERTs (the normal INSERTs you and I do every day) and direct-path INSERTs—used when loading large amounts of data into the database. We'll use AUTOTRACE and the previously created tables T and BIG_TABLE for this simple example. First, we'll load the table using a conventional-path INSERT:

```
SQL> set autotrace traceonly statistics;
SQL> truncate table t;
Table truncated.

SQL> insert into t select * from big_table;
1000000 rows created.

Statistics
----------------------------------------------------------------
         90  recursive calls
     123808  db block gets
      39407  consistent gets
      13847  physical reads
  113875056  redo size
       1177  bytes sent via SQL*Net to client
       1354  bytes received via SQL*Net from client
          4  SQL*Net roundtrips to/from client
          2  sorts (memory)
          0  sorts (disk)
    1000000  rows processed
```

As you can see, that INSERT generated about 113MB of redo.

---

**Note**    The example in this section was performed on a NOARCHIVELOG-mode database. If you are in ARCHIVELOG mode, the table would have to be created or set as NOLOGGING to observe this dramatic change. We will investigate the NOLOGGING attribute in more detail shortly in the section "Setting NOLOGGING in SQL." Please make sure to coordinate all nonlogged operations with your DBA on a "real" system.

---

When we use a direct-path load in a NOARCHIVELOG-mode database, we get the following results:

```
SQL> truncate table t;
Table truncated.

SQL> insert /*+ APPEND */ into t  select * from big_table;
1000000 rows created.
```

Statistics
------------------------------------------------------------
         551   recursive calls
       16645   db block gets
       15242   consistent gets
       13873   physical reads
  **220504**   **redo size**
        1160   bytes sent via SQL*Net to client
        1368   bytes received via SQL*Net from client
           4   SQL*Net roundtrips to/from client
          86   sorts (memory)
           0   sorts (disk)
     1000000   rows processed

SQL> set autotrace off

That INSERT generated only about 220KB—*kilobytes, not megabytes*—of redo. As you can see, the amount of redo generated by a direct-path insert is much less than a conventional insert.

# Can I Turn Off Redo Log Generation?

This question is often asked. The simple short answer is no, since redo logging is crucial for the database; it is not overhead and it is not a waste. You do need it, regardless of whether you believe you do or not. It is a fact of life, and it is the way the database works. If you turned off redo, then any temporary failure of disk drives, power, or a software crash would render the entire database unusable and unrecoverable. That said, however, there are some operations that can be done without generating redo log in some cases.

---

**Note**    Oracle allows you to place your database into FORCE  LOGGING mode. In that case, *all* operations are logged regardless if you specify NOLOGGING. The query SELECT FORCE_LOGGING FROM V$DATABASE will display if logging is forced or not. This feature is in support of Data Guard, a disaster-recovery feature of Oracle that relies on redo to maintain a standby database copy.

---

# Setting NOLOGGING in SQL

Some SQL statements and operations support the use of a NOLOGGING clause. This does not mean that all operations against the object will be performed without generating redo, just that some very *specific* operations will generate *significantly less* redo than normal. Note that I said "significantly less redo," not "no redo." All operations will generate some redo—all data dictionary operations will be logged regardless of the logging mode. The amount of redo generated can be significantly less, however. For this example of the NOLOGGING clause, I ran the following in a database running in ARCHIVELOG mode with no force logging enabled:

```
SQL> select log_mode, force_logging from v$database;

LOG_MODE       FORCE_LOGGING
------------   -----------------
ARCHIVELOG     NO

SQL> drop table t purge;
Table dropped.

SQL> variable redo number
SQL> exec :redo := get_stat_val( 'redo size' );
PL/SQL procedure successfully completed.

SQL> create table t  as  select * from all_objects;
Table created.

SQL> exec dbms_output.put_line( (get_stat_val('redo size')-:redo) ↵
|| ' bytes of redo generated...' );
4487796 bytes of redo generated...
PL/SQL procedure successfully completed.
```

That CREATE TABLE generated about 4MB of redo information (your results will vary depending on how many rows are inserted into table T). We'll drop and re-create the table, in NOLOGGING mode this time:

```
SQL> drop table t;
Table dropped.
```

```
SQL> variable redo number
SQL> exec :redo := get_stat_val( 'redo size' );
PL/SQL procedure successfully completed.

SQL> create table t
       NOLOGGING
     as  select * from all_objects;
Table created.

SQL> exec dbms_output.put_line( (get_stat_val('redo size')-:redo) ↵
|| ' bytes of redo generated...' );
90108 bytes of redo generated...
PL/SQL procedure successfully completed.
```

This time, we generated only 90KB of redo. As you can see, this makes a tremendous difference—4MB of redo vs. 90KB. The 4MB written in the first example is a copy of the actual table data itself; it was written to the redo log when the table was created without the NOLOGGING clause.

If you test this on a NOARCHIVELOG-mode database, you will not see any differences between the two. The CREATE TABLE will not be logged, with the exception of the data dictionary modifications, in a NOARCHIVELOG-mode database. Additionally, if you run this test in a database that has force logging enabled, you will always get redo logged, regardless of the NOLOGGING clause.

These facts point out a valuable tip: test your system in the mode it will be run in production, *as the behavior may be different*. Your production system will be running in ARCHIVELOG mode; if you perform lots of operations that generate redo in this mode, but not in NOARCHIVELOG mode, you'll want to discover this during testing, not during rollout to the users!

Of course, it is now obvious that you will do everything you can with NOLOGGING, right? In fact, the answer is a resounding *no*. You must use this mode very carefully, and only after discussing the issues with the person in charge of backup and recovery. Let's say you create this table and it is now part of your application (e.g., you used a CREATE TABLE AS SELECT NOLOGGING as part of an upgrade script). Your users modify this table over the course of the day. That night, the disk that the table is on fails. "No problem," the DBA says. "We are running in ARCHIVELOG mode and we can perform media recovery." The problem is, however, that the initially created table, since it was not logged, is not recoverable from the archived redo log. This table is unrecoverable and this brings out the most important point about NOLOGGING operations: they must be coordinated with your DBA and the system as a whole. If you use them and others are not aware of that fact, you may compromise the ability of your DBA to recover your database fully after a media failure. NOLOGGING operations must be used judiciously and carefully.

The important things to note about NOLOGGING operations are as follows:

- *Some amount of redo will be generated,* as a matter of fact. This redo is to protect the data dictionary. There is no avoiding this at all. It could be of a significantly lesser amount than before, but there will be some.

- *NOLOGGING does not prevent redo from being generated by all subsequent operations.* In the preceding example, I did not create a table that is never logged. Only the single, individual operation of creating the table was not logged. All subsequent "normal" operations such as INSERTs, UPDATEs, DELETEs, and MERGEs will be logged. Other special operations, such as a direct-path load using SQL*Loader, or a direct-path INSERT using the INSERT /*+ APPEND */ syntax, will not be logged (unless and until you ALTER the table and enable full logging again). In general, however, the operations your application performs against this table *will be logged.*

- After performing NOLOGGING operations in an ARCHIVELOG-mode database, *you must take a new baseline backup of the affected data files as soon as possible,* in order to avoid losing the data created by the NOLOGGING operation due to media failure. Since the data created by the NOLOGGING operation is not in the redo log files, and is not yet in the backups, you have no way of recovering it!

## Setting NOLOGGING on an Index

There are two ways to use the NOLOGGING option. You have already seen one method—embedding the NOLOGGING keyword in the SQL command. The other method, which involves setting the NOLOGGING attribute on the segment (index or table), allows *certain* operations to be performed implicitly in a NOLOGGING mode. For example, I can alter an index or table to be NOLOGGING by default. This means for the index that subsequent rebuilds of this index will not be logged (the index will not generate redo; other indexes and the table itself might, but this index will not). Using the table T we just created, we can observe:

```
SQL> select log_mode, force_logging from v$database;

LOG_MODE      FORCE_LOGGING
------------  -----------------
ARCHIVELOG    NO

SQL> create index t_idx on t(object_name);
Index created.

SQL> variable redo number
SQL> exec :redo := get_stat_val( 'redo size' );
PL/SQL procedure successfully completed.

SQL> alter index t_idx rebuild;
Index altered.

SQL> exec dbms_output.put_line( (get_stat_val('redo size')-:redo)
               || ' bytes of redo generated...');
672264 bytes of redo generated...
PL/SQL procedure successfully completed.
```

> **Note**    Again, this example was performed in an ARCHIVELOG-mode database. You would not see the differences in redo size in a NOARCHIVELOG-mode database as the index CREATE and REBUILD operations are not logged in NOARCHIVELOG mode.

When the index is in LOGGING mode (the default), a rebuild of it generated about 600KB of redo. However, we can alter the index:

```
SQL> alter index t_idx nologging;
Index altered.

SQL> exec :redo := get_stat_val( 'redo size' );
PL/SQL procedure successfully completed.

SQL> alter index t_idx rebuild;
Index altered.
```

```
SQL> exec dbms_output.put_line( (get_stat_val('redo size')-:redo)
                    || ' bytes of redo generated...');
```
**39352 bytes of redo generated...**

```
PL/SQL procedure successfully completed.
```

And now it generates a mere 39KB of redo. But that index is "unprotected" now. If the data files it was located in failed and had to be restored from a backup, we would lose that index data. Understanding that fact is crucial. The index is not recoverable right now—we need a backup to take place. Alternatively, the DBA could just re-create the index as we can re-create the index directly from the table data as well.

# NOLOGGING Wrap-up

The operations that may be performed in a NOLOGGING mode are as follows:

- Index creations and ALTERs (rebuilds).

- Bulk INSERTs into a table using a direct-path INSERT such as that available via the /*+ APPEND */ hint or SQL*Loader direct-path loads. The table data will not generate redo, but all index modifications will (the indexes on this nonlogged table will generate redo).

- LOB operations (updates to large objects do not have to be logged).

- Table creations via CREATE TABLE AS SELECT.

- Various ALTER TABLE operations such as MOVE and SPLIT.

Used appropriately on an ARCHIVELOG-mode database, NOLOGGING can speed up many operations by dramatically reducing the amount of redo log generated. Suppose you have a table you need to move from one tablespace to another. You can schedule this operation to take place immediately before a backup occurs—you would ALTER the table to be NOLOGGING, move it, rebuild the indexes (without logging as well), and then ALTER the table back to logging mode. Now, an operation that might have taken X hours can happen in X/2 hours perhaps (I'm not promising a 50-percent reduction in runtime!). The appropriate use of this feature includes involving the DBA, or whoever is responsible for database backup and recovery or any standby databases. If that person is not aware that you're using this feature and a media failure occurs, you may lose data, or the integrity of the standby database might be compromised. This is something to seriously consider.

# Why Can't I Allocate a New Log?

I get this question all of the time. You are getting warning messages to this effect (this will be found in `alert.log` on your server):

```
Thread 1 cannot allocate new log, sequence 1466
Checkpoint not complete
  Current log# 3 seq# 1465 mem# 0: /.../...redo03.log
```

It might say `Archival required` instead of `Checkpoint not complete`, but the effect is pretty much the same. This is really something the DBA should be looking out for. This message will be written to `alert.log` on the server whenever the database attempts to reuse an online redo log file and finds that it can't. This happens when DBWn has not yet finished checkpointing the data protected by the redo log or ARCn has not finished copying the redo log file to the archive destination. At this point, the database effectively *halts* as far as the end user is concerned. It stops cold. DBWn or ARCn will be given priority to flush the blocks to disk. Upon completion of the checkpoint or archival, everything goes back to normal. The reason the database suspends user activity is that there is simply no place to record the changes the users are making. Oracle is attempting to reuse an online redo log file, but because either the file would be needed to recover the database in the event of a failure (`Checkpoint not complete`), or the archiver has not yet finished copying it (`Archival required`), Oracle must wait (and the end users will wait) until the redo log file can safely be reused.

If you see that your sessions spend a lot of time waiting on a "log file switch," "log buffer space," or "log file switch checkpoint or archival incomplete," you are most likely hitting this. You will notice it during prolonged periods of database modifications if your log files are sized incorrectly, or because DBWn and ARCn need to be tuned by the DBA or system administrator. I frequently see this issue with the "starter" database that has not been customized. The "starter" database typically sizes the redo logs far too small for any significant amount of work (including the initial database build of the data dictionary itself). As soon as you start loading up the database, you will notice that the first 1,000 rows go fast, and then things start going in spurts: 1,000 go fast, then hang, then go fast, then hang, and so on. These are the indications you are hitting this condition.

There are a couple of things you can do to solve this issue:

- *Make DBWn faster*: Have your DBA tune DBWn by enabling ASYNC I/O, using DBWn I/O slaves, or using multiple DBWn processes. Look at the I/O on the system and see if one disk or a set of disks is "hot" and you need to therefore spread the data out. The same general advice applies for ARCn as well. The pros of this are that you get "something for nothing" here—increased performance without really changing any logic/structures/code. There really are no downsides to this approach.

- *Add more redo log files*: This will postpone the Checkpoint not complete in some cases, and after a while, it will postpone the Checkpoint not complete so long that it perhaps doesn't happen (because you gave DBWn enough breathing room to checkpoint). The same applies to the Archival required message. The benefit of this approach is the removal of the "pauses" in your system. The downside is it consumes more disk, but the benefit far outweighs any downside here.

- *Re-create the log files with a larger size*: This will extend the amount of time between the time you fill the online redo log and the time you need to reuse it. The same applies to the Archival required message, if the redo log file usage is "bursty." If you have a period of massive log generation (nightly loads, batch processes) followed by periods of relative calm, then having larger online redo logs can buy enough time for ARCn to catch up during the calm periods. The pros and cons are identical to the preceding approach of adding more files. Additionally, it may postpone a checkpoint from happening until later, since checkpoints happen at each log switch (at least), and the log switches will now be further apart.

- *Make checkpointing happen more frequently and more continuously*: Use a smaller block buffer cache (not entirely desirable) or various parameter settings such as FAST_START_MTTR_TARGET, LOG_CHECKPOINT_INTERVAL, and LOG_CHECKPOINT_TIMEOUT. This will force DBWn to flush dirty blocks more frequently. The benefit to this approach is that recovery time from a failure is reduced.

There will always be less work in the online redo logs to be applied. The downside is that blocks may be written to disk more frequently if they are modified often. The buffer cache will not be as effective as it could be, and it can defeat the block cleanout mechanism discussed in the next section.

The approach you take will depend on your circumstances. This is something that must be fixed at the database level, taking the entire instance into consideration.

# Block Cleanout

In this section, we'll discuss *block cleanouts*, or the removal of "locking"-related information on the database blocks we've modified. This concept is important to understand when we talk about the infamous `ORA-01555: snapshot too old` error in a subsequent section.

If you recall from Chapters 2 and 3, we talked about data locks and how they are managed. I described how they are actually attributes of the data, stored on the block header. A side effect of this is that the next time that block is accessed, we may have to clean it out—in other words, remove the transaction information. This action generates redo and causes the block to become *dirty* if it wasn't already, meaning that a simple `SELECT` *may generate redo* and may cause lots of blocks to be written to disk with the next checkpoint. Under most normal circumstances, however, this will not happen. If you have mostly small- to medium-sized transactions (OLTP), or you have a data warehouse that performs direct-path loads or uses `DBMS_STATS` to analyze tables after load operations, you'll find the blocks are generally cleaned for you. If you recall from Chapter 6, section "What Does a COMMIT Do?", one of the steps of `COMMIT`-time processing is to revisit some blocks if they are still in the SGA and if they are accessible (no one else is modifying them), and then clean them out. This activity is known as a *commit cleanout* and is the activity that cleans out the transaction information on our modified block. Optimally, our `COMMIT` can clean out the blocks so that a subsequent `SELECT` (read) will not have to clean it out. Only an `UPDATE` of this block would truly clean out our residual transaction information, and since the `UPDATE` is already generating redo, the cleanout is not noticeable.

We can force a cleanout to *not* happen, and therefore observe its side effects, by understanding how the commit cleanout works. In a commit list associated with our transaction, Oracle will record lists of blocks we have modified. Each of these lists is 20 blocks long, and Oracle will allocate as many of these lists as it needs—up to a point. If the sum of the blocks we modify exceeds 10 percent of the block buffer cache size, Oracle will stop allocating new lists. For example, if our buffer cache is set to cache 3,000 blocks, Oracle will maintain a list of up to 300 blocks (10 percent of 3,000). Upon COMMIT, Oracle will process each of these lists of 20 block pointers, and if the block is still available, it will perform a fast cleanout. So, as long as the number of blocks we modify does not exceed 10 percent of the number of blocks in the cache *and* our blocks are still in the cache and available to us, Oracle will clean them out upon COMMIT. Otherwise, it just skips them (i.e., does not clean them out).

With this understanding, we can set up artificial conditions to see how the cleanout works. I set my DB_CACHE_SIZE to a low value of 16MB, which is sufficient to hold 2,048 8KB blocks (my block size is 8KB). Next, I create a table such that a row fits on exactly one block—I'll never have two rows per block. Then, I fill this table up with 10,000 rows and COMMIT. We know that 10,000 blocks far exceeds 10% of 2048, so the database will not be able to clean out all of these dirty blocks upon commit—most of them will not even be in the buffer cache anymore. I'll measure the amount of redo I've generated so far, run a SELECT that will visit each block, and then measure the amount of redo that SELECT generated.

---

**Note**   In order for this example to be reproducible and predictable, you'll need to disable SGA automatic memory management. If that is enabled, there is a chance that the database will increase the size of your buffer cache—defeating the "math" I've worked out.

---

Surprisingly to many people, the SELECT will have generated redo. Not only that, but it will also have "dirtied" these modified blocks, causing DBWn to write them again. This is due to the block cleanout. Next, I'll run the SELECT to visit every block once again and see that no redo is generated. This is expected, as the blocks are all "clean" at this point. We'll start by creating our table:

```
SQL> create table t
    ( id number primary key,
      x char(2000),
      y char(2000),
      z char(2000)
    )
    /

Table created.

SQL> exec dbms_stats.set_table_stats( user, 'T', numrows=>10000,
numblks=>10000 );

PL/SQL procedure successfully completed.
```

I used DBMS_STATS to set table statistics so as to avoid any side effects from hard parsing later (Oracle tends to scan objects that have no statistics during a hard parse and this side effect would interfere with my example!). So, this is my table with one row per block (in my 8KB block size database). Next, we'll inspect the block of code we'll be executing against this table:

```
SQL> declare
        l_rec t%rowtype;
    begin
        for i in 1 .. 10000
        loop
            select * into l_rec from t where id=i;
        end loop;
    end;
    /
declare
*
ERROR at line 1:
ORA-01403: no data found
ORA-06512: at line 6
```

That block failed, but that's OK—we knew it would since there is no data in the table yet. I ran that block simply to get the hard parse of the SQL and PL/SQL performed, so when we run it later, we won't have to worry about side effects from hard parsing being counted. Now, we are ready to load the data into our table and commit:

```
SQL> insert into t
    select rownum, 'x', 'y', 'z'
      from all_objects
    where rownum <= 10000;
10000 rows created.

SQL> commit;
Commit complete.
```

And, finally, I'm ready to measure the amount of redo generated during the first read of the data:

```
SQL> variable redo number
SQL> exec :redo := get_stat_val( 'redo size' );
PL/SQL procedure successfully completed.

SQL> declare
        l_rec t%rowtype;
    begin
        for i in 1 .. 10000
        loop
            select * into l_rec from t where id=i;
        end loop;
    end;
    /
PL/SQL procedure successfully completed.

SQL> exec dbms_output.put_line( (get_stat_val('redo size')-:redo)
                        || ' bytes of redo generated...');
802632 bytes of redo generated...
PL/SQL procedure successfully completed.
```

So, this SELECT generated about 802KB of redo during its processing. This represents the block headers it modified during the index read of the primary key index and the subsequent table read of T. DBWn will be writing these modified blocks back out to disk at some point in the future (actually, since the table doesn't fit into the cache, we know that DBWn has already written out at least some of them). Now, if I run the query again

```
SQL> exec :redo := get_stat_val( 'redo size' );
PL/SQL procedure successfully completed.

SQL> declare
        l_rec t%rowtype;
    begin
        for i in 1 .. 10000
        loop
            select * into l_rec from t where id=i;
        end loop;
    end;
    /
PL/SQL procedure successfully completed.

SQL> exec dbms_output.put_line( (get_stat_val('redo size')-:redo)
                || ' bytes of redo generated...');
```
**0 bytes of redo generated...**
```
PL/SQL procedure successfully completed.
```

I see that no redo is generated—the blocks are all clean.

If we were to rerun the preceding example with the buffer cache set to hold a little more than 100,000 blocks, we'd find that we generate little to no redo on any of the SELECTs—we will not have to clean dirty blocks during either of our SELECT statements. This is because the 10,000-plus (remember the index was modified as well) blocks we modified fit comfortably into 10 percent of our buffer cache, and we are the only users. There is no one else mucking around with the data, and no one else is causing our data to be flushed to disk or accessing those blocks. In a live system, it would be normal for at least some of the blocks to not be cleaned out sometimes.

This behavior will most affect you after a large INSERT (as just demonstrated), UPDATE, or DELETE—one that affects many blocks in the database (anything more than 10 percent of the size of the cache will definitely do it). You'll notice that the first query to touch the block after this will generate a little redo and dirty the block, possibly causing it to be rewritten if DBWn had already flushed it or the instance had been shut down, clearing out the buffer cache altogether. There is not too much you can do about it. It is normal and to be expected. If Oracle didn't do this deferred cleanout of a block, a COMMIT could take as long to process as the transaction itself. The COMMIT would have to revisit each and every block, possibly reading them in from disk again (they could have been flushed).

If you are not aware of block cleanouts and how they work, they will be one of those mysterious things that just seem to happen for no reason. For example, say you UPDATE a lot of data and COMMIT. Now you run a query against that data to verify the results. The query appears to generate tons of write I/O and redo. It seems impossible if you are unaware of block cleanouts; it was to me the first time I saw it. You go and get someone to observe this behavior with you, but it is not reproducible as the blocks are now "clean" on the second query. You simply write it off as one of those database mysteries—a mystery that only happens when you are alone.

In an OLTP system, you'll probably never see a block cleanout happening, since those systems are characterized by small, short transactions that affect only a few blocks. By design, all or most of the transactions are short and sweet. Modify a couple of blocks and they all get cleaned out. In a warehouse where you make massive UPDATEs to the data after a load, block cleanouts may be a factor in your design. Some operations will create data on "clean" blocks. For example, CREATE TABLE AS SELECT, direct-path loaded data, and direct-path inserted (using the /* +APPEND */ hint) data will all create clean blocks. An UPDATE, normal INSERT, or DELETE may create blocks that need to be cleaned with the first read. This could really affect you if your processing consists of

- Bulk loading lots of new data into the data warehouse

- Running UPDATEs on all of the data you just loaded (producing blocks that need to be cleaned out)

- Letting people query the data

You have to realize that the first query to touch the data will incur some additional processing if the block needs to be cleaned. Realizing this, you yourself should "touch" the data after the UPDATE. You just loaded or modified a ton of data—you need to analyze it at the very least. Perhaps you need to run some reports to validate the load. This will clean the block out and make it so the next query doesn't have to. Better yet, since you just bulk-loaded the data, you now need to refresh the statistics anyway. Running the DBMS_STATS utility to gather statistics may well clean out all of the blocks as it just uses SQL to query the information and would naturally clean the blocks out as it goes along.

# Log Contention

This, like the cannot allocate new log message, is something the DBA must fix, typically in conjunction with the system administrator. However, it is something a developer might detect as well if the DBA isn't watching closely enough.

If you are faced with log contention, what you might observe is a large wait time on the "log file sync" event and long write times evidenced in the "log file parallel write" event in a Statspack report. If you see this, you may be experiencing contention on the redo logs; they are not being written fast enough. This can happen for many reasons. One application reason (one the DBA can't fix, but the developer must) is that you are committing too frequently—committing inside of a loop doing INSERTs, for example. As demonstrated in the Chapter 6 section, "What Does a COMMIT Do?", committing too frequently, aside from being a bad programming practice, is a surefire way to introduce lots of log file sync waits. Assuming all of your transactions are correctly sized (you are not committing more frequently than your business rules dictate), the most common causes for log file waits that I've seen are as follows:

- *Putting redo on a slow device*: The disks are just performing poorly. It is time to buy faster disks.

- *Putting redo on the same device as other files that are accessed frequently*: Redo is designed to be written with sequential writes and to be on dedicated devices. If other components of your system— even other Oracle components—are attempting to read and write to this device at the same time as LGWR, you will experience some degree of contention. Here, you want to ensure LGWR has exclusive access to these devices if at all possible.

- *Mounting the log devices in a buffered manner*: Here, you are using a "cooked" file system (not RAW disks). The operating system is buffering the data, and the database is also buffering the data (redo log buffer). Double buffering slows things down. If possible, mount the devices in a "direct" fashion. How to do this varies by operating system and device, but it is usually possible.

- *Putting redo on a slow technology, such as RAID-5*: RAID-5 is great for reads, but it is generally terrible for writes. As we saw earlier regarding what happens during a COMMIT, we must wait for LGWR to ensure the data is on disk. Using any technology that slows this down is not a good idea.

If at all possible, you really want at least five dedicated devices for logging and optimally six to mirror your archives as well. In these days of 200GB, 300GB, 1TB, and larger disks, this is getting harder, but if you can set aside four of the smallest, fastest disks you can find and one or two big ones, you can affect LGWR and ARCn in a positive fashion. To lay out the disks, you would break them into three groups (see Figure 7-2):

- *Redo log group 1*: Disks 1 and 3

- *Redo log group 2*: Disks 2 and 4

- *Archive*: Disk 5 and optionally disk 6 (the big disks)

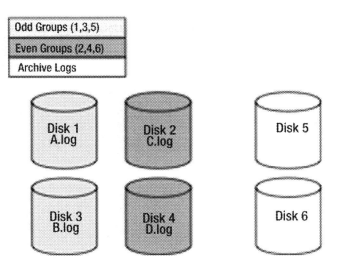

***Figure 7-2.*** *Optimal redo log configuration*

You would place redo log group 1 with members A and B onto disks 1 and 3. You would place redo log group 2 with members C and D onto disks 2 and 4. If you have groups 3, 4, and so on, they'd go onto the odd and even groups of disks, respectively. The effect of this is that LGWR, when the database is currently using group 1, will write to disks 1 and 3 simultaneously. When this group fills up, LGWR will move to disks 2 and 4. When they fill up, LGWR will go back to disks 1 and 3. Meanwhile, ARCn will be processing the full online redo logs and writing them to disks 5 and 6, the big disks. The net effect is neither ARCn nor LGWR is ever reading a disk being written to, or writing to a disk being read from, so there is no contention (see Figure 7-3).

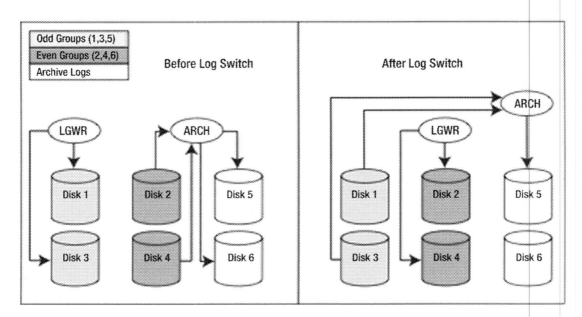

**Figure 7-3.** *Redo log flow*

So, when LGWR is writing group 1, ARCn is reading group 2 and writing to the archive disks. When LGWR is writing group 2, ARCn is reading group 1 and writing to the archive disks. In this fashion, LGWR and ARCn each have their own dedicated devices and will not be contending with anyone, not even each other.

# Temporary Tables and Redo

Oracle comes with two types of temporary tables: global and private. Global temporary tables have been a feature within Oracle for a long time. Global temporary tables are permanent database objects that persist on disk and are visible to all sessions. They are named temporary tables because the data within them only persists for the duration of the transaction or session.

Starting with Oracle 18c, you can create a private temporary table. Unlike a global temporary table, a private temporary table exists only in memory and is only visible to the session that created it. You can define a private temporary table to persist per transaction or session duration, after which the temporary table is automatically dropped.

---

**Note**   If you've worked with other database technologies such as SQL Server or MySQL, a private temporary table aligns more with what you've used in those environments.

---

Even though global temporary tables have been around for a while, there is still some confusion surrounding them, in particular in the area of logging. In this section, we'll also explore the question, "How do temporary tables work with respect to logging of changes?"

In Oracle 12c, the processing of undo for temporary tables is significantly enhanced. Therefore, I'll break this topic into two sections: prior to 12c and starting with 12c. I think it's still important to demonstrate the behavior prior to 12c. This is because the 12c enhancements must be enabled via setting the TEMP_UNDO_ENABLED parameter. By default, this parameter is turned off. This means that even if you're running a version 19 database or later, you may not be getting the performance from temporary tables that you expect because the TEMP_UNDO_ENABLED parameter has been left at the default value.

## Global Temporary Tables Prior to 12c

Temporary tables generate no redo for their blocks. Therefore, an operation on a temporary table is not recoverable. When you modify a block in a temporary table, no record of this change will be made in the redo log files. However, temporary tables do generate undo, *and the undo is logged*. Hence, temporary tables will generate some redo.

At first glance, this doesn't seem to make total sense: Why would they need to generate undo? This is because you can roll back to a SAVEPOINT within a transaction. You might erase the last 50 INSERTs into a temporary table, leaving the first 50. Temporary tables can have constraints and everything else a normal table can have. They might fail a statement on the 500th row of a 500-row INSERT, necessitating a rollback of that statement. Since temporary tables behave in general just like normal tables, temporary tables must generate undo. Since undo data must be logged, temporary tables will generate some redo log for the undo they generate.

This is not nearly as ominous as it seems. The primary SQL statements used against temporary tables are INSERTs and SELECTs. Fortunately, INSERTs generate very little undo (you need to restore the block to "nothing," and it doesn't take very much room to store "nothing"), and SELECTs generate no undo. Hence, if you use temporary tables for INSERTs and SELECTs exclusively, this section means nothing to you. It is only if you UPDATE or DELETE that you might be concerned about this.

I set up a small test to demonstrate the amount of redo generated while working with temporary tables, an indication therefore of the amount of undo generated for temporary tables, since only the undo is logged for them. To demonstrate, I'll take identically configured permanent and temporary tables and then perform the same operations on each, measuring the amount of redo generated each time. The tables I'll use are as follows:

```
SQL> create table perm
     ( x char(2000) ,
       y char(2000) ,
       z char(2000)  )
   /
Table created.

SQL> create global temporary table temp
     ( x char(2000) ,
       y char(2000) ,
       z char(2000)  )
     on commit preserve rows
   /
Table created.
```

I set up a small stored procedure to allow me to perform arbitrary SQL and report the amount of redo generated by that SQL. I'll use this routine to perform INSERTs, UPDATEs, and DELETEs against both the temporary and permanent tables:

```
SQL> create or replace procedure do_sql( p_sql in varchar2 )
    as
        l_start_redo      number;
        l_redo            number;
    begin
            l_start_redo := get_stat_val( 'redo size' );
            execute immediate p_sql;
            commit;
            l_redo := get_stat_val( 'redo size' ) - l_start_redo;
            --
            dbms_output.put_line
            ( to_char(l_redo,'99,999,999') ||' bytes of redo generated for "' ||
              substr( replace( p_sql, chr(10), ' '), 1, 25 ) || '"...' );
    end;
  /
Procedure created.
```

Then, I ran equivalent INSERTs, UPDATEs, and DELETEs against both the PERM and TEMP tables:

```
SQL> set serveroutput on format wrapped
SQL> begin
        do_sql( 'insert into perm
                select 1,1,1
                   from all_objects
                 where rownum <= 500' );

        do_sql( 'insert into temp
                select 1,1,1
                   from all_objects
                 where rownum <= 500' );
        dbms_output.new_line;
```

```
        do_sql( 'update perm set x = 2' );
        do_sql( 'update temp set x = 2' );
        dbms_output.new_line;

        do_sql( 'delete from perm' );
        do_sql( 'delete from temp' );
    end;
/

3,313,088 bytes of redo generated for "insert into perm"...
   72,584 bytes of redo generated for "insert into temp"...

3,268,384 bytes of redo generated for "update perm set x = 2"...
1,946,432 bytes of redo generated for "update temp set x = 2"...

3,245,112 bytes of redo generated for "delete from perm"...
3,224,460 bytes of redo generated for "delete from temp"...

PL/SQL procedure successfully completed.
```

As you can see,

- The INSERT into the "real" table generated a lot of redo, while almost no redo was generated for the temporary table. This makes sense—there is very little undo data generated for INSERTs and only undo data is logged for temporary tables.

- The UPDATE of the real table generated about twice the amount of redo as the temporary table. Again, this makes sense. About half of that UPDATE, the "before image," had to be saved. The "after image" (redo) for the temporary table did not have to be saved.

- The DELETEs each took about the same amount of redo space. This makes sense, because the undo for a DELETE is big, but the redo for the modified blocks is very small. Hence, a DELETE against a temporary table takes place very much in the same fashion as a DELETE against a permanent table.

Therefore, the following generalizations can be made regarding DML activity on temporary tables:

- An INSERT will generate little to no undo/redo activity.

- An UPDATE will generate about half the redo as with a permanent table.

- A DELETE will generate the same amount of redo as with a permanent table.

There are notable exceptions to the next-to-last statement. For example, if I UPDATE a column that is entirely NULL with 2,000 bytes of data, there will be very little undo data generated. This UPDATE will behave like the INSERT. On the other hand, if I UPDATE a column with 2,000 bytes of data to be NULL, it will behave like the DELETE as far as redo generation is concerned. On average, you can expect an UPDATE against a temporary table to produce about 50 percent of the undo/redo you'd experience with a permanent table.

In addition, you must consider any indexes in place on your temporary tables. Index modifications will also generate undo—which in turn generates redo. If you rerun the preceding example with these two indexes in place

```
SQL> create index perm_idx on perm(x);
Index created.

SQL> create index temp_idx on temp(x);
Index created.
```

you will find redo generated in the order of (for brevity, all of the code from the previous example is not repeated here)

```
    ...
    end;
  /
```

```
11,735,576 bytes of redo generated for "insert into perm"...
 3,351,864 bytes of redo generated for "insert into temp"...

 9,257,748 bytes of redo generated for "update perm set x = 2"...
 5,465,868 bytes of redo generated for "update temp set x = 2"...

 4,434,992 bytes of redo generated for "delete from perm"...
 4,371,620 bytes of redo generated for "delete from temp"...

PL/SQL procedure successfully completed.
```

The numbers hold true from what we saw before—but you can see that the index definitely added to the redo generated. The INSERT into the global temporary table went from generating almost no redo to generating 3.3MB of redo. All of this additional redo was related to the undo produced for the index maintenance.

---

**Note**    This is an exaggerated example. The index in question was on a CHAR(2000) column; the index key is much larger than you'll normally see in real life. Don't expect this much additional redo typically.

---

In general, common sense prevails in estimating the amount of redo created. If the operation you perform causes undo data to be created, then determine how easy or hard it will be to reverse (undo) the effect of your operation. If you INSERT 2,000 bytes, the reverse of this is easy. You simply go back to no bytes. If you DELETE 2,000 bytes, the reverse is INSERTing 2,000 bytes. In this case, the redo is substantial.

Armed with this knowledge, you will avoid deleting from temporary tables. You can use TRUNCATE, bearing in mind, of course, that TRUNCATE is DDL that will commit your transaction. Or just let the temporary tables empty themselves automatically after a COMMIT or when your session terminates. All of these methods generate no undo and, therefore, no redo. You should try to avoid updating a temporary table unless you really have to for some reason. You should use temporary tables mostly as something to be INSERTed into and SELECTed from. In this fashion, you'll make optimum use of their unique ability to not generate redo.

## Global Temporary Tables Starting with 12c

As you saw in the previous section, when issuing INSERT, UPDATE, and DELETE statements in a temporary table, the undo for those changes is recorded in the undo tablespace, which in turn will generate redo. With the advent of Oracle 12c, you can instruct Oracle to store the undo for a temporary table in a temporary tablespace via the TEMP_UNDO_ENABLED parameter. When blocks are modified in a temporary tablespace, no redo is generated. Therefore, when TEMP_UNDO_ENABLED is set to TRUE, any DML issued against a temporary table will generate little or no redo.

---

**Note**    By default, TEMP_UNDO_ENABLED is set to FALSE. So, unless otherwise configured, temporary tables will generate the same amount of redo in 12*c* as in prior releases.

---

The TEMP_UNDO_ENABLED parameter can be set at the session or system level. Here's an example of setting it to TRUE at the session level:

```
SQL> alter session set temp_undo_enabled=true;
```

Once enabled for a session, any modifications to data in a temporary table in that session will have a subsequent undo logged to the temporary tablespace. Any modifications to permanent tables will still have undo logged to the undo tablespace. To see the impact of this, I'll rerun the exact same code (from the "Prior to 12c" section) that displays the amount of redo generated when issuing transactions against a permanent table and a temporary table—with the only addition being that TEMP_UNDO_ENABLED is set to TRUE. Here is the output:

```
3,312,148 bytes of redo generated for "insert into perm"...
      376 bytes of redo generated for "insert into temp"...

2,203,788 bytes of redo generated for "update perm set x = 2"...
      376 bytes of redo generated for "update temp set x = 2"...

3,243,412 bytes of redo generated for "delete from perm"...
      376 bytes of redo generated for "delete from temp"...
```

The results are dramatic: a trivial amount of redo is generated by the INSERT, UPDATE, and DELETE statements in a temporary table. For environments where you perform large batch operations that transact against temporary tables, you can expect to see a significant reduction in the amount of redo generated.

---

**Note**    You may be wondering why there were 376 bytes of redo generated in the prior example's output. As processes consume space within the database, Oracle does some internal housekeeping. These changes are recorded in the data dictionary, which in turn generates some redo and undo.

---

Starting with Oracle12c, in an Oracle Active Data Guard configuration, you can issue DML statements directly on a temporary table that exists in a standby database. We can view the amount of redo generated for a temporary table in a standby database by running the same code (from the "Prior to 12c" section) against a standby database. The only difference being the statements issuing transactions against permanent tables must be removed (because you cannot issue DML on a permanent table in a standby database). Here is the output showing that 0 bytes of redo are generated:

```
0 bytes of redo generated for "insert into temp"...
0 bytes of redo generated for "update temp set x = 2"...
0 bytes of redo generated for "delete from temp"...
```

> **Note**    There's no need to set TEMP_UNDO_ENABLED in the standby database. This is because temporary undo is always enabled in an Oracle Active Data Guard standby database.

Global temporary tables are often used for reporting purposes—like generating and storing intermediate query results. Oracle Active Data Guard is often used to offload reporting applications to the standby database. Couple global temporary tables with Oracle Active Data Guard, and you have a more powerful tool to address your reporting requirements.

# Private Temporary Tables

In regard to undo generation, private temporary tables behave similar to global temporary tables. We can see that by running the same tests from the prior section to measure the amount of undo generated when using a temporary table. First, let's create the permanent and the private temporary tables:

```
create table perm
  ( x char(2000) ,
    y char(2000) ,
    z char(2000)  )
/
```

```
CREATE PRIVATE TEMPORARY TABLE ora$ptt_temp
  ( x char(2000) ,
    y char(2000) ,
    z char(2000)
)
ON COMMIT PRESERVE DEFINITION;
```

Next, let's measure the amount of redo generated when transacting against both of the prior tables:

```
set serveroutput on format wrapped
begin
     do_sql( 'insert into perm
             select 1,1,1
             from all_objects
             where rownum <= 500' );

     do_sql( 'insert into ora$ptt_temp
             select 1,1,1
             from all_objects
             where rownum <= 500' );
     dbms_output.new_line;

     do_sql( 'update perm set x = 2' );
     do_sql( 'update ora$ptt_temp set x = 2' );
     dbms_output.new_line;

     do_sql( 'delete from perm' );
     do_sql( 'delete from ora$ptt_temp' );
end;
/
```

As you can see, the redo generated is identical to the behavior of a global temporary table with TEMP_UNDO_ENABLED set to FALSE:

```
3,324,888 bytes of redo generated for "insert into perm          "...
   72,548 bytes of redo generated for "insert into ora$ptt_temp "...
```

```
5,408,292 bytes of redo generated for "update perm set x = 2"...
1,937,060 bytes of redo generated for "update ora$ptt_temp set x"...

3,252,296 bytes of redo generated for "delete from perm"...
3,225,464 bytes of redo generated for "delete from ora$ptt_temp"...
```

If we run the same tests with TEMP_UNDO_ENABLED set to TRUE, you can see the dramatic difference in undo generation:

```
3,324,828 bytes of redo generated for "insert into perm          "...
      384 bytes of redo generated for "insert into ora$ptt_temp "...

2,201,092 bytes of redo generated for "update perm set x = 2"...
      384 bytes of redo generated for "update ora$ptt_temp set x"...

3,251,936 bytes of redo generated for "delete from perm"...
      384 bytes of redo generated for "delete from ora$ptt_temp"...
```

The bottom line is that when you use either global temporary tables or private temporary tables, if you want to minimize undo generation, set TEMP_UNDO_ENABLED to TRUE.

# Summary

In this chapter, we investigated how to measure redo. We also looked at the impact that NOLOGGING has on redo generation. When used in combination with direct-path operations (e.g., direct-path insert), the generation of redo can be reduced dramatically. However, for regular DML statements, the NOLOGGING clause has no effect.

We explored the reasons why a log switch might be delayed. Oracle won't allow a redo log to be overwritten in the event that DBWn has not yet finished checkpointing the data protected by the redo log or ARCn has not finished copying the redo log file to the archive destination. This is mainly a problem for the DBA to detect (inspect the alert. log) and manage.

Lastly, we discussed how redo is handled with transactions that occur in temporary tables. In 12c and above, the amount of redo can be reduced to nearly nothing. For applications that use temporary tables, this can have a positive impact on performance.

# CHAPTER 8

# Investigating Undo

The Oracle database creates and manages information used to roll back (or undo) changes to the database. The most obvious use of undo is when you issue a ROLLBACK statement to undo changes to data that you don't want committed. Here is the complete list of uses of undo:

- Roll back transactions via the ROLLBACK statement

- Enable read consistency

- Recover the database

- Analyze data as of a prior point in time using Oracle Flashback Query

- Recover from logical corruptions using Oracle Flashback features

In the previous couple of chapters, we discussed several of the prior undo segment topics. We've seen how they are used during recovery, how they interact with the redo logs, and how they are used for consistent reads, and nonblocking reads of data. In this chapter, we'll look at the most frequently raised issues with undo segments.

The bulk of our time will be spent on the infamous ORA-01555: snapshot too old error, as this single issue causes more confusion than any other topic in the entire set of database topics. Before we do this, however, we'll investigate one other undo-related issue: the question of what type of DML operation generates the most and least undo (you might already be able to answer that yourself, given the examples in the preceding chapter with temporary tables).

## What Generates the Most and Least Undo?

This is a frequently asked but easily answered question. The presence of indexes (or the fact that a table is an index-organized table) may affect the amount of undo generated dramatically, as indexes are complex data structures and may generate copious amounts of undo information.

219

© Darl Kuhn and Thomas Kyte 2021
D. Kuhn and T. Kyte, *Oracle Database Transactions and Locking Revealed*,
https://doi.org/10.1007/978-1-4842-6425-6_8

That said, an INSERT will, in general, generate the least amount of undo, since all Oracle needs to record for this is a rowid to "delete." An UPDATE is typically second in the race (in most cases). All that needs to be recorded is the changed bytes. It is most common that you UPDATE some small fraction of the entire row's data. Therefore, a small fraction of the row must be remembered in the undo. Many of the previous examples run counter to this rule of thumb, but that's because they update large, fixed-sized rows and they update the entire row. It is much more common to UPDATE a row and change a small percentage of the total row. A DELETE will, in general, generate the most undo. For a DELETE, Oracle must record the entire row's before image into the undo segment. The previous temporary table example (in Chapter 7), with regard to redo generation, demonstrated that fact: the DELETE generated the most redo, and since the only logged element of the DML operation on a temporary table is the undo, we in fact observed that the DELETE generated the most undo. The INSERT generated very little undo that needed to be logged. The UPDATE generated an amount equal to the before image of the data that was changed, and the DELETE generated the entire set of data written to the undo segment.

As previously mentioned, you must also take into consideration the work performed on an index. You'll find that an update of an unindexed column not only executes much faster, it also tends to generate significantly less undo than an update of an indexed column. For example, we'll create a table with two columns, both containing the same information, and index one of them:

```
SQL> create table t
     as
     select object_name unindexed,
            object_name indexed
       from all_objects
   /
Table created.

SQL> create index t_idx on t(indexed);
Index created.

SQL> exec dbms_stats.gather_table_stats(user,'T');
PL/SQL procedure successfully completed.
```

> **Note**    You will not see the exact same results when you run these tests on your database. It will depend on the number of objects in your database, which will be different from database to database.

Now, we'll update the table, first updating the unindexed column and then the indexed column. We'll need a new V$ query to measure the amount of undo we've generated in each case. The following query accomplishes this for us. It works by getting our session ID (SID) from V$MYSTAT, using that to find our record in the V$SESSION view, and retrieving the transaction address (TADDR). It uses the TADDR to pull up our V$TRANSACTION record (if any) and selects the USED_UBLK column—the number of used undo blocks. Since we currently are not in a transaction, we expect it to return zero rows right now:

```sql
SQL> select used_ublk
       from v$transaction
      where addr = (select taddr
                      from v$session
                     where sid = (select sid
                                    from v$mystat
                                   where rownum = 1
                                 )
                   )
  /

no rows selected
```

But the query will return a row after the UPDATE starts a transaction:

```sql
SQL> update t set unindexed = lower(unindexed);
72522 rows updated.

SQL> select used_ublk
       from v$transaction
      where addr = (select taddr
                      from v$session
                     where sid = (select sid
                                    from v$mystat
```

```
                                    where rownum = 1
                                   )
                      )
    /

USED_UBLK
----------
      1369

SQL> commit;
Commit complete.
```

That UPDATE used 1369 blocks to store its undo. The commit would free that up, or release it, so if we rerun the query against V$TRANSACTION, it would once again show us no rows selected. When we update the same data—only indexed this time—we'll observe the following:

```
SQL> update t set indexed = lower(indexed);
72522 rows updated.

SQL> select used_ublk
       from v$transaction
      where addr = (select taddr
                      from v$session
                     where sid = (select sid
                                    from v$mystat
                                   where rownum = 1
                                  )
                    )
    /

USED_UBLK
----------
      3154
```

As you can see, updating that indexed column in this example generated several times as much undo. This is due to the inherit complexity of the index structure itself and the fact that we updated every single row in the table—moving every single index key value in this structure.

# ORA-01555: Snapshot Too Old Error

In Chapter 5, we briefly investigated the ORA-01555 error and looked at one cause of it: committing too frequently. Here, we'll take a much more detailed look at the causes and solutions for the ORA-01555 error. ORA-01555 is one of those errors that confound people. It is the foundation for many myths, inaccuracies, and suppositions.

---

**Note**   ORA-01555 is not related to data corruption or data loss at all. It is a "safe" error in that regard; the only outcome is that the query that received this error is unable to continue processing.

---

The error is actually straightforward and has only two real causes, but since there's a special case of one of them that happens so frequently, I'll say that there are three:

- The undo segments are too small for the work you perform on your system.

- Your programs fetch across COMMITs (actually a variation on the preceding point). We covered this in Chapter 5.

- Block cleanout.

The first two points are directly related to Oracle's read-consistency model. As you recall from Chapter 4, the results of your query are *preordained*, meaning they are well defined before Oracle goes to retrieve even the first row. Oracle provides this consistent point in time "snapshot" of the database by using the undo segments to roll back blocks that have changed since your query began. Every statement you execute, such as the following

```
update t set x = 5 where x = 2;
insert into t select * from t where x = 2;
delete from t where x = 2;
select * from t where x = 2;
```

will see a read-consistent view of T and the set of rows where X=2, regardless of any other concurrent activity in the database.

> **Note**    The four statements presented here are just examples of the types of statements that would see a read-consistent view of T. They are not meant to be run as a single transaction in the database, as the first update would cause the following three statements to see no records. They are purely illustrative.

All statements that "read" the table take advantage of this read consistency. In the example just shown, the UPDATE reads the table to find rows where x=2 (and then UPDATEs them). The INSERT reads the table to find rows where X=2, and then INSERTs them, and so on. It is this dual use of the undo segments, both to roll back failed transactions and to provide for read consistency that results in the ORA-01555 error.

The third item in the previous list is a more insidious cause of ORA-01555 in that it can happen in a database where there is a single session, and this session is not modifying the tables that are being queried when the ORA-01555 error is raised! This doesn't seem possible—why would we need undo data for a table we can guarantee is not being modified? We'll find out shortly.

Before we take a look at all three cases with illustrations, I'd like to share with you the solutions to the ORA-01555 error, in general:

- If your undo tablespaces has autoextend enabled, set the parameter UNDO_RETENTION properly (larger than the amount of time it takes to execute your longest-running transaction or the longest expected flashback operation). V$UNDOSTAT can be used to determine the duration of your long-running queries. Also, ensure sufficient space on disk has been set aside so the undo segments are allowed to grow to the size they need to be based on the requested UNDO_RETENTION.

- If your undo tablespace is a fixed size, then the UNDO_RETENTION parameter is ignored, and Oracle automatically tunes undo. For fixed-size undo tablespaces, choose a size sufficiently large enough to accommodate long-running queries and flashback operations.

- Reduce the runtime of your query (tune it). This is always a good thing if possible, so it might be the first thing you try. It reduces the need for larger undo segments. This method goes toward solving the previous points.

- Gather statistics on related objects. This helps avoid the block cleanout point listed earlier. Since the block cleanout is the result of a very large mass UPDATE or INSERT, statistics-gathering needs to be done anyway after a mass UPDATE or large load.

We'll come back to these solutions, as they are important to know. It seemed appropriate to display them prominently before we begin.

## Undo Segments Are in Fact Too Small

The scenario is this: you have a system where the transactions are small. As a result, you need very little undo segment space allocated. Say, for example, the following is true:

- Each transaction generates 8KB of undo on average.

- You do five of these transactions per second on average (40KB of undo per second, 2,400KB per minute).

- You have a transaction that generates 1MB of undo that occurs once per minute on average. In total, you generate about 3.5MB of undo per minute.

- You have an exceedingly small amount of undo configured for your system.

That is more than sufficient undo for this database when processing transactions. The undo segments will wrap around and reuse space about every three to four minutes or so, on average. If you sized undo segments based on your transactions that do modifications, you did all right.

In this same environment, however, you have some reporting needs. Some of these queries take a really long time to run—five minutes, perhaps. Here is where the problem comes in. If these queries take five minutes to execute *and* they need a view of the data as it existed when the query began, you have a very good probability of the ORA-01555 error occurring. Since your undo segments will wrap during this query execution, you know that some undo information generated since your query began is gone—it has been overwritten. If you hit a block that was modified near the time you started your query, the undo information for this block will be missing, and you will receive the ORA-01555 error.

Here's a small example. Let's say we have a table with blocks 1, 2, 3, … 1,000,000 in it. Table 8-1 shows a sequence of events that could occur.

***Table 8-1.*** *Long-Running Query Timeline*

| Time (Minutes:Seconds) | Action |
| --- | --- |
| 0:00 | Our query begins. |
| 0:01 | Another session UPDATEs block 1,000,000. Undo information for this is recorded into some undo segment. |
| 0:01 | This UPDATE session COMMITs. The undo data it generated is still there but is now subject to being overwritten if we need the space. |
| 1:00 | Our query is still chugging along. It is at block 200,000. |
| 1:01 | Lots of activity going on. We have generated a little over 14MB of undo by now. |
| 3:00 | Our query is still going strong. We are at block 600,000 or so by now. |
| 4:00 | Our undo segments start to wrap around and reuse the space that was active when our query began at time 0:00. Specifically, we have just reused the undo segment space that the UPDATE used to block 1,000,000 back at time 0:01. |
| 5:00 | Our query finally gets to block 1,000,000. It finds it has been modified since the query began. It goes to the undo segment and attempts to find the undo for that block to get a consistent read on it. At this point, it discovers the information it needs no longer exists. ORA-01555 is raised and the query fails. |

This is all it takes. If your undo segments are sized such that they have a good chance of being reused during the execution of your queries, and your queries access data that will probably be modified, you stand a very good chance of hitting the ORA-01555 error on a recurring basis. If this is the case, you must set your UNDO_RETENTION parameter higher and let Oracle take care of figuring out how much undo to retain (this is the suggested approach; it's much easier than trying to figure out the perfect undo size yourself) or resize your undo segments and make them larger (or have more of them). You need enough undo configured to last as long as your long-running queries. The system was sized for the transactions that modify data—you forgot to size for the other components of the system.

With Oracle9*i* and above, there are two methods to manage undo in the system:

- *Automatic undo management*: Here, Oracle is told how long to retain undo for, via the UNDO_RETENTION parameter. Oracle will determine how many undo segments to create based on concurrent workload and how big each should be. The database can even reallocate extents between individual undo segments at runtime to meet the UNDO_RETENTION goal set by the DBA. This is the recommended approach for undo management.

- *Manual undo management*: Don't use this method. This is a relic of the early versions of Oracle.

With manual undo management, DBAs had the choice of manually setting the size and number of the undo segments. Don't use the manual method. Knowledge of this topic is really only relevant when trying to impress older DBAs on the team.

Under automatic undo management, things are much easier from the ORA-01555 perspective. The DBA first creates an autoextending undo tablespace and then tells the database how long the longest-running query (or flashback operation) is and sets that value in the UNDO_RETENTION parameter. Oracle will attempt to preserve undo for at least that duration of time. If sufficient space to grow has been allocated, Oracle will extend an undo segment and not wrap around—in trying to obey the UNDO_RETENTION period. This is in direct contrast to manually managed undo, which will wrap around and reuse undo space as soon as it can. It is primarily for this reason, the support of the UNDO_RETENTION parameter, that I highly recommend *automatic undo management* whenever possible. That single parameter reduces the possibility of an ORA-01555 error greatly (when it is set appropriately).

If you have a fixed-size undo tablespace, then the UNDO_RETENTION parameter is ignored by Oracle. In this configuration, you can use tools such as the Undo Advisor to help you appropriately size your undo tablespace. The undo advisor is accessible via Enterprise Manager or the DBMS_ADVISOR PL/SQL packages. The two most important considerations in sizing your undo are the length of the longest-running query and the longest interval you require for flashback operations.

I am getting a little too deep into the DBA role at this point, so we'll move on to the next case. It's just important that you understand that the ORA-01555 error in this case is due to the system not being sized correctly for your workload. The only solution is to size correctly for your workload. It is not your fault, but it is your problem since you hit it. It's the same as if you run out of temporary space during a query. You either configure sufficient temporary space for the system, or you rewrite the queries so they use a plan that does not require temporary space.

To demonstrate this effect, we can set up a small but somewhat artificial test. We'll create a very small undo tablespace with one session that will generate many small transactions, virtually assuring us that it will wrap around and reuse its allocated space many times—regardless of the UNDO_RETENTION setting, since we are not permitting the undo tablespace to grow. The session that uses this undo segment will be modifying a table, T. It will use a full scan of T and read it from "top" to "bottom." In another session, we will execute a query that will read the table T via an index. In this fashion, it will read the table somewhat randomly: it will read row 1, then row 1,000, then row 500, then row 20,001, and so on. In this way, we will tend to visit blocks very randomly and perhaps many times during the processing of our query. The odds of getting an ORA-01555 error in this case are virtually 100 percent.

So, in one session we start by connecting to the pluggable database (not the root container) and creating a new undo tablespace within it:

```
SQL> create undo tablespace undo_small
     datafile '/tmp/undo.dbf' size 2m
     autoextend off
     /
Tablespace created.

SQL> alter system set undo_tablespace = undo_small;
System altered.
```

Now, we'll set up the table T to query and modify. Note that we are ordering the data randomly in this table. The CREATE TABLE AS SELECT tends to put the rows in the blocks in the order it fetches them from the query. We'll just scramble the rows up so they are not artificially sorted in any order, randomizing their distribution:

```
SQL> drop table t purge;
Table dropped.

SQL> create table t
    as
    select *
      from all_objects
     order by dbms_random.random;
Table created.

SQL> alter table t add constraint t_pk primary key(object_id);
Table altered.

SQL> exec dbms_stats.gather_table_stats( user, 'T', cascade=> true );
PL/SQL procedure successfully completed.
```

And now we are ready to do our modifications:

```
SQL> begin
        for x in ( select rowid rid from t )
        loop
            update t set object_name = lower(object_name) where rowid = x.rid;
            commit;
        end loop;
   end;
  /
```

Now, while that PL/SQL block of code is running, we will run a query in another session. That other query will read table T and process each record. It will spend about 1/100 of a second processing each record before fetching the next (simulated using DBMS_LOCK.SLEEP(0.01)). We will use the FIRST_ROWS hint in the query to have it use the index we created to read the rows out of the table via the index sorted by OBJECT_ID. Since the data was randomly inserted into the table, we would tend to query blocks in the table rather randomly. This block will only run for a couple of seconds before failing:

```
SQL> declare
          cursor c is
          select /*+ first_rows */ object_name
            from t
           order by object_id;

          l_object_name t.object_name%type;
          l_rowcnt      number := 0;
     begin
        open c;
        loop
            fetch c into l_object_name;
            exit when c%notfound;
            dbms_lock.sleep( 0.01 );
            l_rowcnt := l_rowcnt+1;
        end loop;
        close c;
     exception
        when others then
            dbms_output.put_line( 'rows fetched = ' || l_rowcnt );
            raise;
  end;
  /
rows fetched = 191
declare
*
ERROR at line 1:
ORA-01555: snapshot too old: rollback segment number 39 with name
"_SYSSMU39_2997928315$" too small
```

As you can see, it processed only a handful of records before failing with the ORA-01555: snapshot too old error. To correct this, we want to make sure two things are done:

- UNDO_RETENTION is set in the database to be at least long enough for this read process to complete. That will allow the database to grow the undo tablespace to hold sufficient undo for us to complete.

- The undo tablespace is allowed to grow or you manually allocate more disk space to it.

For this example, I have determined my long-running process takes about 720 seconds to complete (I have about 72,000 records in the table, so at 0.01 seconds per row we have 720 seconds). My UNDO_RETENTION is set to 900 (this is in seconds, so the undo retention is about 15 minutes). I altered the undo tablespace's data file to permit it to grow by 1MB at a time, up to 2GB in size:

```
SQL> alter database
     datafile '/tmp/undo.dbf'
     autoextend on
     next 1m
     maxsize 2048m;
Database altered.
```

When I ran the processes concurrently again, both ran to completion. The undo tablespace's data file grew this time, because it was allowed to and the undo retention I set up said to.

```
SQL> select bytes/1024/1024
       from dba_data_files
     where tablespace_name = 'UNDO_SMALL';

BYTES/1024/1024
---------------
             21
```

So, instead of receiving an error, we completed successfully, and the undo grew to be large enough to accommodate our needs. It is true that in this example, getting the error was purely due to the fact that we read the table T via the index and performed random reads all over the table. If we had rapidly full-scanned the table instead, there is a good chance we would not have received the ORA-01555 error *in this particular case*. This is because both the SELECT and UPDATE would have been full-scanning T, and the SELECT could most likely race ahead of the UPDATE during its scan (the SELECT just has to read, but the UPDATE must read and update and therefore could go slower). By doing the random reads, we increase the probability that the SELECT will need to read a block, which the UPDATE modified and committed many rows ago. This just demonstrates the somewhat insidious nature of the ORA-01555 error. Its occurrence depends on how concurrent sessions access and manipulate the underlying tables.

# Delayed Block Cleanout

This cause of the ORA-01555 error is hard to eliminate entirely, but it is rare anyway, as the circumstances under which it occurs do not happen frequently. We have already discussed the block cleanout mechanism (in Chapter 7), but to summarize, it is the process whereby the next session to access a block after it has been modified may have to check to see if the transaction that last modified the block is still active. Once the process determines that the transaction is not active, it cleans out the block so that the next session to access it does not have to go through the same process again. To clean out the block, Oracle determines the undo segment used for the previous transaction (from the block's header) and then determines whether the undo header indicates that the transaction has been committed and, if so, when it committed. This confirmation is accomplished in one of two ways. One way is that Oracle can determine that the transaction committed a long time ago, even though its transaction slot has been overwritten in the undo segment transaction table. The other way is that the COMMIT SCN is still in the transaction table of the undo segment, meaning the transaction committed a short time ago, and its transaction slot hasn't been overwritten.

To receive the ORA-01555 error from a delayed block cleanout, all of the following conditions must be met:

- A modification is made and COMMITed, and the blocks are not cleaned out automatically (e.g., the transaction modified more blocks than can fit in 10 percent of the SGA block buffer cache).

- These blocks are not touched by another session and will not be touched until our unfortunate query (displayed shortly) hits it.

- A long-running query begins. This query will ultimately read some of those blocks from earlier. This query starts at SCN t1, the read-consistent SCN it must roll data back to in order to achieve read consistency. The transaction entry for the modification transaction is still in the undo segment transaction table when we begin.

- During the query, many commits are made in the system. These transactions don't touch the blocks in question (if they did, we wouldn't have the impending problem as they would clean out the old transaction—solving the cleanout issue).

- The transaction tables in the undo segments roll around and reuse slots due to the high degree of COMMITs. Most important, the transaction entry for the original modification transaction is cycled over and reused. In addition, the system has reused undo segment extents, preventing a consistent read on the undo segment header block itself.

- Additionally, the lowest SCN recorded in the undo segment now exceeds t1 (it is higher than the read-consistent SCN of the query), due to the large number of commits.

When our query gets to the block that was modified and committed before it began, it is in trouble. Normally, it would go to the undo segment pointed to by the block and find the status of the transaction that modified it (in other words, it would find the COMMIT SCN of that transaction). If the COMMIT SCN is less than t1, our query can use this block. If the COMMIT SCN is greater than t1, our query must roll back that block. The problem is, however, that our query is unable to determine in this particular case if the COMMIT SCN of the block is greater than or less than t1. It is unsure as to whether it can use that block image or not. The ORA-01555 error then results.

To see this, we will create many blocks in a table that need to be cleaned out. We will then open a cursor on that table and allow many small transactions to take place against some other table—not the table we just updated and opened the cursor on. Finally, we will attempt to fetch the data for the cursor. Now, we *know* that the data required by the cursor will be "OK"—we should be able to see all of it since the modifications to the table would have taken place and been committed *before* we open the cursor. When we get an ORA-01555 error this time, it will be because of the previously described issue with delayed block cleanout. To set up for this example, we'll use

- The 4MB UNDO_SMALL undo tablespace

- A 300MB SGA, this is so we can get some dirty blocks flushed to disk to observe this phenomenon

Before we start, we'll create the undo tablespace and the "big" table we'll be querying:

```
SQL> create undo tablespace undo_small
    datafile '/tmp/undo.dbf' size 4m
    autoextend off
    /
Tablespace created.
```

```
SQL> create table big  as
     select a.*, rpad('*',1000,'*') data
      from all_objects a;
Table created.

SQL> alter table big add constraint big_pk  primary key(object_id);
Table altered.

SQL> exec dbms_stats.gather_table_stats( user, 'BIG' );
PL/SQL procedure successfully completed.
```

---

**Note**    You might wonder why I didn't use CASCADE=>TRUE on the gather-statistics call to gather statistics on the index created by default by the primary key constraint. That is because since Oracle 10*g*, a CREATE  INDEX or ALTER  INDEX REBUILD has implicit compute statistics added to it already whenever the table it is indexing is not empty. So, the very act of creating the index has the side effect of gathering statistics on itself. There's no need to regather the statistics we already have.

---

The previous table will have lots of blocks as we get about six or seven rows per block using that big data field, and my ALL_OBJECTS table has over 70,000 rows. Next, we'll create the small table the many little transactions will modify:

```
SQL> create table small ( x int, y char(500) );
Table created.

SQL> insert into small select rownum, 'x' from all_users;
25 rows created.

SQL> commit;
Commit complete.

SQL> exec dbms_stats.gather_table_stats( user, 'SMALL' );
PL/SQL procedure successfully completed.
```

Now, we'll dirty up that big table. We have a very small undo tablespace, so we'll want to update as many blocks of this big table as possible, all while generating the least amount of undo possible. We'll use a fancy UPDATE statement to do that. Basically, the following subquery is finding the "first" rowid of a row on every block. That subquery will return a rowid for every database block identifying a single row on it. We'll update that row, setting a VARCHAR2(1) field. This will let us update all of the blocks in the table (some 8,000 plus in the example), flooding the buffer cache with dirty blocks that will have to be written out. We'll make sure we are using that small undo tablespace as well. To accomplish this and not exceed the capacity of our undo tablespace, we'll craft an UPDATE statement that will update just the "first row" on each block. The ROW_NUMBER() built-in analytic function is instrumental in this operation; it assigns the number 1 to the "first row" by database block in the table, which would be the single row on the block we would update:

```
SQL> alter system set undo_tablespace = undo_small;
System altered.

SQL> update big
        set temporary = temporary
      where rowid in
      (
      select r
        from (
      select rowid r, row_number() over
              (partition by dbms_rowid.rowid_block_number(rowid) order by
               rowid) rn
        from big
            )
      where rn = 1
      )
  /
3064 rows updated.

SQL> commit;
Commit complete.
```

OK, so now we know that we have lots of dirty blocks on disk. We definitely wrote some of them out, because we just didn't have the room to hold them all. Next, we will open a cursor, but it won't yet fetch a single row. Remember, when we open the cursor, the resultset is preordained, so even though Oracle did not actually process a row of data, the act of opening that resultset fixed the point in time the results must be "as of." Now since we'll be fetching the data we just updated and committed, and we know no one else is modifying the data, we should be able to retrieve the rows without needing any undo at all. But that's where the delayed block cleanout rears its head. The transaction that modified these blocks is so new that Oracle will be obliged to verify that it committed before we begin, and if we overwrite that information (also stored in the undo tablespace), the query will fail. So, here is the opening of the cursor:

```
SQL> variable x refcursor
SQL> exec open :x for select * from big where object_id < 100;
PL/SQL procedure successfully completed.

SQL> !./run.sh
```

The run.sh file is a shell script; it simply fired off twenty SQL*Plus sessions using a command:

```
$ORACLE_HOME/bin/sqlplus yoda/foo@localhost:1521/orcl @test2 1   &
$ORACLE_HOME/bin/sqlplus yoda/foo@localhost:1521/orcl @test2 2   &
$ORACLE_HOME/bin/sqlplus yoda/foo@localhost:1521/orcl @test2 3   &
...
$ORACLE_HOME/bin/sqlplus yoda/foo@localhost:1521/orcl @test2 19   &
$ORACLE_HOME/bin/sqlplus yoda/foo@localhost:1521/orcl @test2 20   &
```

In the prior code, each SQL*Plus session was passed a different number (that was number 1; there was a 2, 3, and so on). In the prior script, ensure you replace the username and password with the username and password for your environment. The script test2.sql they each ran is as follows:

```
begin
    for i in 1 .. 5000
    loop
        update small set y = i where x= &1;
        commit;
```

```
    end loop;
end;
/
exit
```

So, we had nine sessions inside of a tight loop initiate many transactions. The `run.`
`sh` script waited for the nine SQL*Plus sessions to complete their work, and then we
returned to our session, the one with the open cursor. Upon attempting to print it out, we
observe the following:

```
SQL> print x
ORA-01555: snapshot too old: rollback segment number 44 with name
"_SYSSMU44_3913812538$" too small
no rows selected
```

As I said, the preceding is a rare case. It took a lot of conditions, all of which must
exist simultaneously to occur. We needed blocks that were in need of a cleanout to exist,
and these blocks are rare in Oracle8*i* and above. A `DBMS_STATS` call to collect statistics
gets rid of them so the most common causes—large mass updates and bulk loads—
should not be a concern, since the tables need to be analyzed after such operations
anyway. Most transactions tend to touch less than 10 percent of the blocks in the buffer
cache; hence, they do not generate blocks that need to be cleaned out. If you believe
you've encountered this issue, in which a `SELECT` against a table that has no other DML
applied to it is raising the `ORA-01555 error`, try the following solutions:

- Ensure you are using "right-sized" transactions in the first place.
  Make sure you are not committing more frequently than you should.

- Use `DBMS_STATS` to scan the related objects, cleaning them out after
  the load. Since the block cleanout is the result of a very large mass
  `UPDATE` or `INSERT`, this needs to be done anyway.

- Allow the undo tablespace to grow by giving it the room to extend
  and increasing the undo retention. This decreases the likelihood of
  an undo segment transaction table slot being overwritten during
  the course of your long-running query. This is the same as the
  solution for other cause of an `ORA-01555` error (the two are very much

related; you experience undo segment reuse during the processing
of your query). In fact, I reran the preceding example with the undo
tablespace set to autoextend 1MB at a time, with an undo retention of
900 seconds. The query against the table BIG completed successfully.

- Reduce the runtime of your query—tune it. This is always good if
  possible, so it might be the first thing you try.

One last comment, in the database that you ran the prior experiment in, don't forget
to set your undo tablespace back to the original one, for example:

```
SQL> alter system set undo_tablespace=undotbs2;
SQL> drop tablespace undo_small including contents and datafiles;
```

That way you ensure you're not running your database with an extremely small undo
tablespace.

# Summary

In this chapter, we investigated which statements generate the least and most undo. In
general, an INSERT generates the least amount, an UPDATE generates more than INSERT,
and a DELETE generates the most undo.

The bulk of this chapter explored the causes of the infamous ORA-01555 error
(snapshot too old). This error can occur because the undo tablespace has been sized too
small. The DBA must ensure that the undo tablespace is sized large enough to mostly
eliminate this as a cause for the error. We also looked at how a delayed block cleanout
can cause issues. If you've correctly sized your transactions and your undo tablespace,
you will probably rarely run into this error. Tuning the query that throws the ORA-01555
error should always be one of the first methods employed to resolve the issue.

# CHAPTER 9

# Troubleshooting

In this book, we have covered various themes such as transactions, locking, blocking, redo, and undo. As we went along, we touched on basic troubleshooting techniques related to these subjects. In this chapter, we dive deeper into diagnosing issues related to these topics. Specifically, we'll look at the following:

- Detecting unindexed foreign key columns
- Displaying blocking sessions
- Killing sessions
- Reporting top consumers of undo and redo
- Inspecting log switching and redo generation

Having said that, the goal of this chapter is not to present you with a bunch of SQL scripts that report on various problem aspects of your database. You can do an Internet search and find dozens of such scripts. Rather what is presented in this chapter will be the types of issues to look for and the thought process of using a script to solve the problem at hand. Having worked in many different production support environments, I'll add some insight as to what is important to look for.

Additionally, there are many graphical tools available that can assist with identifying issues related to topics in this book. This chapter doesn't focus on using graphical tools to identify the pain points. Rather, we focus on thought process and views underpinning the scripts. I strongly believe that understanding the underlying views and how to query them will greatly enhance your ability to troubleshoot problems.

© Darl Kuhn and Thomas Kyte 2021
D. Kuhn and T. Kyte, *Oracle Database Transactions and Locking Revealed*,
https://doi.org/10.1007/978-1-4842-6425-6_9

# Detecting Unindexed Foreign Keys

In chapter 2, we touched on issues related to unindexed foreign key columns and how this can cause unnecessary locks. To that end, when someone complains of deadlocks in the database, I have them run a script that detects unindexed foreign keys; 99 percent of the time, we locate an offending table. By simply indexing that foreign key, the deadlocks—and lots of other contention issues—go away. The following example demonstrates the use of this script to locate the unindexed foreign key. First, log in as your schema and then create a couple of tables (based off of the SCOTT schema) and define a foreign key constraint:

```
sqlplus yoda/foo@localhost:1521/orcl
```

```
SQL> create table dept
  as select * from scott.dept;
```

```
SQL> create table emp
  as select * from scott.emp;
```

```
SQL> alter table dept
  add constraint dept_pk
  primary key(deptno);
```

```
SQL> alter table emp
  add constraint emp_pk
  primary key(empno);
```

```
SQL> alter table emp
  add constraint emp_fk_dept
  foreign key (deptno)
  references dept(deptno);
```

Now, we have a parent and child table with a foreign key constraint defined, but no index created on the foreign key column. Let's run our script to check for this occurrence:

```
SQL> select table_name, constraint_name,
cname1 || nvl2(cname2,','||cname2,null) ||
nvl2(cname3,','||cname3,null) || nvl2(cname4,','||cname4,null) ||
```

```
nvl2(cname5,','||cname5,null) || nvl2(cname6,','||cname6,null) ||
nvl2(cname7,','||cname7,null) || nvl2(cname8,','||cname8,null)
   columns
from ( select b.table_name,
         b.constraint_name,
         max(decode( position, 1, column_name, null )) cname1,
         max(decode( position, 2, column_name, null )) cname2,
         max(decode( position, 3, column_name, null )) cname3,
         max(decode( position, 4, column_name, null )) cname4,
         max(decode( position, 5, column_name, null )) cname5,
         max(decode( position, 6, column_name, null )) cname6,
         max(decode( position, 7, column_name, null )) cname7,
         max(decode( position, 8, column_name, null )) cname8,
         count(*) col_cnt
         from (select substr(table_name,1,30) table_name,
                  substr(constraint_name,1,30) constraint_name,
                  substr(column_name,1,30) column_name,
                     position
                   from user_cons_columns ) a,
                 user_constraints b
            where a.constraint_name = b.constraint_name
              and b.constraint_type = 'R'
            group by b.table_name, b.constraint_name
          ) cons
      where col_cnt > ALL
              ( select count(*)
                 from user_ind_columns i,
                      user_indexes      ui
                where i.table_name = cons.table_name
                  and i.column_name in
                    (cname1, cname2, cname3, cname4,
                     cname5, cname6, cname7, cname8 )
                  and i.column_position <= cons.col_cnt
                  and ui.table_name = i.table_name
                  and ui.index_name = i.index_name
```

```
                    and ui.index_type IN ('NORMAL','NORMAL/REV')
                group by i.index_name
            );
```

Here is the output for this example:

```
TABLE_NAME        CONSTRAINT_NAME COLUMNS
--------------    --------------- -------------------------------
EMP               EMP_FK_DEPT     DEPTNO
```

Now, let's add an index to the foreign key column:

```
SQL> create index empfkidx on emp(deptno);
```

And rerunning the prior query to check for foreign keys returns no rows now:

```
no rows selected
```

This script works on foreign key constraints that have up to eight columns in them (if you have more than that, you probably want to rethink your design). It starts by building an inline view named CONS in the previous query. This inline view transposes the appropriate column names in the constraint from rows into columns, with the result being a row per constraint and up to eight columns that have the names of the columns in the constraint. Additionally, there is a column, COL_CNT, which contains the number of columns in the foreign key constraint itself. For each row returned from the inline view, we execute a correlated subquery that checks all of the indexes on the table currently being processed. It counts the columns in that index that match columns in the foreign key constraint and then groups them by index name. So, it generates a set of numbers, each of which is a count of matching columns in some index on that table. If the original COL_CNT is greater than all of these numbers, then there is no index on that table that supports that constraint. If COL_CNT is less than all of these numbers, then there is at least one index that supports that constraint. Note the use of the NVL2 function, which we used to "glue" the list of column names into a comma-separated list. This function takes three arguments: A, B, and C. If argument A is not null, then it returns argument B; otherwise, it returns argument C. This query assumes that the owner of the constraint is the owner of the table and index as well. If another user indexed the table or the table is in another schema (both rare events), it will not work correctly.

The prior script also checks to see if the index type is a B*Tree index (NORMAL or NORMAL/REV). We're checking to see if it's a B*Tree index because a bitmap index on a foreign key column does not prevent the locking issue.

---

**Note**   In data warehouse environments, it's common to create bitmap indexes on a fact table's foreign key columns. However, in data warehouse environments, usually the loading of data is done in an orderly manner through scheduled ETL processes and, therefore, would not encounter the situation of inserting into a child table as one process while concurrently deleting from a parent table from another process (like you might encounter in an OLTP application).

---

So, the prior script shows that table C has a foreign key on the column X but no index. By creating a B*Tree index on X, we can remove this locking issue all together. In addition to this table lock, an unindexed foreign key can also be problematic in the following cases:

- When you have an ON DELETE CASCADE and have not indexed the child table. For example, EMP is child of DEPT. DELETE DEPTNO = 10 should CASCADE to EMP. If DEPTNO in EMP is not indexed, you will get a full table scan of EMP for each row deleted from the DEPT table. This full scan is probably undesirable, and if you delete many rows from the parent table, the child table will be scanned once for each parent row deleted.

- When you query from the parent to the child. Consider the EMP/DEPT example again. It is very common to query the EMP table in the context of a DEPTNO. If you frequently run the following query (say, to generate a report), you'll find that not having the index in place will slow down the queries:

```
select * from dept, emp
where emp.deptno = dept.deptno and dept.deptno = :X;
```

When do you not need to index a foreign key? The answer is, in general, when the following conditions are met:

- You do not delete from the parent table.

- You do not update the parent table's unique/primary key value (watch for unintended updates to the primary key by tools).

- You do not join from the parent to the child (like DEPT to EMP).

If you satisfy all three conditions, feel free to skip the index; it's not needed. If you meet any of the preceding conditions, be aware of the consequences. This is the one rare instance when Oracle tends to overlock data.

# Examining Blocking

I have been on dozens of troubleshooting calls that start out something like this: "The database is hung, can you investigate why my session isn't processing?" The reality is that the database is not "hung" but is functioning as it is supposed to. The more probable issue is that there is some blocking going on in the database that is causing a session to wait for a resource that is tied up (locked). For example, if one user is updating a row in the dataset and has not committed or rolled back the transaction, then any other users in the database will not be able to modify the row. This of course is the expected behavior (Oracle will only let one user at a time modify a row of data). When dealing with situations like this, you should check for any sessions that are being blocked.

## Blocking Basics

One simple way to check for blocking sessions is to query the V$SESSION view and check to see if the BLOCKING_SESSION column has a value (e.g., is not null). For example, say you start two SQL*Plus sessions—first, in one terminal, you start a session as the CHEWY user:

```
sqlplus chewy/foo@localhost:1521/orcl

SQL> select username, sid, serial#
from v$session where username=(USER);

USERNAME            SID    SERIAL#
----------- ---------- ----------
CHEWY                22       4437
```

Then, in the second terminal, connect as the DARTH user:

```
sqlplus darth/foo@localhost:1521/orcl

SQL> select username, sid, serial#
from v$session where username=(USER);

USERNAME            SID    SERIAL#
------------ ---------- ----------
DARTH                31        561
```

Now, suppose both users want to update the same row in the DEPT table. The user CHEWY updates the row first:

```
SQL> update dept set loc='DENVER' where loc='BOSTON';
1 row updated.
```

Now, at this point, the CHEWY user has a row-level lock on the row being updated in the DEPT table. Next, in the second session, the DARTH user attempts to update the same row:

```
SQL> update dept set loc='LA' where loc='BOSTON';
```

Notice that this statement appears to hang. In reality, the second session is waiting for the lock on that row (held by CHEWY) to be released before it can proceed with its update. The simplest way to view this is to query the data dictionary as follows:

```
select
 username AS blked_user
,serial#  AS blked_serial#
,sid       AS blked_sid
,blocking_session AS blking_sid
,seconds_in_wait AS sec_in_wait
from v$session
where blocking_session is not NULL
order by blocking_session;
```

Here is the output showing DARTH is the blocked user:

```
BLKED_USER   BLKED_SERIAL#  BLKED_SID BLKING_SID SEC_IN_WAIT
------------ -------------- ---------- ---------- -----------
DARTH                   561         31         22          70
```

With the blocking session identifier, you can dig deeper into the details of the blocking session with the following query:

```
select
 username
,sid
,serial#
from v$session
where sid=&sid;
```

In this example, the blocking session identifier is 22, so we enter that when prompted and get the following:

```
USERNAME             SID    SERIAL#
------------ ---------- ----------
CHEWY                 22       4437
```

With this information, you could try to contact the user and see if they have done some processing without issuing a COMMIT or ROLLBACK. However, when working in large systems with thousands of users and a myriad of mid-tier machines between the user and the database, it will be difficult to identify somebody you could call and ask them to finish their transaction. You may be able to identify a business owner who can confidently tell you that it's okay to kill the user holding the lock. If you have that approval, then armed with the SID and SERIAL#, you can kill the blocking session as follows:

```
SQL> alter system kill session '22,4437';
```

That will kill the blocking session and release the lock and allow the session that was being blocked to continue processing.

## Advanced Blocking Examples

Recall this query from Chapter 3; we introduced this basic query to display blocking sessions:

```
select
 (select username from v$session where sid=a.sid) blocker,
  a.sid,' is blocking ',
```

```
(select username from v$session where sid=b.sid) blockee,
 b.sid
   from v$lock a, v$lock b
  where a.block = 1
    and b.request > 0
    and a.id1 = b.id1
    and a.id2 = b.id2;
```

Let's run the prior query using the blocking example in the prior section. The output shows clearly the CHEWY user is blocking the DARTH user:

```
BLOCKER          SID 'ISBLOCKING'  BLOCKEE          SID
---------  ----------  -------------  ---------  ----------
CHEWY             22  is blocking   DARTH             31
```

The key to understanding the prior query is that when blocking occurs, there will be a row in V$LOCK that has a value of 1 for the BLOCK column. This is the session that is blocking. There will also be an additional row in V$LOCK that has a value greater than 0 for the REQUST column. This is the session being blocked. The two rows in V$LOCK (one row for blocking and one row for being blocked) are related by a common ID1, and ID2 columns (the columns to join on).

We can build on that query to display more information to assist with troubleshooting what session is causing the blocking and which session is being blocked. For example, we can add to it useful information such as the SERIAL# of the blocking session and for how many seconds the blocking activity has taken:

```
select
  sblocker.username AS blocker
 ,blocker.sid
 ,sblocker.serial#
 ,'is blocking '
 ,sblockee.username AS blockee
 ,blockee.sid
 ,sblockee.seconds_in_wait secondsWait
from v$lock     blocker
    ,v$session sblocker
    ,v$lock     blockee
```

```
    ,v$session sblockee
where blocker.block = 1
and    blockee.request > 0
and    blocker.id1 = blockee.id1
and    blocker.id2 = blockee.id2
and    blocker.sid = sblocker.sid
and    blockee.sid = sblockee.sid;
```

Here is an example of the output:

```
BLOCKER    SID    SERIAL# 'ISBLOCKING' BLOCKEE    SID SECONDSWAIT
-------  ------  ---------- ------------ -------  ------ -----------
CHEWY      22      45611 is blocking  DARTH       31         312
```

This gives you enough information to determine who is blocking and who is being blocked. With the SID and SERIAL#, you can terminate a session if required. Terminating (or killing) sessions will be covered in detail in the next section.

# Killing Sessions

We touched briefly on killing sessions in a prior section in this chapter. The basic idea is that in some scenarios you have a blocked session that cannot continue to process until a resource is released. For whatever reason, the session that is doing the blocking has not committed or rolled back the transaction, and this causes bottlenecks within the application. In my experience, terminating a session is usually the last resort. Ideally, you'd be able to find the root cause of the blocking within the application and not have to resort to manual intervention. In reality, sometimes you will have to intercede and terminate a session holding resources.

We've shown in prior sections how to identify the session responsible for blocking. Once you have the SID and SERIAL#, you can log in to the database as a privileged DBA account and issue the following command with this basic syntax:

```
alter system kill session '<SID>,<SERIAL#>';
```

If the session isn't currently performing an operation such as a rollback, then any open transactions are rolled back and locks on objects are released. At this point, any blocked sessions should be able to proceed normally.

If the session is currently performing an operation such as waiting for a response from a remote database or rolling back a transaction, Oracle will wait for the rollback operation to complete, mark the session as terminated, and return control back to you. If the waiting lasts more than a minute, Oracle marks the session as terminated and then returns control back to you with a message that the session has been marked for termination.

If you wish for Oracle to immediately return back to you after issuing the KILL SESSION command, then you can use the IMMEDIATE clause:

```
alter system kill session '<SID>,<SERIAL#>' immediate;
```

The prior command doesn't immediately terminate the session, rather it immediately returns control back to you at the SQL prompt. After which, Oracle will roll back ongoing transactions, release all locks held by the session, and recover the entire session state.

If you're in a RAC environment (e.g., more than one instance per databases), then you can use the instance identifier to terminate a session running in a specific instance. For example, you may wish to terminate a session that is connected to a different instance than the one that you're logged into. In this scenario, you must specify the INST_ID, shown when querying the GV$SESSION view. This allows you to kill a session running on a specific RAC node:

```
alter system kill session  '<SID>,<SERIAL#>,@INST_ID';
```

If you're working in a more recent version of Oracle (18c and above), you can also kill a specific SQL statement via the CANCEL  SQL clause. This has the basic syntax as follows:

```
alter system cancel sql '<SID>,<SERIAL#>[,@<INST_ID>][,<SQL_ID>]';
```

You'll need the SID, SERIAL#, and the SQL_ID to terminate a specific SQL statement, for example:

```
alter system cancel sql '467,52828,cfna18y8xjwzb';
```

There's one last small topic I want to cover in this section regarding killing sessions. I've been in production environments where an application schema may have dozens of connections to a database, and all of these sessions are causing blocking. In these scenarios, it's handy to have a script to generate the SQL you'll need to kill multiple sessions. For example, if you want to kill all sessions of a particular schema, you can use a script like this:

```
select 'ALTER SYSTEM KILL SESSION ' || '''' || sid || ',' || serial# ||
'''' || ';'
from v$session
where username=UPPER('&schema');
```

You'll be prompted for a schema name; after which, you'll get the kill statements for each session connected as that schema:

```
ALTER SYSTEM KILL SESSION '467,30699';
ALTER SYSTEM KILL SESSION '469,14524';
```

You can then take the output and cut and paste it into a SQL session and run the statements, or you can spool the output to a file and execute the file. This will save you a great deal of time if you have to kill more than a few sessions.

# Dealing with ORA-00054 Resource Busy

The ORA-00054 error is often encountered when you're attempting to modify a table only to find out that there's some sort of a lock on the object which prevents you from running your DDL statement, for example:

```
SQL> drop table dept;
drop table dept
          *
ERROR at line 1:
ORA-00054: resource busy and acquire with NOWAIT specified or timeout
expired
```

One way of handling the ORA-00054 error is to give the process that is trying to acquire the lock more time to complete its operation. To this end, you can use the DDL_LOCK_TIMEOUT parameter. This will instruct your process to wait a specified amount of time for the lock to be released. If you're working in an environment where locks are acquired and released fairly quickly, this is a good approach. For example, you can instruct your process to wait for 60 seconds for the lock to be released:

```
SQL> alter session set ddl_lock_timeout=60;
```

In this scenario, your session will continuously try to acquire the lock it needs for 60 seconds. If the lock isn't released within that time, you'll get the ORA-00054 error again.

If you're blocked for a considerable amount of time, then there may be some other transaction that is modifying data within the table that hasn't committed or rolled back yet. To identify the blocking session, you can query the DBA_DML_LOCKS view, for example:

```
select session_id
,owner
,mode_held
,mode_requested
from dba_dml_locks;
```

Here is some sample output:

```
SESSION_ID OWNER       MODE_HELD  MODE_REQUESTED
---------- ---------- ---------- ----------------
        12 DARTH      Row-X (SX) None
```

If you want to kill the blocking session, you'll also need the SERIAL# of the blocker. You can view that via the following query:

```
select a.sid, a.serial#
from v$session a
    ,v$locked_object b
    ,dba_objects c
where b.object_id = c.object_id
and a.sid = b.session_id
and object_name='DEPT';
```

Here is some sample output:

```
USERNAME              SID    SERIAL#
------------ ---------- ----------
CHEWY                  12       4021
```

With that information, you can decide whether or not it's okay to attempt to kill the blocking session (see the prior section in this chapter for examples). Other techniques for avoiding the ORA-00054 error would be to

- Only run DDL during off-peak processing hours (if possible)

- Run the DDL during a specified maintenance window in which users are typically not processing data

One final note on the ORA-00054 error, I did work in an environment where we could not identify the root cause of the block. We searched all of the views for the relevant blocking session information and came up empty handed. In this scenario, we ended up bouncing (stopping/starting) the instance to resolve the issue. This is an extreme example, but I thought it would be worth mentioning here. Our best guess was there was some sort of internal database lock being held that wasn't visible to us.

# Troubleshooting Undo

In an Oracle database, recall that undo refers to the mechanism by which Oracle can roll back a transaction. When you make a change to a row of data, Oracle will make a copy of the data. This copy is appropriately referred to as undo because you can undo the change via a ROLLBACK statement. Oracle stores the before image copy of the record in the undo tablespace.

One thing to keep in mind when inspecting undo is that each pluggable database can have its own undo tablespaces within the container database. So when you're digging into undo issues, ensure that you connect to the correct pluggable database. I've had issues attempting to diagnose undo problems because I was connected to the root container when running troubleshooting queries that were reporting off of the root container undo tablespaces. In these scenarios, it's important to connect to the appropriate pluggable database and investigate the undo there. If the pluggable database does not have its own undo tablespace, then ensure you look at the undo tablespace in the root container.

Additionally, if you're in a RAC environment, each instance has its own undo tablespaces. If you're querying the data dictionary in a RAC environment, ensure that you use the GV$ views (and not the single instance V$ views).

# Reporting Top Undo Consumers

Problems with undo are usually manifested in a couple of different ways:

- You receive ORA-30036 unable to extend segment in undo tablespace.

- You get an ORA-01555 snapshot too old message while running a query.

CHAPTER 9  TROUBLESHOOTING

When you see these error messages related to undo, one of the first ways to troubleshoot this is to determine which user is consuming resources in the undo tablespace. If you're using a container database, ensure to connect to the pluggable database where the undo is being consumed (e.g., if you're connected to the root container, then you won't see any information). This next query will display the USERNAME, SID, and SERIAL# of users consuming undo:

```
SELECT  s.username,
        s.sid,
        s.serial#,
        t.used_ublk,
        t.used_urec,
        rs.segment_name,
        r.rssize,
        r.status
FROM    v$transaction t,
        v$session s,
        v$rollstat r,
        dba_rollback_segs rs
WHERE   s.saddr = t.ses_addr
AND     t.xidusn = r.usn
AND     rs.segment_id = t.xidusn
ORDER BY t.used_ublk;
```

Here is some sample output:

```
USERNAME SID  SERIAL# USED_UBLK USED_UREC SEGMENT_NAME            RSSIZE STATUS
-------- ---- ------- --------- --------- ---------------------- ------ -------
YODA     454  50603           1         5 _SYSSMU41_3266304675$  122880 ONLINE
```

With the prior information, you can determine who is consuming the undo and further enhance the query by adding columns such as MACHINE and PROGRAM to the output to help you track down the offending user.

# Showing Transactions Consuming Undo

Usually when tracking down issues with undo, you're looking for a big transaction, such as an INSERT, UPDATE, or DELETE statement that is consuming large amounts of undo. The following query will show details such as the SQL_ID of the DML statement, time the transaction was started, number of seconds the transaction has been running, and amount of undo being used:

```
SELECT
  s.inst_id,
  s.username,
  s.sid,
  s.serial#,
  s.machine,
  NVL(s.client_info,'nada') client_info,
  NVL(s.sql_id, s.prev_sql_id) sql_id,
  NVL(sqlcom.command_name,'nada') sqlcommand,
  s.module,
  s.action,
  s.program,
  t.status,
  t.start_date,
  ROUND((SYSDATE-t.start_date)*24*60*60) AS secondsopen,
  SUM(t.used_urec) as undorecordsinuse,
  SUM(t.used_ublk) as undoblocksinuse
FROM
  gv$transaction t,
  gv$session s,
  gv$sqlcommand sqlcom
WHERE t.addr = s.taddr
AND sqlcom.command_type=s.command
AND t.inst_id = s.inst_id
GROUP BY
  s.inst_id,
  s.username,
  s.sid,
```

```
  s.serial#,
  s.machine,
  s.client_info,
  NVL(s.sql_id, s.prev_sql_id),
  NVL(sqlcom.command_name,'nada'),
  s.module,
  s.action,
  s.program,
  t.status,
  t.start_date,
  (SYSDATE-t.start_date)*24*60*60
ORDER BY
  undoblocksinuse DESC;
```

I'm not going to list any sample output from this query as there are too many columns to fit nicely on the page. When you run the prior query on your database, if the value of undo blocks in use is greater than 10,000, then you might have an issue. If that number is greater than 100,000, then you should definitely investigate further. Using the SQL_ID in the output, you can track down the DML statement in the V$SQL view.

# Displaying Snapshot Tool Old Occurrences

You can use the query in this section to determine if your database is throwing the ORA-01555 snapshot too old error. You must run this query while connected to the pluggable database (not the root container):

```
SELECT
  TO_CHAR(begin_time,'YYYY-MM-DD HH24:MI:SS') "Begin",
  TO_CHAR(end_time,'YYYY-MM-DD HH24:MI:SS') "End ",
  undoblks "UndoBlocks",
  ssolderrcnt "ORA-01555"
FROM gv$undostat
WHERE ssolderrcnt > 0;
```

Here is some sample output:

```
Begin               End                 UndoBlocks   ORA-01555
------------------- ------------------- ----------   ----------
2020-06-17 18:49:04 2020-06-17 18:59:04       1886            1
```

When you detect occurrences of the ORA-01555 error, then you should investigate the database alert log for further details. For example, here's a partial listing of the alert log details:

```
ORCL(3):ORA-01555 caused by SQL statement below (SQL ID: d8c267bvx6rn9,
Query Duration=45 sec, SCN:
ORCL(3):0x000000000094c661
```

If there's a corresponding trace file listed, you should also open that to get complete details of the issue that caused the problem.

# Inspecting Redo

Recall that when any data is changed in the database, Oracle will keep a record of how the data changed. This redo audit trail allows Oracle to recover a database in the event you had a disk failure and need to restore the data files and then apply redo to them to ensure they have all of the database changes up until the point of the failure.

Usually issues with redo express themselves in a couple of different ways. Namely, you'll see messages in the database alert log related to

- Checkpoint not complete

- Log switches occurring very frequently (every two minutes or less)

When you see these messages, it could be an indication that your log files are too small, or you need to add more log groups. The next subsections in this chapter discuss techniques for displaying excessive log switching and pinpointing which user is responsible for generating redo.

# Log Switching Frequency

The first step in troubleshooting redo issues is to determine how frequently your online redo logs are switching. Here is the most basic query to display log switching:

```
SELECT
 TRUNC(completion_time) as DAY
,COUNT(1)
,TRUNC(sum(blocks*block_size)/1024/1024) as MB
FROM gv$archived_log
WHERE first_time > TRUNC(sysdate-7)
GROUP BY TRUNC(completion_time)
ORDER BY TRUNC(completion_time);
```

The prior query is inadequate for several reasons:

- If you're in a RAC environment, you need to know which thread of redo is switching.

- If you have Data Guard enabled, you don't want to count switching that occurs in the standby database to be counted with your primary database.

The following query adds the thread number and logic to remove counting switching on the standby:

```
SELECT
 thread#
,TRUNC(completion_time) as DAY
,COUNT(1)
,TRUNC(sum(blocks*block_size)/1024/1024/1024) as GB
,TRUNC(sum(blocks*block_size)/1024/1024) as MB
FROM gv$archived_log
WHERE first_time > TRUNC(sysdate-7)
AND dest_id = (SELECT dest_id FROM gv$archive_dest_status WHERE
status='VALID' AND type='LOCAL')
GROUP BY thread#, TRUNC(completion_time)
ORDER BY thread#, TRUNC(completion_time);
```

Here is some sample output:

| THREAD# | DAY | COUNT(1) | GB | MB |
|---------|-----------|----------|----|------|
| 1 | 11-JUN-20 | 19 | 7 | 8119 |
| 1 | 12-JUN-20 | 47 | 18 | 19294 |
| 1 | 13-JUN-20 | 4 | 1 | 1696 |
| 1 | 14-JUN-20 | 7 | 2 | 2509 |
| 1 | 15-JUN-20 | 12 | 5 | 5236 |
| 1 | 16-JUN-20 | 18 | 7 | 7620 |
| 1 | 17-JUN-20 | 22 | 8 | 9013 |
| 1 | 18-JUN-20 | 5 | 2 | 2097 |

Usually when troubleshooting log switching issues, you'll need a report that displays hourly switching rates. This will better help you determine if your logs are sized appropriately or if you have large intermittent spikes of transactions. Ideally, you do not want your logs switching more than ten times in an hour. Here is a script that reports on the hourly rate of switching:

```
SELECT
  thread#,
  TO_CHAR(first_time,'YYYY-MM-DD') DAY,
  TO_CHAR(first_time,'HH24') HOUR,
  COUNT(*) TOTAL
FROM gv$log_history
WHERE first_time >= SYSDATE-2
GROUP BY thread#, TO_CHAR(first_time,'YYYY-MM-DD'),TO_CHAR(first_
time,'HH24')
ORDER BY thread#, DAY ASC, HOUR ASC
/
```

Here is some sample output:

| THREAD# | DAY | HOUR | TOTAL |
|---------|------------|------|-------|
| 1 | 2020-06-16 | 15 | 5 |
| 1 | 2020-06-16 | 16 | 6 |
| 1 | 2020-06-16 | 17 | 4 |

| | | | |
|---|---|---|---|
| 1 | 2020-06-16 | 19 | 1 |
| 1 | 2020-06-17 | 08 | 4 |
| 1 | 2020-06-17 | 11 | 3 |
| 1 | 2020-06-17 | 12 | 3 |
| 1 | 2020-06-17 | 13 | 3 |
| 1 | 2020-06-17 | 14 | 3 |

These basic queries will quickly give you an accurate reporting of log switching. If you consistently see values of over ten log switches per hour, then you need to consider resizing the logs to a larger value.

# Determining Who Is Generating Redo

In the prior section of this chapter, we demonstrated how to determine if there is a large amount of redo being generated (e.g., very frequent log switching). When you notice large amounts of redo being generated, the next question is which user is generating the redo? To answer that question, run the following query:

```
select
    s.username,
    s.sid,
    s.serial#,
    ss.value AS redoSize,
    s.program,
    s.module
from v$statname sn,
     v$sesstat ss,
     v$session s
where ss.statistic#=sn.statistic#
and sn.name='redo size'
and s.sid=ss.sid
and ss.value>0
and s.username is not null
order by ss.value;
```

This will identify the user and program generating the most redo. Here is some sample output (truncated so that it will fit on the page):

```
USERNAME          SID    SERIAL#   REDOSIZE PROGRAM
---------- ---------- ---------- ---------- -------
YODA                2     56822      35944 sqlplus
```

With this information, you can contact the user or application team and work with them to understand what is generating the redo and if it's normal or required.

Another way to look at the problem of who is generating redo is to display which tables are experiencing excessive insert, update, and delete statements. To determine this, you can query the DBA_TAB_MODIFICATIONS view, for example:

```
select table_owner, table_name, inserts, updates, deletes
from dba_tab_modifications
where table_owner !='SYS';
```

Here is some output:

```
TABLE_OWNE TABLE_NAME             INSERTS    UPDATES    DELETES
---------- -------------------- ---------- ---------- ----------
SCOTT      DEPT                    234480          0          0
SCOTT      EMP                      17372          0         10
```

This will give you an idea of what application tables are the most heavily used and what types of statements are generating the redo.

# Summary

This chapter showed various techniques for troubleshooting issues related to topics covered in this book. We started with a query to report on unindexed foreign keys. This helps identifying where you can add indexes to mitigate excessive locks being taken by Oracle. Next, we covered how to report on blocking sessions. Blocking sessions are a frequent problem, and being able to quickly identify blocks and resolve them is critical for maintaining a healthy database. The last two topics were troubleshooting undo and redo issues. We covered many queries to help identify who is generating excessive undo and redo. This information will help you quickly diagnose issues related to transactions and locking, which in turn will help you keep your database running more smoothly and efficiently.

# Index

## A

Archived redo log files, 162
Atomicity
    DDL, 126, 127
    procedure-level, 121–126
    statement-level, 118–121
    transaction-level, 126
Autonomous
        transactions, 152
    procedure, 155
    use, 156, 157, 159
    working, 153, 154

## B

Blocking
    DML statements, 31
    INSERT, 31, 32, 34
    locked resource, 31
    UPDATE, 35

## C

Checksum
    approach universal, 29
    database functionality, 26
    hash function, 26
    hash value, 28
    optimistic locking, 30

    ORA_HASH built-in function, 27
    PL/SQL packages, 26
Concurrency controls, 3, 4
    lock, 81
    multiversioning, 82
    statement level, 83
    transaction isolation levels, 83
    TX transaction, 82
Cost of latching, shared pool
    bind variables, 69, 71, 74, 76, 77
    CPU machine, 68
    performance/scalability
        comparison, 77
    SGA configuration, 72
    Statspack report, 67, 73, 74
    test, setup, 68, 69

## D

Data definition language
    (DDL), 22, 41, 126
Data manipulation language (DML), 41
DBMS_LOCK package, 79, 80
Database writer (DBWR), 163
DDL locks
    ALTER TABLE T, 58
    breakable parse lock, 59, 63
    CREATE action, 60
    CREATE INDEX ONLINE
        command, 61

261

Printed in the United States
By Bookmasters